CONDUCTING OPERA

Where Theater Meets Music

by
Joseph Rescigno

University of North Texas Press
Denton, Texas

Printed in the United States of America.

10 9 8 7 6 5 4 3 2 1

Permissions:
University of North Texas Press
1155 Union Circle #311336
Denton, TX 76203-5017

The paper used in this book meets the minimum requirements of the American National Standard for Permanence of Paper for Printed Library Materials, z39.48.1984. Binding materials have been chosen for durability.

Library of Congress Cataloging-in-Publication Data

Rescigno, Joseph, author.
Conducting opera: where theater meets music / by Joseph Rescigno.
Pages cm
Includes bibliographical references and index.
ISBN-13 978-1-57441-793-7 (cloth : alk. paper)
ISBN-13 978-1-57441-804-0 (ebook)
1. Conducting. 2.Opera—Production and direction. 3. Musical theater—Production and direction.

MT85 .R39 2020
782.1/145–dc23

2019057915

The electronic edition of this book was made possible by the support of the Vick Family Foundation. Typeset by vPrompt eServices.

For Grandpa

My dear young friend, I have lived a long while, and I have known all the chefs d'orchestre. There are two kinds: one takes the music too fast, and the other too slow. There is no third!

—Camille Saint-Saëns to Thomas Beecham[1]

Contents

Preface

So the conductor is a kind of sculptor whose element is time instead of marble . . .

—Leonard Bernstein[2]

There are many worthy manuals about how to conduct music, as well as interesting histories of the conducting profession. There are invaluable scholarly treatises about the evolution and performance history of individual works and exhaustive anatomical studies of those works. Biographies of conductors and composers tell the reader something, more or less, about their subjects' music making. These books have something to offer the professional musician, the student, and the music-loving public alike.

This book is none of the above. It is about one musician's approach to conducting a sampling of masterworks of the operatic literature. My goal is to illuminate how we can realize what opera can uniquely achieve: a fusion of music and drama such that the whole is greater than the sum of its parts. In more concrete terms and depending on the specific opera, this book includes practical advice about propelling a story forward, supporting singers, navigating through problematic passages, and remaining true to the style of a work.

In other words, this book is one performer's take on the masterpieces that some of the great composers have given us, and the challenges they have set for us, rather than a work of history or musicology. It deals with the operas and composers that have dominated my career in professional opera companies around the world and especially in North America for over four decades: Mozart to Richard Strauss with an emphasis on those beloved works that opera-goers encounter most often.

"Most beloved" and "most performed" characterizations are not as straightforward as they may sound, however. If nothing else, fashions and tastes change; and companies legitimately need to vary their offerings to the ticket-buying public. Therefore, some industry resources have been allocated to works by contemporary composers; some to resurrection of neglected works; and some to works from countries other than Italy, Germany, and France, which so completely dominated the opera world for many years. All of this is positive, and I have been privileged to participate in such productions.

Within the standard repertory, however, the sheer number of productions of some operas over others cannot be explained without acknowledging the difference in the cost of mounting the bigger, longer, and more expensive operas. In some cases, operas that were once wildly popular are now pretty hard to find in the season brochures. *Madama Butterfly* and *Ariadne auf Naxos* are fine operas that I would not want to see drop out of sight. But it would be nice to see just a few performances of them give way to a few more of the once-ubiquitous *Il trovatore* and *Manon* of Jules Massenet.

Furthermore, I will offer insights and suggestions only on operas in German and the Romance languages since I conduct complete operas only in languages that I can at least read. This is because it is helpful to have a good grasp of what is being said onstage if one wishes to truly lead in lyric theater. Much as beginning conductors and singers might like to divine meaning from the notes, it is a bit of an illusion that we can get better guidance from our own visceral reaction to the glorious sounds we work with than we can from the words to which the composer set the music. Music of the Romantic period—where almost anything can sound like a love song—presents the greatest dangers. Performers need to dig below what composer Aaron Copland calls the sensuous plane of listening and arrive at a reasoned interpretation, and in lyric theater, that reasoning begins with the words in the score.[3]

Competence with the language also helps the conductor remember the music. While I place no emphasis on memorization for its own sake, it is critically important to know large swaths of music so well that they are virtually memorized. There are moments when there simply is not enough time to look down, let alone turn the page.

Thus, in order for an opera to be included here: It must be something I have performed, something with issues and challenges worth discussing, and something that is produced frequently enough to be a topic of more than purely academic interest.

The reader who is a conductor is assumed to come to this book with competence in podium technique and score study; the singer and stage director, similarly, with a foundation in their respective crafts and an interest in understanding the kind of issues that drive the conductors they have to work with; and the music lover, with a craving to get behind the scenes (or into the pit) in this most complex and demanding art form.

Chapters will address individual operas with, broadly, an introduction and then more in-depth discussion of the technical issues and problems on which I can give useful advice to conductors and helpful insight to others. This changes across the repertory. Decoration and ornamentation of the vocal line is a subject of vital importance in the first few chapters and not even considered in Richard Strauss's music. Motives are *structurally* important in some operas, interesting—even fun—in others, and effectively nonexistent in still others. Tempo discussions change when a composer supplies metronome markings. Through-composition changes the conductor's job. Casting is certainly important and influences some conductorial choices, but it is never among the technical problems or issues in a chapter.

So there will be some variability in which topics are addressed in each chapter, how much weight they get, and even whether they appear at the beginning, middle, or the end of a chapter. Before we get to individual operas, however, Chapter 1 addresses the analysis and planning that takes place long before opening night, or even the first rehearsal call, in more general terms.

About Scores

Citations in the text reference orchestra scores that are described in detail in the Appendix. We use rehearsal numbers or letters when possible, but page numbers are given when such markings are absent or difficult to use.

Whenever possible, we are citing scores that are available free on-line and mention others only when they are directly pertinent to some citation or example. This is not to disparage any number of scores that I have worked with and own. Even when I disagree with editors' choices, I value knowing about their research and the issues they find. (For perspective about this work, I recommend Philip Gossett's discussion of "The Romance of the Critical Edition" to any serious music lover.[4]) I would urge those studying conducting, in particular, to do their best to review multiple versions of a work where they exist as well as new editions.

References to piano-vocal reductions are included because many readers will have greater access to them than to orchestra scores. But our primary source is the orchestra score. Any indications mentioned in the text and tables, including metronome indications, are those printed in the orchestra scores, unless identified as being my recommended or suggested speeds.

Irrespective of cost or date, there can be variations in the organization of different editions. (This is more important in older works and less important in operas from later in the nineteenth century and beyond.) Readers with access to scores should check the Appendix for information that may be helpful in locating citations.

Chapter 1

Step into My Study

. . . there are conductors who destroy the unity of a work that is one and indivisible, and others who can shape the *apparently* fragmentary into a unity.

—Felix Weingartner[1]

In studying a work for the first time, I begin with the piano-vocal score. In addition to the melodies, rhythms, and harmonies, this reduced score tells me about most of the structure, or how all of work's sections fit together sequentially. The success of a performance depends on a clear exposition of this structure, even if the listener is not consciously aware of it. Connections and propulsion are felt; motives and themes are set in relief.

Destinations

By the time that I have gotten most of what I can out of the piano-vocal score and begun a systematic review of the complete orchestration, I have determined the emotional high point of the work and what should be its loudest moments. The purpose of this analysis is to keep both emotion and dynamics under control. It is a truism that, if everything is loud, nothing is loud—or that nothing will stand out as loud*er*. If, dramatically, we chew up the scenery all night, where is the climax for the audience? At first, one might think that the dynamic and emotional high points are the same thing, and sometimes they are. In *Carmen*, for example, the emotional and dynamic climaxes coincide in the final duet when José murders Carmen (No. 27). But in other cases, the two climaxes may not coincide. Two examples are Mozart's *Le nozze di Figaro* and Richard Strauss's *Elektra*.

In *Le nozze di Figaro*, I find two dynamic high points. One is in the final 16 measures of the PRESTISSIMO section of the Act II finale (beginning at m. 924 in No. 16, p. 338 [vocal 133]), and the other in the finale of Act IV on the words "di tormenti" in the ALLEGRO ASSAI section (No. 29, at m. 451, p. 582 [vocal 228]). Not only is this second climax sudden, but we also have the exquisite dissonance of G-sharp against A-natural. The emotional climax, on the other hand, is near—but not at—the end of Act IV, when the humiliated count asks his wife for forgiveness with "Contessa perdona" at ANDANTE (No. 29, m. 420, p. 578 [vocal 226]). His request is written *piano*. His wife grants forgiveness, still *piano*, and I like the Countess's reply to be even softer than the Count's phrase. Then everyone sings in a whisper commenting on this astonishing reversal.

In *Elektra*, the loudest point should be the end of the Elektra-Klytämnestra duet (at [259]) while the emotional high point is Elektra's recognition of her brother Orest (at [144a]). In this recognition scene, when Elektra cries out Orest's name, the orchestra comes in very loud and then plays a long DIMINUENDO as she repeats his name three times and finally sings "Es rührt sich niemand."

Identifying one or two dynamic high points becomes increasingly important in big works with lots of orchestral sound throughout, works that could be loud for most of their running time. Admittedly, an "emotional" high point may be hard to pinpoint in some works like some comedies or particularly fragmented works. Furthermore, in a work that is dominated by a single character, the drama and emotional high point are going to hinge in some measure on the star's approach. *La traviata*, *Madama Butterfly*, and *Lucia di Lammermoor* come to mind readily. In preparing to perform any work in music theater, however, it will pay to look for one or two moments toward which much of the musical action will build.

This, then, is the conductor's job, which is not unlike that of a pilot: to have a destination and ensure that the musical and dramatic aircraft lands on the runway and not on some field nearby.

While I may offer suggestions of many kinds, the principal way in which I simultaneously set the rules and give all of the performers expressive breathing room is through pacing. Certainly, I can emphasize some tone or harmony—by means of articulation and balance within the orchestra, for example. The use and control of dynamics is very important. The right volume can supply drama and pathos while, conversely, the wrong volume can sabotage a soloist. Unflagging attention to the words of the libretto is absolutely essential. And of course, I support the singers, by letting them shine or helping them out. But the most important thing a conductor does is pace a performance.

To the question of whether there is a single right tempo for a piece of music, the answer is no, but there is certainly a correct *range* of tempos for a given piece. Igor Stravinsky tells us that the relation of tempo and meaning is "a primary question of musical order," even asserting that he could not compose until he was sure he had found the right tempo.[2]

We should note that pacing an entire opera or other large work like a symphony or oratorio is about more than simple speed at any given moment, however. It is also a matter of the sweep from scene to scene and even section to section within a scene. In a three-hour opera, there may be a difference of only a few minutes between two performances that are perceived as very different. Excitement or boredom is frequently the result of how the sections of a piece hang together and move forward with some sense of inevitability, not to mention how free all of the performers are to do their best.

Example 1.1 From Zerlina's "Batti, batti" in *Don Giovanni* (Act I, No. 12, from m. 58, p. 169 [vocal 108]).

Of course, nothing above or below rules out expressive tempo bending—or *rubato*—without which music would be mechanical and thus less interesting than it can and should be. Composers may suggest some flexibility for a phrase with indications like RITARDANDO or ACCELERANDO. In Example 1.1,

Mozart suggests some rubato, as well as decoration, with a simple fermata.[3] Sometimes we employ rubato with no indications, however. It is partly a matter of style; more rubato is appropriate and acceptable in Puccini's music than in that of Mozart, for example. But it exists in all music.

The Flight Plan

Planning a successful performance requires more than envisioning the big picture, the one or more climactic moments, and the work's gestalt. It next requires that I work my way backward from those key moments that will have the maximum effect and develop a plan for how we get there smoothly.

The way to achieve a smooth and seamless performance is to execute most transitions between adjacent sections of music with tempos that are mathematically related. The simplest examples are double time or half time. There are subtler transitions, and some require a little arithmetic. But often, far more study time is spent head-scratching and pondering than figuring out the math. In any case, sweeping from one tempo to another mathematically related tempo is usually the way the pit can illuminate the greatness in the score as well as help propel the opera's story forward. If I want the audience breathless—and the performers grinning—at the end of a great Mozart or Rossini finale, I need to execute transitions between sections that even experienced listeners are barely aware of. The textbook case lies in the finale of *Le nozze di Figaro's* Act II, which is discussed at length in Chapter 2. A few other notable or knotty scenes are analyzed in detail in this book, but the concept of tempo relationships will appear in every chapter.

While focusing on arithmetic may sound confining, in fact, it works in quite the opposite way. That is, freedom has its pleasures, but self-discipline can pay big dividends—especially where continuity is necessary to reach some distant goal. For example, in the Act IV finale of *Le nozze di Figaro* there is a shift to a LARGHETTO that can be made both slower than one might expect *and* smoother when we get the proportions exactly right (also discussed in Chapter 2).

In some of Wagner's scores, relationships may govern hundreds of measures containing multiple tempo digressions in many minutes of music; this is true in the Act II, Scene 2, duet in *Tristan und Isolde*, for example (Chapter 5). On the other hand, in many Mozart, bel canto, and French operas, discrete sections are separated by recitative or spoken dialogue. In such instances no relationships are intended, and we should not invent them. Inventing them usually means imposing accelerations and decelerations in order to sweep from one section to the next. This can get quite anti-dramatic, and to the musically sophisticated listener, it can be downright distracting. When I attack a new section after recitative or dialogue, I judge the tempo in terms of the style of the composer and era, as well as the drama onstage.

To be sure, it would be wrong to suggest that there are no moments when discontinuity is right. Verdi expresses the unhinged Otello's rage and delusions with tempos that are a little jerky, as discussed in Chapter 4. Richard Strauss comically interrupts in a manner that is meant to be jarring as The Composer is about to kiss Zerbinetta in *Ariadne auf Naxos* (Chapter 8).

Nonetheless, in most operas written from the eighteenth century through the early twentieth century, when we encounter a scene or an entire act that contains continuous melody, the relationships between discrete but interlocking parts require analysis and rigor. Throughout this book, the reader will find three fundamental and interrelated principles that are critical to this analysis: Absent reason to do otherwise, transitions should be made seamless. The way to achieve this seamlessness is to find a mathematical relationship between any tempo and the tempo that immediately precedes it. And to achieve this proportionality when a meter changes from simple to compound or vice versa, a constant pulse, or beat, is usually appropriate.

Example 1.1 affords a miniature case study. A tradition of making a rather noticeable change of tempo at the change to $\frac{6}{8}$ goes back a very long way. Indeed, for years, editors have added ALLEGRETTO or ALLEGRO at this change of time signature, even the editors of the 1968 "urtext" from Bärenreiter. I have always felt that choosing to make an extreme contrast between the two sections is at least questionable. I grew up with older scores (like the Dover reprint of the C.F. Peters score also available for download) that are consistent with the autograph manuscript in omitting any tempo indication at the meter change. (This is on p. 152 in Dover. It is also the leaf labeled 97 by hand in the autograph [physical p. 193]).

Mozart knew that the music would speed up naturally because of the meter change as long as the beat remained unchanged. His fermata allows Zerlina some time to act and creates some separation between the two sections of music. But an unrelated faster tempo after the fermata, or even a related tempo that is much faster, draws a bolder line separating the two sections. The aria also has greater elegance with a constant pulse than it does with a big bump-up in speed. That is, a constant pulse lends the aria unity and elegance.

Technical texts on conducting skills endorse smooth connections between sections of music and lay out the arithmetic involved when crunching a few numbers is required, so all conductors learn about these relationships. (See Box 1.1, "Watching the Meter.") But acting on that knowledge is variable. As my career has progressed and I have both tackled diverse repertory and conducted some of music's greatest masterpieces many times, I have become ever more convinced of the wisdom of those of my elders who emphasized this kind of analysis to me for the kind of music that is the subject of this book. For those looking to make their performances flow and cohere better (and we can always do better), it is my intention to supply some models in the chapters that follow.

Box 1.1 Watching the Meter

A concept fundamental to the music discussed in this book is that, as a rule, music should be played and conducted with a constant pulse, or beat. It was the default assumption of Mozart and other composers well into the nineteenth century. Later composers, including some of those in this book, may clarify tempo and meter changes with some statement about the mathematical relationship between notes on either side of the indication. And when a meter changes from simple to compound or vice versa, the two approaches result in two different tempos. For example, assuming we begin at 60 quarter notes per minute:

Constant value means ♪ = ♪ and therefore, ♩ = 60 and ♩. = 40.

Constant pulse means ♩ = ♩. and therefore, ♩ = 60 and ♩. = 60 (or, two ♪ = three ♪).

The first disclaimer to be made is that there is considerable inconsistency among musicians and educators in the use of the relevant words here. For the purposes of this book, constant value—often called constant tempo—means that notes of any given relative duration, like the eighth note, take the same length of time throughout. It follows, then, that after a shift between simple and compound meters, the beat and the bar will take more time or less time than they had previously. The constant pulse means that the beat never changes; the beat takes the same length of time throughout, as does the bar. It follows, then, that notes of the same relative duration must speed up or slow down in order to fit into the unchanging beat.

In addition, some want to reserve the term "tempo change" for places in a score that include tempo indications in words or metronome indications; they consider meter changes to be a different subject. However at a compound-to-simple or simple-to-compound meter change, music is going to sound slower or faster, a lot or a little, even if I do not want to make any change beyond what inevitably results from the meter change. In Example 1.1 for instance, assuming that I start in the neighborhood of 60 quarter notes per minute, the music may sound barely perceptibly slower or clearly faster after the meter change. It will sound slower if notes of any given duration take the same length of time throughout. It will sound faster if the length of time that my beat takes remains the same throughout. And neither of those choices involves a conscious or purposeful *additional* adjustment. So I do not want to lose the importance of the choice a conductor makes at a point like this or pretend that "only" the rhythm changes for the listener. A meter change of this kind results in a change in how fast the notes are arriving at our ears and brains.

Finally, composers and editors also have used equations like these inconsistently. In many scores that we reference in this book, ♩. = ♩ means that the dotted quarter note in the upcoming music lasts as long as the quarter note in the preceding measures. But in other scores it may mean the opposite (the previous dotted quarter equals the new quarter). Happily, the musical context can make the meaning of the equation clear. Usually. That is, such relationships should always be considered carefully, and there will be instances in which some extra scrutiny is warranted.

For numerous exercises and examples of these relationships, see Chapter 28 of Max Rudolf's *The Grammar of Conducting* (New York: G. Schirmer, Inc., 1950) as well as Chapter 2 of Gustav Meier's *The Score, the Orchestra, and the Conductor* (New York: Oxford Univ. Press, 2009).

Charted and Uncharted Territory

As I absorb the basics in the piano-vocal score, come to some conclusion about how the entire performance builds to its most important moments, and begin looking at the orchestration, I need to make a host of small choices. "Small" is relative of course, and dozens of small choices can combine into something quite significant. Ultimately, such choices will be driven by my understanding of tradition, my assessment of the talent that will be available in the upcoming production, and my own artistic sensibility.

Tradition

Every work a musician picks up sits on a continuum: at one end there is little or no accumulated tradition, and at the other end there are steamer trunks of tradition of every kind. There is an adage that says that tradition can be nothing more than the memory of the last bad performance, but that is simplistic and unhelpful for the decision-making musician. There are really two kinds of tradition: The first is a body of unwritten law, conventions that a composer took for granted and therefore *influenced the act of composition*, in the words of conductor Erich Leinsdorf. The second is customary practices and habits that date from performances in some later period. No book contains the last word on this subject since scholarship continues, but Leinsdorf's *The Composer's Advocate* is worth any musician's attention.[4]

The sheer quantity and durability of many traditions in the standard operatic repertory tracks closely with how popular works are and how often they have been performed. A couple of hundred years of performing will allow considerable accretion of practices never envisioned by a work's composer. Therefore, many of the operas discussed in this book carry a hefty load of traditions, and in some cases those traditions have become virtually sacrosanct. I'll address a number of traditions that I eschew in this book.

Yet all tradition is certainly not to be condemned. For one thing, we should note that there are corners of the repertory where we have relatively less reliable scholarship to consider in forming judgments. In these cases, we workaday performers lean in part on tradition handed down to us by our elders, including guidance about taste. We should lean gingerly, but if nothing else, tradition can serve as food for thought.

How do I separate the good from the (at least) questionable? My first duty is to notice when something I expect to find in the score is not there. This sounds simpler than it is. When you think something is there in the score—when it is already part of your planned performance, usually because that is the way you have always heard it—it is easy to miss the fact that it is, in fact, not on the page. But for example, there is no ritard in the 2 measures at the end of the brief orchestral introduction to Act I of *Madama Butterfly* (from m. 2 before [5]).

My second duty is to consider stylistic integrity, dramatic suitability, and moderation. This, in turn, suggests approaching a score having some acquaintance with the context in which it was written. Context includes the performance practices of the time, the nature of the instruments used, the language of the libretto, and the composer's individual style in theater music, concert music, and chamber music to the extent possible. Any reader may disagree about which traditions should be excised and which should be retained. My only caution is that choices of this nature should be made in a thoughtful manner. In the chapters that follow, traditions of a few kinds will be discussed.

Singing: Traditions for singers involve decoration, variation, note holding, interpolated high notes and, to a lesser extent, tempos. Stylistically inappropriate alterations can be jarring to the educated listener. Some may actually change harmonies or rhythms or both. Wrong tempos have left us with musical lines distorted by excessive breathing and the text sometimes reduced to "ah." And too much decoration risks turning a drama into a series of vocal stunts.

In this book, I will point to traditions I think are good ideas, bad ideas for a variety of reasons, and bad ideas for some singers sometimes. Entrenched traditions can be pernicious: singers may shoot themselves in the foot with tempos that they cannot sing beautifully or risk notes that are ill advised, in both cases because of supposed audience expectations. There are often alternatives that will have an equivalent impact, some of which I will suggest in the chapters that follow.

Finally, some transpositions have been around for a very long time, often to accommodate high notes that were added to the score after the composer laid down his pen. "Di quella pira" for Manrico in *Il trovatore's* Act III is a case in point (in No. 11, from p. 307 [vocal 170]), and there are many across the bel canto literature. (A delightful legend was told to me at the beginning of my career: During the *Risorgimento*, a tenor who felt that he could not hit the expected high C in "Di quella pira" chose instead to shout *Evviva Garibaldi!* Naturally, the audience could do nothing but applaud.)

If a singer sings the part well except for a single note or very few, I want to accommodate him or her without risking a disaster at the top of an exciting scene. If I have to transpose, I try to go back to a point in the opera that allows for the same progression of harmonies in relative terms to avoid losing the excitement in the original. Alas, this can require rewriting the orchestra parts for many pages, something that is not always feasible.

Conducting: There are some tempo adjustments that seem necessary to virtually all of us. But there are also numerous instances of speeding up and slowing down that make little sense dramatically, musically, and sometimes even vocally. I would only urge the developing conductor to give the indicated tempo a chance. Meanwhile, I also endorse a little more attention to some bedrock conducting conventions—conventions such as the constant pulse (discussed above), the stretto (Chapter 3), and the singer-friendly *dopo la parola* (Chapters 7 and 8).

Cuts: Conductors, stage directors, and managements sometimes seem wedded to traditional cuts. Usually, the reason they give is saving money. But often enough, money has little to do with it; some cuts save a very few minutes. Sometimes, there is a that's-the-way-it's-done or the-audience-will-be-bored rationale underneath the proposals and decisions. Reasons like this only tell me that the decision maker is unfamiliar with the music in question or does not like it. This is unfortunate. After a while, we lose our collective memory of some wonderful music with little to show for our ax-wielding. In the following chapters, I will point to a number of passages that are worth restoring.

This is not to condemn all cuts, however. Even with an unlimited budget, fine singers, and complete faith in the music, cuts are needed in some operas.

Richard Wagner himself sanctioned some cutting in *Tristan und Isolde,* although he left no specific instructions. And even in Verdi's day, *Il trovatore's* Act IV cabaletta for Leonora, "Tu vedrai che amore in terra" was often cut (from ALLEGRO AGITATO in No. 12, p. 349 [vocal 191]). Decisions about this class of cuts hinge on the singer's stamina more than budget or even singing difficulty.

Corner-cutting: As in any enterprise, it is possible to trim a little cost here and trim a little cost there. Often, individual snips are not noticeable to most of the customers until, finally, the product is unrecognizable. In an opera, cutting scenes or parts of scenes probably comes to mind first, and it is fair to ask why one would produce a four-hour opera only to cut it to well under three hours. But actually, a moderate amount of judicious cutting is not always the worst alternative. Cheesy sets are instantly noticed, of course. Surrounding a big star with lackluster supporting singers may sell some tickets, but it will not result in the greatest listener satisfaction or customer loyalty. Trimming the number of musicians operates in a similar manner since it limits the thrills and joys we should be delivering.

But one of the most unfortunate corners being cut—at least from a musical perspective—is the mishandling of music written to be played backstage and onstage. In operas of the bel canto era and those of Giuseppe Verdi's early to middle years, one of these ensembles of ten to fourteen instruments, usually wind instruments, was called a "banda." But backstage musicians (sometimes with chorus) or costumed musicians onstage exist in a very large number of operas across the repertory.

This music is not cut, but it is moved into the pit. Doing so has become something of a tradition in my lifetime, and it has crept into more and more operas. I say it has become a tradition because, with respect to some operas, the intended effect is virtually forgotten outside the biggest and richest companies. There are directors and singers who have never worked with the Act I banda of *La traviata* where it belongs, backstage. (This bookends the "Valzer-Duetto" that continues No. 2, beginning at ALLEGRO BRILLANTE on p. 48 [vocal 33].) They are unfamiliar with its theatrically appropriately distant sound or even with how much easier it is to sing conversationally and be heard easily when this background music is, well, in the background. I feel like The Old Man indeed when these artists express their surprise and delight upon discovering this sound.

Beyond audibility, the theatrical effect is palpable when sound comes from a separate location, and nothing can quite match it. Sound coming from diverse locations is one of the things that live theater—without the mediation of amplification—can uniquely supply.

In some operas, the dramatic effect of this kind of ensemble is so essential that it cannot reasonably be moved to the pit. A wind banda after the tenor's aria "Ma se m'è forza perderti" in the third act finale of *Un ballo in maschera* is a case in point (from [41] ALLEGRO VIVISSIMO, p. 450 [vocal 217]); the alternation of banda and orchestra is dramatically essential. Moving the musicians of *La bohème's* Act II parade into the pit cheats the audience both dramatically and musically (from [27] [vocal p. 155, third beat of m. 5). And the three onstage ensembles of *Don Giovanni's* Act I finale can sound dissonant in the extreme if they are not separated in space (No. 13). Sadly, however, paying the additional musicians for rehearsals and performances has become increasingly difficult. In the United States, only the largest companies still employ a banda for *La traviata* or *Rigoletto*, for example (through much of the first scene of *Rigoletto*, No. 2 [vocal No. 1]).

If compromise is necessary and feasible and the music is to be played in the pit, the music in question can sound too loud because of both the shortened distance to the listeners' ears and the retention of too many players given that changed distance. Some instrument substitutions may also be in order. Muted strings can give a faraway sound that would not be needed if the musicians were actually backstage but can be very useful when they are playing in the pit. With respect to earlier operas at least, it is worth remembering that the reason that the orchestration of a banda is rarely included in the conductor's score and we can only study its details in the parts, is that bandas were generally played by whatever extra musicians could be rounded up. So substituting instruments, even if the banda is played outside the pit as it should be, is not without precedent.

In these cases, a conductor needs to look at the number of musicians available and whether they are playing against the main music in the pit or playing alone. Then the appropriate arrangement can be devised, which may involve reducing the number of players. The string banda of *Ballo's* Act III, for example, can be transferred to the pit more successfully than the earlier wind banda, and can be effective with relatively few strings playing (beginning at 63, ASSAI MODERATO, p. 490 [vocal 237]).

Taste and Judgment

All conductors need to make adjustments from time to time, and even the purest of the pure do so. The doubting reader may wish to consider a revealing survey of modifications made to Beethoven's Ninth Symphony by five prominent conductors (most of whom, as it happens, are as well known for composing as conducting) in Leonard Slatkin's *Conducting Business*.[5]

In my experience, one set of reasons arises out of a singer's or instrumentalist's strengths or weaknesses. We make adjustments in order to give the audience the best show possible. Sometimes a theater's acoustics or the instruments available require a tweak—just to get back to the sound we believe is closer to what the composer meant us to hear. (And there is plenty of room for debate when that subject comes up.) Moreover, expression is needed in all music; and particularly in the earliest scores in this book, we know that nobody expected a strict reading of the music without any expressive touches.

Making choices about how the strings play is an essential part of the conductor's job, for example. Strings have the greatest range of expression in the orchestra by far, with dozens of possible ways to produce their sound, so it is impossible to remain neutral. Making no choice is simply defaulting to what the string players themselves think (especially the first violin). Knowing something about the exigencies of all instruments is a laudable goal, but paying very close attention to a lot of string playing is one of the better uses of a developing conductor's time and energies. Sometimes specific circumstances (like the size of the section, for example) may help me decide which techniques will suit. At other times, I may consider tradition; but sometimes, I have to rely on my own taste and my own sense of the composer's style.

When I am not choosing among a widely accepted, standard repertory of articulations, how do I resolve the tension between fidelity to the score and the need for some expression? When an idea comes to mind, the questions I ask myself parallel those I ask about those traditional practices that have been handed down to me: What makes sense and honors the work and what does not? When I consider a change, I hold that any touches I might add should help clarify the music for the listener, the way polish brings out the inherent beauty of an object or the right frame enhances our perception of a picture. But any personal touch that I might introduce into a performance must stop short of obscuring the composer's idea or diverting attention away from the central idea in the passage.

In the interest of emphasis for example, I may ask one instrument to reinforce the notes of another. The reinforcing instrument is either idle for the moment or is playing notes that are played by others who are audible enough. I find such an opportunity for emphasis in the last measures of *Il trovatore's* Act III, Scene 1, for example, where some of the instruments have trills (from m. 13 before the end of No. 10, p. 288 [vocal 160]). Although Verdi used trumpet trills in other operas (*Macbeth*, *Aida*, *Otello*, and *Falstaff*, for example), there are none here, and I do not pretend to know why. What I can say is that they can add a surge of energy that seems stylistically appropriate and dramatically apt at this moment in *Il trovatore*. Therefore, I ask the first trumpet to trill the same F and E that others are trilling for 8 measures while the second trumpet plays what is written (notes that are also supported by other instruments). That is, the trills in the trumpet are reinforcing the trills in other instruments, not introducing trills where none exist, and the notes assigned to the trumpet and others are still played with the same variety of timbres.

All of this said, I try to keep in mind Hector Berlioz's caution that the conductor's artistic flourishes not resemble the affections of the ass in the fable who crushes his master in trying to caress him.[6]

Conclusion

Performers may disagree about where we find the climaxes in individual works; and that is to be expected. Some dismiss the need for arithmetically related tempo changes entirely, or almost so; there, I can only say that we will agree to disagree. And all bets are off when it comes to the myriad small decisions about traditional practices and expressive touches supplied by performers, including conductors; in those cases, too much agreement might not even be desirable.

For one conductor's insights and experience, however, I invite you into my study.

My favorite things

Like most performers, I am often asked about my favorite work. The more immersed you become in music, however, the harder that gets. There are too many apples-and-oranges comparisons or, more, too many steak-versus-ice cream choices. However, what is somewhat easier to choose is favorite moments in a given work. So I will share those with respect to each work discussed in depth in this book.

Chapter 2

Mozart

> I beg of you do your best that we may go to Italy. You know my greatest longing—to write operas. . . . I am envious of every man who composes one; I could almost weep from chagrin whenever I hear or see an aria. But Italian, not German: *seria* not *buffa*.
>
> —Wolfgang Amadeus Mozart[1]

Claudio Monteverdi may have invented Western opera, but Wolfgang Amadeus Mozart did more to shape the bulk of the standard repertory than any other composer. Among other things, Mozart created a model for the vocal ensembles that would become the backbone of what we call Italian grand opera: that is, for the next century up to Verdi's middle period.

Richard Wagner and Giuseppe Verdi both strove to make opera dramatically satisfying, more like theater and more realistic. It may have been Mozart, however, who made the greatest strides in this direction relative to what came before. Mozart, especially in the operas composed to Lorenzo Da Ponte's librettos, uses contemporary stories. There are more vocal lines singing independent or even conflicting thoughts in different moods than in operas of earlier eras. There are more tempo shifts that must be knitted together as seamlessly as possible, which is the conductor's main contribution to achieving a satisfying, even thrilling, climax. Tension is built for longer periods and then resolved.

In addition, Mozart's masterful orchestration supplies color and emotion. When we think of the great orchestrators, we usually think of Maurice Ravel, Nikolai Rimsky-Korsakov, or Richard Strauss. Mozart, however, may be the greatest orchestrator in Western music. With the simplest of means, he creates incredible colors.

Nonetheless, the sometimes-elliptical nature of the scores of his time means that the conductor should exercise some imagination and expressiveness after thoroughly studying the style appropriate to the work. Thus, preparing to perform these operas includes looking for the moments where the orchestra can reinforce the drama or just render the music more clearly, all without changing a note. As discussed below, contrasting articulation can go a long way toward increasing the transparency in the sound and maintaining the interest of the listener. Control of dynamics is, of course, fundamental in this endeavor as well.

Preparation also includes mapping out multiple series of tempos that interlock and dovetail in a manner that propels the action forward throughout the duration of the opera. In addition, of course, it requires working with the singers to find out where they need support and where they can soar, but also to get the style right.

In mapping out a tempo plan, I encounter two related issues that require analysis before the first downbeat as well as discipline thereafter. They are finding the pulse for connected sections of music (especially in the finales) and pacing long sections of orchestral recitative. In order for multi-sectioned finales to build to a climax, the right approach is usually to maintain a constant pulse. Therefore, the first task is to determine what that pulse should be in scores with no metronome indications. This means I have to take a step back and determine the pulse that allows me to move smoothly from beginning to end without pauses, accelerate and decelerate as needed, and yet keep the music at a singable speed throughout. When I cannot find a series of relationships among the sections, as a rule, I redouble my efforts because they are almost certainly there in Mozart's music. As discussed at Example 2.2, there is one relationship near the end of *Le nozze di Figaro* that it took me years to discern.

The second task is to decide upon the right amount of variety and flexibility in long passages of orchestral recitative. While we cannot go much faster than speech, going too slowly will put the audience to sleep. The longer the passage, the larger this issue looms, of course. Ideally, the text between orchestral punctuation should flow naturally, like the dialogue in a play. In the three operas discussed in this chapter, the long discussions between Tamino and the Priest in the Act I finale of *Die Zauberflöte* are the knottiest for a conductor (for example, from the ADAGIO at m. 85 in No. 8, p. 138 [vocal 57]); two conversations between Donna Anna and Don Ottavio in *Don Giovanni* require a similar analysis (Nos. 2 and 10). These sections are, in fact, reminiscent of the *opere serie* where even longer passages of this type exist.

Finally, preparing to perform the earlier works in the repertory requires at least some meeting of the minds with singers regarding embellishment and decoration. My interest is in helping all of the performers do their best. At the end of the day—or, more precisely, during the performance—there is no room for debate and no more time for coaching. Before and during rehearsals, I will do my best to guide them regarding style, while learning what support they need and how to showcase their strengths. This may even entail the fashioning of new variations and cadenzas, which is always gratifying.

A body of scholarship exists regarding varying the vocal line in this music. This does not mean that there is widespread agreement, however. What can be said of the vigorous debates in the literature is that they supply considerable food for thought and plenty of grounds for humility. From my perspective, the danger here is in not finding the middle of the road. It is preferable to do no embellishments at all rather than to clutter this glorious music with too many. I feel they should be far less frequent in Mozart's music than in Handel's or in bel canto music.

An in-depth discussion laying out assumptions, documentary evidence, and reasoning is beyond the scope of this book. For the purpose of this discussion, however, the questions come down to: "What does a grace note mean?" and "When should we consider altering the pitch of a note?" and "Which more extensive variations (like cadenzas) are suitable?"

The Meaning of a Grace Note

Grace notes may be written with or without a slash and, while modern publishers may try to bring some consistency to the table, there may be little or nothing in an older score that directs us about what a slash means or how a grace note is to be executed. So, however helpful an editor tries to be, choosing between appoggiaturas and acciaccaturas is a matter of taste and tradition and continuing scholarship. In the best critical editions of operas, we can get a sense of what evidence exists in the editors' sources, what reasoning has been brought to bear, and whatever unanswered questions remain. Nonetheless, even editors of critical editions have been known to include later traditions without making that clear.

Example 2.1 Variation by Mozart: Zerlina's "Batti, batti" in *Don Giovanni* (Act I, No. 12).

In addition, it may be helpful to bear in mind that the appoggiatura is not any particular symbol in the notation but, rather, a discordant note that precedes and resolves to a note in the chord. The acciaccatura—that little hiccup, generally before the beat, that many of us first think of at the sight of a grace note—has also been called the "short appoggiatura." But a less-short ornament, sung on the beat, is known only as an "appoggiatura" and may also be indicated with a grace note. Example 2.1 illustrates such a grace note on the last syllable of "povera," in the reprise, and how it is executed.

In a Mozart vocal line, the appoggiatura is usually the more appropriate treatment for a grace note. This is one of those small details that can loom quite large as a listener acquires some sophistication. Hearing a Rossinian ornament in the midst of Mozart, or vice versa, can be somewhat jarring. But styles and traditions change. For example, the grace notes in the second and third movements of his "Haffner" Symphony have been performed and recorded in a variety of ways over the decades: as acciaccaturas played either before or on the beat, but also as simpler and more melodic appoggiaturas.

Altering Pitches (as an Embellishment)

When two notes of the same pitch are written at the end of a phrase, the first may be sung a half or whole step higher (the general rule) or lower, with the whole or half tone being a matter of harmonic context. So while the grace-note appoggiatura asks the singer to interpret a written grace note of a particular pitch, this unwritten, pitch-changing appoggiatura is more improvisational. Scholars also call this unwritten appoggiatura the "prosodic appoggiatura" because of its relationship to prosody, or the pattern of rhythm and stress in verse.

While the legitimacy of the practice is not disputed, debates revolve around the where-and-when. The discussion starts with the pattern of stressed syllables in the poetry being sung, but beyond that, reasonable people will disagree about what is purely "decorative," thus inessential, versus what is mandated by the poetry.

I resist the notion that rules can be formulated with certainty in this arena. That said, we are all obliged to stay informed about both tradition and evolving scholarship (with new-old materials being unearthed with surprising and delightful regularity). The cardinal rule is to strive for tasteful results.

In the past, altering the first of two identical notes appearing side-by-side became downright excessive in some quarters. Since actions can be expected to provoke equal and opposite reactions, there came a time in the twentieth century when they were almost never observed, and that was surely about as wrong. Now, in the early years of the twenty-first century, the pendulum has swung so far that some seem to want to employ them always. They should, in fact, be observed when melodically interesting, usually from the note above, but avoided when they would weaken the musical line or interfere with hearing a melody. That is, from where I stand, I would not by any means want to hear a singer alter every pair of notes of the same pitch.

There is a perfect example of this need for discretion at the beginning of Donna Anna's Act I aria in *Don Giovanni*. In "Or sai chi l'onore," there are three instances of two notes of the same pitch in the course of 6 measures: a pair of Gs, a pair of As, and a pair of Bs (No. 10, from the ANDANTE at m. 70, p. 143 [vocal 90]). Making an appoggiatura each time seems excessive and even distracting. It is better if the soprano sings two notes of the same pitch in the first and second instance, and executes an appoggiatura in the third instance, on the last two syllables of "traditore." She might sing C-sharp followed by B. A more dramatic and dissonant effect can be achieved if she executes the appoggiatura from the note below, singing A-sharp and B, which emphasizes the word "traditore." Other approaches are possible, but this is an instance in which stepping back and asking the question can only help.

Suitable Cadenzas and Other Variations

These too were almost never heard in Mozart's operas forty or fifty years ago. Thanks to increased scholarship, we have learned that the practice of decorating reprises or inserting cadenzas was often employed in Mozart's time.

I always try to use the variations that Mozart wrote as a guide in formulating new ones. An example is in the aria "Batti, batti." Example 2.1 illustrates the melody as first sung and then Mozart's variation on the reprise. The variation is simple and perfectly captures the teasing nature of the situation. The melody begins with four descending eighth notes. In the variation, each is shortened and decorated with an ascending interval of a second. Decorating the descending melody with these little upticks gives the effect of little sobs in Zerlina's voice. In addition, it may be argued that the grace note a little later in the variation, performed as an appoggiatura, gives the tune a little more mock seriousness than would an acciaccatura. In any case, what is very clear is that the decorations for *Die Zauberflöte's* Queen of the Night are quite different, and a faithful interpreter takes those different styles into account.

Le Nozze di Figaro

There is a special place in my heart for *Le nozze di Figaro* (1786). It was the first opera that I conducted with a full orchestra and fully staged. Even if this were not so, however, the work would remain a treasure to me for its engaging characters and story, its riot of inspired melody and orchestration, and its groundbreaking architecture. It can also be enjoyed on many levels and by listeners at every stage of their education since it contains heartfelt sentiment, romantic comedy, and farce, as well as a subversive streak. It is therefore perennially on the most-often-produced lists well over two centuries after its premiere. Among other things, this opera's popularity proves that the death of civilization is exaggerated.

As in all music, the conductor may make adjustments to illuminate what is on the printed page. For example, the Act I Duettino between Susanna and Marcellina offers an opportunity to reinforce contrasts with articulation in the orchestra as the two characters engage in teasing and one-upsmanship (No. 5). I like to ask the violins to articulate their parts differently, with spiccato in the second violins' triplets and legato in the first violins' ordinary notes. This is in keeping with the style of this era and allows the listener to follow two thoughts simultaneously and appreciate their interplay even better.

In addition, sometimes I need to make volume adjustments in order to establish the right balance within a modern orchestra with its bigger string section than Mozart had in mind. Near the end of the overture for example, there are measures after a crescendo where the woodwinds might not be heard (from m. 262, which is m. 35 from the end, p. 26 [vocal 10]). The horns, trumpets, and strings should attack their first notes aggressively but immediately soften in order to ensure that the woodwinds' final descending scales can register with the listener.

At other times, I may use dynamics to create dramatic emphasis. For example, during the Act II finale, there is a passage in which Susanna, Figaro, and the Countess implore the Count to allow the wedding to proceed without interference (No. 16 from m. 449, p. 267 [vocal 104]). The section begins SOTTO VOCE with double basses playing a "pedal point"—a low sustained C—which they will do through almost all of 14 measures. At the Count's vocal entrance, in which he angrily wonders why Marcellina has not shown up in support of his plot, there is an *f* indication for everyone except the basses (middle of m. 453). They play *f* a beat earlier, at the beginning of that measure, and I ask them to rearticulate for maximum effect. This extra prominence underscores the drama and the contrasting emotions.

For the singers, there is opportunity to vary the vocal line in *Le nozze di Figaro*. Cherubino's love song to the Countess, for example, is an ardent "performance" within the opera and is repeated (No. 12 [vocal No. 11]). Thus, while the first statement of the melody of "Voi che sapete" should be set out in a straightforward manner, the repeat merits extra romantic flourishes (from m. 62). A very dramatic moment, too, may justify some embellishment. One instance occurs with the Count's angry outburst in the duet that opens the Act II finale. A fermata over the second through fourth beat of "Vel leggo in volto!" suggests some freedom to take the time needed to maximize the dramatic effect. This intent is clearer in the orchestra score than in the vocal score (m. 80 in No. 16, p. 229 [vocal 87]).

Anomalous tempos have crept into some Mozart arias, however. For example, over the years, performers have drifted toward interpreting Susanna's words in her Act IV recitative before "Deh vieni non tardar" too romantically and, therefore, taking the recitative too slowly (No. 28). First, it is marked ALLEGRO VIVACE ASSAI, so taking it at an ANDANTE is suspect on its face. Second, looking back a half-dozen measures confirms Mozart's humorous intention. This brief recitative before the aria, in which Susanna feigns passionate yearning for the Count, is a tease meant to torment Figaro. On the other hand, the aria proper is marked ANDANTE and should be taken seriously and romantically. Perhaps Susanna cannot help but think of her true love once she begins this aria. The transition and contrast can be very affecting with the right singing actress.

Step into My Study . . .

Mozart's gift for structure influenced virtually all of the composers who followed him, right up until the present. He set the standard. And part of what makes his structures special is his magnificent, multi-sectioned finales.

Act II Finale

For me, the textbook case for Mozart's genius and the value of getting tempo relationships right, lies in the Act II finale of *Le nozze di Figaro*, a transcendent sequence in ten sections with nine tempo changes and ending in the dynamic high point of the opera. In this finale, a duet becomes a trio, then a quartet, a quintet, and then finally a septet. Mozart's indications with suggested metronome speeds are summarized in Table 2.1. Readers seeking a much more in-depth analysis of this finale can do no better than pick up a copy of *The Composer's Advocate* by Erich Leinsdorf, one of the best books on music that I have ever read.[2]

Table 2.1 *Figaro's* Act II finale (No. 16 [vocal No. 15]).

Scene	At...	Page*	Meter/Tempo	Suggestion
6	m. 1	222 (84)	$\frac{4}{4}$ ALLEGRO	𝅗𝅥 = 80
7	m. 126, *trio*	233 (89)	$\frac{3}{8}$ MOLTO ANDANTE	♪ = 80
8	m. 167	236 (91)	$\frac{4}{4}$ ALLEGRO	𝅗𝅥 = 80
9	m. 328, *quartet*	253 (98)	$\frac{3}{8}$ ALLEGRO	♩. = 80
	m. 398	259 (101)	$\frac{2}{4}$ ANDANTE	♪ = 80
10	m. 467, *quintet*	270 (105)	$\frac{4}{4}$ ALLEGRO MOLTO	𝅗𝅥 = 80
	m. 603	290 (113)	COLLA VOCE AD LIBITUM	𝅗𝅥 = 60 (approx.)
	m. 605	291 (113)	$\frac{6}{8}$ ANDANTE	♩. = 60
11	m. 697, *septet*	305 (118)	$\frac{4}{4}$ ALLEGRO ASSAI	𝅗𝅥 = 120
	m. 783	316 (122)	PIÙ ALLEGRO	𝅗𝅥 = 132
	m. 907	336 (132)	PRESTISSIMO	𝅝 = 80

* Vocal score page in parentheses.

The finale begins with a duet between the Count and Countess in $\frac{4}{4}$ meter, marked ALLEGRO, for which a pace of approximately 80 half notes per minute works. Although a relatively quick speed for an ALLEGRO (though it is often performed even faster), it works to express the Count's anger and the

Countess's anxiety. As importantly, it will work as a foundation as the music flows to a bravura conclusion. Typically, in $\frac{4}{4}$ meter, the quickest notes are sixteenths. The fact that the quick notes are eighth notes suggests that the section should be conducted in two rather than in four. Trying to beat four times per measure at this speed would be unhelpful at best. My beat would be moving too fast for the musicians to follow for any length of time.

With the entrance of Susanna, the duet becomes a trio in $\frac{3}{8}$ meter, MOLTO ANDANTE. This means very moderately slow, or slower than a normal andante, so 80 eighth notes per minute, conducting three beats per measure, works. Another way to express this relationship is that the eighth note of the MOLTO ANDANTE is about equal in duration to the half note of the previous ALLEGRO.

(It is to be noted that some editors have changed this MOLTO ANDANTE to ANDANTE CON MOTO. This is because there is a debate about whether *molto andante* is slower or faster than a normal andante, and *andante con moto* is considered a less ambiguous term for a fast andante. I have never been persuaded that *molto andante* is faster than andante. In any case, Mozart spoke Italian and knew how to say *andante con moto* if that is what he intended.)

The trio concludes with a $\frac{4}{4}$ section again marked ALLEGRO, so I can return to the first tempo (80 half notes per minute, conducted in two). The half note approximately equals the preceding eighth note.

With the arrival of Figaro, the trio becomes a quartet written in $\frac{3}{8}$ meter marked ALLEGRO. Here, I give myself 80 dotted quarter notes per minute; and I conduct one beat per measure. Why is this ALLEGRO slower than both of the earlier ALLEGRO passages? The answer is that in the earlier ALLEGRO passages, the singers are singing in quarter notes whereas here they are singing in eighth notes. They simply have more words per measure to get across, so I can and should give them just a little more time. In fact, the eighth and thirty-second notes of this ALLEGRO would be perceived as faster than the quarter notes of the previous ALLEGRO even if played by a machine at a tempo that is verifiably identical.

The quartet concludes with a $\frac{2}{4}$ ANDANTE (80 eighth notes per minute). Some conductors feel that the transition to ANDANTE can be discontinuous, that the tempo is not necessarily related to what comes before, because of the dramatic situation. (The Count has unexpectedly produced the letter that the other characters did not know he had.) A smooth proportional relationship makes more sense to me for a couple of reasons: First, this slower andante reflects the Count's sarcasm. Second, Mozart supplies one indication to follow the singer in this finale, a very short while later (COLLA VOCE AD LIBITUM, m. 603). In my opinion, one disruption in the flow is enough in this music.

With Antonio's entrance, the quartet becomes a quintet (although he leaves a little before the end). This stretch begins in $\frac{4}{4}$ meter marked ALLEGRO MOLTO. Eighty half notes per minute, conducted in two, makes sense.

Next is the COLLA VOCE AD LIBITUM as Figaro pretends to have hurt his foot. When I look ahead, I also see that there is an ANDANTE only 2 measures hence, so it is wise to get ready for a slower tempo. This suggests that I slow the COLLA VOCE AD LIBITUM to about 60 half notes a minute (still conducting in two), and maintain that pulse, with 60 dotted quarter notes per minute for the $\frac{6}{8}$ section marked ANDANTE, still beating twice per measure.

The finale ends with a septet that begins with the entrance of Bartolo, Basilio, and Marcellina. The septet is composed of three sections, all in $\frac{4}{4}$ meter, each with a different and progressively faster tempo (ALLEGRO ASSAI, PIÙ ALLEGRO, and finally PRESTISSIMO). This final septet ends at a very fast tempo, that is. So, looking ahead, as I observe indications to go progressively faster, I will, in fact, reassert the pulse of 80 with which the finale began. And 80 whole notes a minute is extremely fast.

The septet begins with an ALLEGRO ASSAI. This is very upbeat, more so than the earlier MOLTO ALLEGRO. I can create quite a rush from the ANDANTE to ALLEGRO ASSAI with a tempo of about 120 half notes per minute. It would be inadvisable to increase speed any more than that at this juncture since this is more than doubling the tempo and the music gets faster still.

This is followed by a PIÙ ALLEGRO, which permits me to push slightly faster on my way to the fastest tempo at the PRESTISSIMO. Note that I am already going quite fast when I get to PIÙ ALLEGRO and, in fact, at faster speeds changes in tempo are less perceptible. So I can nudge the tempo from 120 to about 132 half notes per minute and it barely will be felt.

The increase to PRESTISSIMO results in a tempo so fast that the only way to conduct it is with one beat per measure. With a tempo of 80 whole notes per minute, I have returned to my starting pulse of 80.

Mozart has built six scenes composed of ten sections in which it is possible to maintain a single pulse with only a brief pullback where he directs and, thereafter, use the PIÙ ALLEGRO to reestablish the original pulse. Formulating tempos that follow proportionally from those that went before results in considerable propulsion towards a satisfying—and singable—climax.

Act IV Finale

There is a more problematic intersection in the Act IV finale, however. Mozart begins with Cherubino and the Countess singing at an initial ANDANTE, which works well at about 60 quarter notes per minute. The composer also writes CON UN POCO PIÙ DI MOTO toward the end of the section after the Count, Susanna, and Figaro have joined in. An increase to about 80 quarter notes a minute makes sense at the end of this section.

But the next section presents a dilemma. Example 2.2 illustrates 5 measures. The following LARGHETTO, where only Figaro is singing, is written in $\frac{3}{4}$ meter. The new section is obviously slower than the preceding ANDANTE CON UN POCO PIÙ DI MOTO. But by how much?

A common approach to slowing down is to make a rallentando near the end of the first section. There are three problems with this approach: First, rallentando implies some relaxation, which is inconsistent with what is happening onstage. Second, there is no such indication here, whereas Mozart does supply such indications elsewhere. It is not very Mozartean to slow down gradually like that. It is unsatisfying for those who believe as I do that he knew what he was doing and meant something different. There must be a relationship that he saw readily but is less obvious to most of us. And it was less than obvious to me for many years, I will admit.

Third, and ironically, with a rallentando, we can end up not slowing enough. Most of us hesitate to bend a tempo too much with techniques like rallentando when we have no real justification for doing so and no particular target toward which we are heading. Most of us will slow down

Example 2.2 A tempo change in *Figaro's* Act IV finale (No. 29, from m. 106, p. 545 [vocal 214]).

a bit but not slow down as much as we could and as much as we should if we want the transition to the LARGHETTO to have the maximum effect but still feel seamless.

A clue lies in the way the parts differ. Most instruments playing across this transition continue with quarter and eighth notes. But the violins diverge. They go from eighth and quarter notes to triplet eighths in Example 2.2. If the eighth notes in the violins do not change, the beat is stretched. The violins play three unchanged eighth notes per beat, while those playing quarter notes and duple eighth notes slow down to the new beat. If I take my cue from the violins, that is, the pace is reset from 80 quarter notes (160 eighth notes) to roughly 53 quarter notes per minute (160 ÷ 3). This is not only slower than the ANDANTE CON UN POCO PIÙ DI MOTO section, but even a bit slower than the beginning of that ANDANTE section (60 quarter notes minute). The music is slower but the tempo is related, and the transition is smooth. This creates continuity between the sections and also ends the LARGHETTO at a singable tempo.

The LARGHETTO lasts just a dozen measures, followed by ALLEGRO DI MOLTO, which is a direction to go very fast. If the pace of LARGHETTO was 53 quarter notes in a minute, then this section should be three times faster (or 53 dotted half notes per minute).

My favorite things

The pedal point in the double basses at about half way through the Act II finale and particularly the *f* in the basses just before the melody repeats (m. 453 as discussed above). They are unexpected at that moment, and so apt dramatically as they underline the opposite sentiment in the line the Count is about to sing.

Don Giovanni

People ask me about my favorite opera and that is a hard question to answer. What I can say is that *Don Giovanni* (1787) is one that I have never tired of and one that rewards my revisiting it year-in and year-out. Mozart set Lorenzo Da Ponte's libretto to magnificent and suitably revolutionary music.

Il dissoluto punito, ossia il Don Giovanni is one of many works based on the Don Juan legend, but surely one of the best and most influential.

This work has its full share of Mozartean tone painting. In the Act II sextet, for example, the entrance of trumpets before Ottavio's first line immediately signals the nobility of this character (No. 19). The Bärenreiter score indicates *clarino*, an early valveless trumpet which, like many things Baroque, has enjoyed some resurgence in recent decades. In modern productions with modern orchestras however, the part is usually played by the standard trumpet.

When Anna enters, the key of D major becomes D minor. With this key shift and a soft timpani roll, Mozart suggests clouds over the grieving woman's first phrase. Another example: whenever the ghost of the Commendatore sings in Act II, he is accompanied by trombones. These lower brass instruments are heard nowhere else in the opera, not even where the same themes are sounded in the overture and Act I. They give his spirit an otherworldly power. On the lighter side, the staccato articulation that accompanies Leporello's "Catalogue Aria" positively sparkles, particularly in the woodwinds (No. 4).

There are instances in which singers want to go too slowly in *Don Giovanni*. One is in Zerlina's "Batti, batti" in Act I (No. 12), and another comes in the "La ci darem la mano" duet of Giovanni and Zerlina in the same act (No. 7). If the main body of the music is too slow, performers will want to go much faster at the $\frac{6}{8}$ sections of these numbers, creating an extreme contrast. In fact, they should start a little faster and keep the same pulse at the $\frac{6}{8}$ meter change; the $\frac{6}{8}$ will naturally be faster. In both cases, the result will be more suitable dramatically while the transition itself will be appropriately smooth and subtle. (As discussed at Example 1.1, there is no tempo indication in the manuscript at No. 12's change of time signature [physical p. 193]. The same is true in No. 7 [physical p. 122].)

On the other hand, two arias are frequently performed too fast: "Il mio tesoro" of Don Ottavio and the first part of Leporello's Catalogue Aria. Ottavio's "Il mio tesoro" is marked ANDANTE GRAZIOSO, moderately slow and gracefully (No. 21). Taking it at too lively a pace results in something far from *grazioso*. About 58 half notes per minute is a good tempo, but in this aria, Don Ottavio must sing the word "tornar" across 6 measures. Breathing in the middle of a word is to be avoided, of course. But the alternative is that tenors and conductors sometimes accelerate a lot across those measures in order to get through the word. This is unfortunate and, at the end of the day, I find breathing in the middle of a word preferable to distorting the music.

Leporello's aria is marked ALLEGRO, and singing it too fast is more a matter of misguidance than a symptom of vocal difficulty (No. 4). It should not be confused with other arias in which a baritone is called upon to rattle off lists (for example, the far more purely comic "Largo al factotum" of Rossini's Figaro). A bravura display of the baritone's elocution misses an important part of the drama here. The words are those of calm, laid-back sarcasm, as Leporello tells Donna Elvira of all of Giovanni's many conquests. He is certainly teasing, if not humiliating Elvira, so this should not be very fast. A more moderate tempo also permits a smooth transition into the next ANDANTE CON MOTO section. Taking it quickly, but not at a rousing PRESTO or VIVACE, allows the audience to enjoy the sparkle in the orchestra mentioned above.

While restraint is a good idea in Mozart vocal practice, there is at least one instance in which discreet embellishment is eminently appropriate. It is in Ottavio's aria "Dalla sua pace" (Appendix, No. 10a [vocal No. 10b]. In the score, the melody is simply repeated at the reprise (from m. 36).

Step into My Study . . .

Though the orchestration for the duet "La ci darem la mano" is light, it is masterful (No. 7). Note that Mozart gives Giovanni and the flute the same melody at times and similarly doubles Zerlina's part with the bassoon momentarily. Any garden-variety composer would have doubled Zerlina with a flute and Giovanni with the bassoon. The fact that the accompaniment is sparing allows me to ensure that each pairing stands out for the audience. The oboe and horn enter briefly just for punctuation, perhaps stressing Giovanni's insistence, but the accompaniment throughout is almost entirely in the five string parts. I like to build on Mozart's musical characterization by varying the accompanying figure in the strings. The strings can reasonably use long and smooth bowing for Giovanni the sophisticate, but lighter and staccato articulation to accompany the hesitant Zerlina's "Vorrei, e non vorrei."

Similarly, when Elvira, Anna, and Ottavio enter the finale of Act I, I like to employ a variety of both on-the-string and off-the-string playing where Mozart only gives staccato and legato indications but not instrument-specific articulations. It works beautifully to have very short notes played spiccato in the violins, while the violas slur their longer legato notes (No. 13, m. 173, p. 193 [vocal 121]). For further contrast, the cellos and basses can play their few eighth notes off the string in the opening measures, while playing their quarter notes on the string.

I feel duty bound to share one tip since I can take no credit for it. Gustav Mahler showed it to Bruno Walter who passed it along to my uncle Nicola who shared it with me: In the opening passage of the first scene, there is a pattern that continues under Leporello's text when he enters and sings "Notte e giorno faticar" with the emphasis on "faticar" (No. 1 from m. 10, p. 28 [vocal 8]). I have the violins play the first five soft notes up-bow, and then play down-bow on the louder phrase that ends in the final, full-value quarter note. This decisive difference where Leporello and the violins come together seems just right for Leporello's angry complaint.

More problematic, and unfortunate, are the few instances in which it is possible to lose some instrumental line when a modern orchestra plays *Don Giovanni*. An example is in the finale of Act II, during the confrontation between Giovanni and the Commendatore. There the trumpets, trombones, and timpani can drown out the cellos and double basses. The brass and timpani should play what is written FORTE as forte subito mezzo forte so that the audience can enjoy the fast ascending scales in the lower strings (No. 24, from m. 525, p. 440 [vocal 278]).

Something similar goes on at the beginning of the overture (in mm. 13 and 14). In this instance, I ask the second violins to play mezzo forte, bowing twice per measure for maximum sound. In this manner, we not only hear the main theme in the first violins' syncopated quarter notes, with their irregular accents, but the second violins' accompaniment in sixteenth notes as well.

In this opera however, the greatest challenge to the conductor trying to balance multiple elements is to be found in the finale of Act I, a party at Giovanni's place with musical entertainment (No. 13). This is more than a question of decibels. The scene is an adventurous passage for Mozart's time, really quite astonishing. He sets up three instrumental ensembles, each playing a different dance simultaneously: a minuet, an allemande, and a folie, with all three onstage. While this is ideal, it is not always practical. Nonetheless, it is imperative that at least some players be outside the pit. Playing all three dances from the pit results in chaos. The problem is physics. Simply put, when the groups are physically separated, the three melodies come through. When they are playing from the same location, the listener will find the melodies difficult or impossible to distinguish (e.g., in the MENUETTO, from m. 439, p. 221 [vocal 137]).

Playing one dance in the pit works satisfactorily, and Orchestra I makes sense because it has the greatest number of players. But the second and third groups should be on either side of the stage. If the physical production does not make putting two groups onstage possible, then the best arrangement is to put the two other ensembles in opposite wings of the stage. And, yes, a little bit of amplification may be necessary. Even in a concert, the groups should be separated somehow.

Relationships

A less than obvious tempo relationship is found in *Don Giovanni.* The beginning of the overture contains the same music as is heard at the arrival of the Commendatore near the end of the opera. In Act II, it comes when Giovanni's banquet is in progress and there comes a knock on the door. Giovanni opens the door; the Commendatore calls out "Don Giovanni" a few measures later; and their final confrontation—containing the opera's dynamic high point—begins.

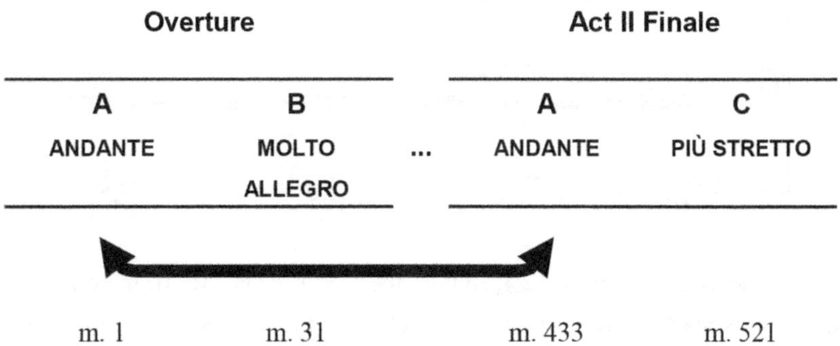

Figure 2.1 Parallels in *Don Giovanni's* Overture and Act II finale (No. 24). The Act II finale ANDANTE is on p. 273 in the vocal score; m. 1 on p. 278 should have the indication PIÙ STRETTO.

Example 2.3A From *Don Giovanni's* overture. The tempo is ANDANTE from the top of the overture.

As described in Figure 2.1, in both the overture and Act II, the music in question is marked ANDANTE and, in each case, the ANDANTE is followed by a faster tempo. If either ANDANTE is too fast, the subsequent faster tempo can turn out to be something unplayable or, more likely, disjointed as the conductor is compelled to slow to an unrelated tempo at the intersection.

Example 2.3B (Continued)

If the problem arises, it is rooted in part in the use of cut time and its running up against conducting habits. The problem is that too many musicians interpret ¢ or ALLA BREVE to mean that a passage should always be conducted in two and, absent enough discipline, they tend to conduct too fast. This lets the beat pattern drive the tempo which is getting things exactly backwards. It happens because beating a "slow two" requires an extra dollop of skill and discipline; it is simply more difficult.

So before I can think about a beat pattern, I must arrive at a tempo. If there were a metronome mark at the top of the overture, this would be easier. Being given no starting tempo however, there is a two-part puzzle: What is the relationship between the ANDANTE and the faster music that follows it in each place? And what, if any, are the implications of the fact that the same theme practically bookends the opera? It is reasonable to think that Mozart is foreshadowing Giovanni's second-act downfall in the overture and that, therefore, the ANDANTE should be pretty similar in the two instances.

Given this premise, the problem becomes finding a tempo for ANDANTE that permits a smooth transition to the next tempo in each instance. So I look at these two intersections for a relationship. For me, the key to finding the right tempo for the ANDANTE is its relationship to the MOLTO ALLEGRO in the overture. How much faster is MOLTO ALLEGRO than ANDANTE in the overture? Having established the tempo of the ANDANTE in the overture, I can transfer my analysis to the tempos of ANDANTE and PIÙ STRETTO in Act II.

In the overture (Example 2.3), the second violins and violas have an accompanying figure in thirty-second notes that begins in m. 23 of the ANDANTE. The violas continue this figure in the first 5 measures of the MOLTO ALLEGRO as eighth notes. For a connection and a smooth transition between the sections, it is reasonable to make the violas' thirty-second notes in the ANDANTE introduction equal to their eighth notes in the subsequent MOLTO ALLEGRO.[3]

The speed of the MOLTO ALLEGRO really cannot be much faster than 144 half notes a minute. A tempo much faster than that is rushed and graceless, and some orchestras will be unable to execute it cleanly. If the new eighth notes are to take the same time as the earlier thirty-seconds, it follows that the ANDANTE introduction must be in the neighborhood of 72 quarter notes a minute. This is unusually slow to conduct in two (i.e., beating twice per measure), which is the inclination when we see cut time. If it is uncomfortable or, more important, not working for the orchestra, a different beat pattern should be employed to hold the tempo where it needs to be.

Taking this introductory music too fast also creates problems in Act II. The introduction plays under the Commendatore, marked ANDANTE. The next indication is PIÙ STRETTO, and doubling the tempo generally works well at that indication, at least in Mozart's music and that of the bel canto school, including Verdi's early works. PIÙ STRETTO is not as fast as the MOLTO ALLEGRO that follows the ANDANTE in the overture, however. So, if I allow 72 half notes to the minute for this PIÙ STRETTO, which is pretty fast, then a pace of 72 quarter notes per minute works perfectly for the introductory ANDANTE.

In summary, my approach to resolving these questions is to look forward and then work backward. I start with a tradition that suggests doubling the tempo at PIÙ STRETTO and maintaining a constant pulse in order to make smooth transitions from section to section. Can it be an accident that when I observe the traditions and work the math, the same music, marked ANDANTE, works beautifully at about the same tempo of 72 quarter notes per minute at opposite ends of the opera? It might be a quirky coincidence—a great trivia question—in some instances. But when the music of the overture reappears at so important a dramatic moment as Giovanni's comeuppance, it seems unlikely to be accidental.

A bit later in No. 24, an ALLEGRO appears and, there, the music can move almost imperceptibly faster (m. 554, p. 444 [vocal 279]). To go much faster would be to leave the concept of *allegro*. And increasing speed only slightly seems right as Giovanni sings "Da qual tremore insolito."

My favorite things

The lyricism in the trumpet of the Act II sextet. It foretells what a composer like Richard Strauss would do in *Der Rosenkavalier* over a century later. (This is identified as the clarino part where Don Antonio enters in No. 19, at m. 28, p. 312 [vocal 189].)

Die Zauberflöte

There are few if any other works that portray childlike wonder in quite the way that *Die Zauberflöte* (1791) does. Childlike simplicity in the theater is not child's play, however. This opera in particular requires a great deal of planning to keep it flowing. It can rather easily bog down. First, since the two-act work can run almost three and a half hours, most North American companies do substantial cutting in the dialogue. The first things to go are usually some racism and misogyny in Emanuel Schikaneder's libretto that have not aged nearly as well as have the timeless fable of love triumphant and the sublime music Mozart wrote.

Some parts are a bit harder to cast than others. The Queen of the Night sings two of the highest and most difficult arias in the standard operatic repertory (Nos. 4 and 14). It is a relatively short role but it is all fireworks and there is no place to hide any vocal deficiencies. Sarastro requires a true bass, with strong low notes. The Three Spirits are called *Knäbchen* (boys of about ten to twelve years of age), but finding three excellent boys of this age, one soprano and two altos, is often very difficult outside of the biggest cities. Moreover, their extended scene with Pamina at the beginning of the finale of Act II is difficult to sing. Using young women for the Three Spirits is sometimes necessary to ensure the best results, just as we sometimes use a woman to sing the Shepherd Boy's aria in Act III of Puccini's *Tosca*.

The music is so consistent with the childlike simplicity of the story that I discourage adding ornaments and interpolating high notes. Note the difference between the fireworks of the Queen of the Night and the heroine Pamina's heartfelt and straightforward melodies. More of the music follows Pamina's lead than that of the Queen of the Night. That said, there is a tradition that Sarastro sing an optional low note on his last two words in "In diesen heil'gen Hallen" and this is acceptable as it does no great violence to the music or the mood (No. 15 [vocal p. 108]).

However, another tradition lingers around Pamina's aria, "Ach, ich fühl's," in which singers perform it far more slowly than seems consistent with her age or character (No. 17). It is an ANDANTE written in the same meter as Susanna's "Deh vieni non tardar" (*Le nozze di Figaro*, No. 28). Conventionally, though, Pamina's ANDANTE is taken more than twice as slowly as Susanna's. The scholarship that today informs so much performance of the music of Mozart and earlier composers seems to have passed Pamina by. There is no particular reason that Pamina's music seems simply stuck in the much slower "traditional" tempos that prevailed during the first half of the twentieth century.

In addition to many gorgeous ensembles and virtuoso showpieces, the score is a study in imaginative and evocative orchestration. In two instances, these choices support important themes, making them all the more salient. If not quite motives in the Wagnerian sense, they are reprised to excellent dramatic effect: First, Mozart wrote a very simple pan flute part for Papageno to perform onstage; it is introduced at his entrance (No. 2) and reappears frequently. The interplay between the flute in the pit, representing Tamino's flute, and Papageno's pan flute is particularly charming (No. 8, m. 207, p. 149 [vocal 63]).

Second, the trombones add solemnity to the motive of the priests, both at the beginning of the overture and in the opening of Act II (No. 9, from ADAGIO, p. 193 [vocal 84]). This is true for modern audiences but even truer for Mozart's since the trombone was not part of the Classical orchestra but was commonly heard in liturgical music. For them, the association with religion was inescapable.

The glockenspiel has an honored place in this opera. The part requires a keyboard glockenspiel in the pit, but this is not very commonly available so many companies substitute a celesta. The celesta is admittedly the closest relative to the glockenspiel, but it produces a softer and subtler sound that is less like bells. All other things being equal, it is better to get a good sampler into the pit to produce a bell-like sound than to substitute the celesta.

Getting this right is worth the effort. The glockenspiel portrays Papageno's magic bells. They hypnotize Monostatos's henchmen in Act I (No. 8 from m. 293, p. 157 [vocal 68]). They also play a big role in bringing Papagena to him in Act II where his aria is introduced by the glockenspiel with a statement, a variation, and a second variation that includes magic-invoking filigree (No. 20). The bell-like sound of the glock really makes a difference.

Step into My Study . . .

After I know that I have a production and singers that will permit stage magic, my first concern is pacing. Taking it too fast can cheapen this elegant music; but when so much elegant and gentle music is too slow, the audience may be put to sleep. It is imperative that in such a long opera, with spoken dialogue, each jewel-like musical number stop time but that the whole not be permitted to bog down. Yet, we have no precise knowledge of the tempo Mozart took on opening night. We have to depend on our own study, judgment, and informed taste in coming up with a game plan for presenting this masterpiece to our audiences.

Nowhere is this more important than in the long finales. The components of each finale are interrelated, but both finales are more flexible than the two in *Figaro*. In the case of the Act II *Figaro* finale, for example, the drama is continuous. It all takes place in one room and people enter and exit as the musical and dramatic conversations dovetail. It is a realistic sequence of scenes occurring in real time. In fact, at this point *Figaro* is a domestic farce, and a farce needs to be tight and seamless indeed or else it falls very flat.

By contrast, during the finales of *Die Zauberflöte*, the characters are moving in space and time. It is more "open" dramatically and this calls for a little more flexibility about the tempo relationships. Let it be said, however, that seamlessness is definitely an ideal to reach for in this opera. As a rule, I will not make adjustments as sudden as when Figaro momentarily stops the action in the Act II finale of *Figaro*. They will be subtler. They will also be more numerous.

An unusually large proportion of the first scene of the Act I finale (No. 8) is given to recitative, first Tamino's, then a dialogue between Tamino and the Priest, and then another solo by Tamino. This whole sequence is both forward looking, anticipating some of the musical dialogues of Wagner, but also backward looking to the music of Gluck and even Monteverdi. And recitative, approximating speech, is traditionally performed in a freer manner than arias and ensembles.

The sequence of recitatives presents a challenge because it is so long. I pay attention to the words in a search for dramatic tension and clues about how I might build toward a climax at PRESTO (No. 8, m. 518, p. 181 [vocal 79]). First, it is reasonable to contrast the overall impetuosity of Tamino with the more restrained demeanor of the Priest. In addition, while the Priest's tempo is generally slower than Tamino's, a certain urgency is nonetheless implied in some of his words as, for example, when he tells Tamino to stay and explain himself with "Wenn du dein Leben liebst . . ." (mm. 111–112, p. 140 [vocal 58]). In that same middle section there are also syncopations that, if taken too slowly, fail to express Tamino's anxiety and the conflict between his respect for what the Priest is saying and his desire to free Pamina. An example of this syncopation may be found beginning at m. 102, for example.

So extended recitative is at the heart of the Act I finale, and going too slowly can be a mistake. In the somewhat longer and more complicated Act II finale, going too slowly can be close to fatal. A chorale with Tamino and the two Armored Men holds the secret to the structure. It is based on Bach's "Ach Gott, vom Himmel sieh' darein." (See the First Armored Man's line at m. 206 of No. 21, p. 288 [vocal 136]. It should be noted, however, that scholars differ on whether Mozart was paying direct homage to Bach or whether they were both basing their work on what was a well-known hymn with a text by Martin Luther.)

Though marked ADAGIO, it should be performed at about 48 to 50 half notes per minute; and further, it should be conducted alla breve—with two beats per measure. This is the speed of most chorales and will permit us to maintain a still-dignified tempo at the following ALLEGRETTO. If the audience has trouble discerning a melody, the chorale is too slow and the finale will seem interminable.

Table 2.2 outlines the Act II finale's tempo changes, which are anchored, first, in the tempo of the Chorale (about 48 half notes per minute). Another anchoring tempo is the ALLEGRO that includes a glockenspiel solo and ends with a duet at the end of the second garden scene (Scene 29). Determining the tempo for that ALLEGRO requires no reference to anything external to the opera such as a recognized form like a chorale. I start my thinking with 112 half notes per minute in mind, but note that this tempo is dependent on the specific singers and staging. So Table 2.2 eschews specific metronome indications and only gives relationships.

Table 2.2 Act II finale, *Die Zauberflöte* (No. 21).

Scene	At...	Page*	Meter/Tempo	Suggestion
26	m. 1, *Garden: Three Spirits*	267 (125)	2/2 ANDANTE	
27	m. 45, + *Pamina*	272 (127)		
	m. 94	277 (131)	3/4 ALLEGRO	
28	m. 190, *Mountains: Tamino, Two Armored Men*	287 (135)	**2/2 ADAGIO**	**Roughly the tempo of a chorale.**
	m. 247 + *Pamina*	295 (138)		
	m. 249	295 (138)	2/2 ALLEGRETTO	
	m. 278	299 (141)	3/4 ANDANTE	
	m. 362, March	304 (144)	4/4 ADAGIO	Half speed.
	m. 389, + *Chorus*	308 (146)	4/4 ALLEGRO	
29	m. 413, *Garden: Papageno*	314 (148)	6/8 ALLEGRO	♪ = ♪
	m. 533	323 (153)	6/8 ANDANTE	Somewhat slower.
	m. 543, + *Three Spirits*	324 (153)	**2/2 ALLEGRETTO**	**Close to 𝅗𝅥 = ♩.**
	m. 576, glockenspiel solo m. 613-615, *Spirits leave* m. 626, + *Papagena*	329 (155) 331 (156) 332 (157)	2/2 ALLEGRO	𝅗𝅥 = ♩
30	m. 745, *Monostatos, Queen, Ladies*	342 (164)	4/4 PIÙ MODERATO	Somewhat slower.
	m. 824 m. 826	354 (169)	RECITATIVE MAESTOSO	
	m. 828, *Chorus and others*	355 (169)	4/4 ANDANTE	
	m. 846	358 (170)	2/4 ALLEGRO	Twice as fast.

* Vocal score page in parentheses.

Based upon a couple of target tempos (boldface in Table 2.2), I build a plan in which I make every effort to make smooth transitions while on the lookout for opportunities to reinforce the drama onstage with subtle adjustments. The finale is flexible for the same reasons that the Act I finale is: it is "open" dramatically. In fact, multiple story lines come to their conclusions in multiple locations. (It is worth mentioning that the unity of this finale also rests on an harmonic architecture, an analysis well worth the effort but beyond the scope of this book.)

The finale takes place in three locations: the garden, the mountains, back in the garden, and then in the temple. Since the opening ANDANTE (in the garden) must be at least a little faster than an ADAGIO—and the chorale should be one of the slowest and most majestic sections of the finale—I aim for a Scene 26 opening ANDANTE that is a bit faster than the ADAGIO that follows. Toward the end of the ADAGIO section, I slow a bit more for one measure to facilitate doubling the speed at the ALLEGRETTO that comes next. I do not impose rubato at an intersection between two tempos, but since Pamina stops Tamino with her words from offstage, taking her line at an altered tempo that facilitates the next tempo change is reasonable. So, up to and including the ALLEGRETTO in Scene 28, I may reasonably be said to have a relatively constant pulse, or for purists, at least a tempo theme based on the ADAGIO chorale.

When Pamina enters and Tamino rapturously recognizes her at the ANDANTE of Scene 28, a new mood is introduced. Given the dramatic turn, it is fair to allow some shift in the pulse, but this ANDANTE (conducted in three) connects seamlessly to the subsequent ADAGIO by way of a constant pulse (twice as slow). There is another shift in mood when the chorus praises the two lovers, ending the section in the mountains (ALLEGRO). This too may reasonably have a distinct pulse, but it should not get too fast. (I conduct it in four.)

The new scene in the garden (Scene 29) begins ALLEGRO, like the final section in the mountains, but with a new meter $\frac{6}{8}$. If I impose a constant pulse at this juncture, the speed-up at the new meter will seem a bit excessive. If I keep the eighth note constant on the other hand, the result will be a completely seamless, virtually cinematic transition between the mountains and the second scene in the garden.

Having established the speed of the opening ALLEGRO in the second garden scene, however, I am not out of the woods, as it were. With the beginning ALLEGRO and the next ANDANTE both bearing a time signature of $\frac{6}{8}$ (and both conducted in two), I do not have much to go on in deciding how much slower the ANDANTE in the garden should be. However, what I do know is that Papageno has just tried playing his pan flute to summon Papagena, to no avail, and decided that there is no reason to go on living. His despair (short-lived) will give way to the energetic (and successful) efforts of the Three Spirits to get him to soldier on. So, at the entrance of the Three

Spirits (the ALLEGRETTO of Scene 29) a change in pulse is in keeping with Papageno's melodrama. However, such a change should not be excessive. If the new half note is roughly equal to the preceding dotted quarter note, the shift in mood is felt yet continuity is maintained.

The last section in the second garden scene includes the magical glockenspiel solo and ends with a reunion and duet between Papagena and Papageno. An exact doubling of the tempo supplies a surge of joy and energy that is thoroughly apt for this ALLEGRO section.

The finale ends with Scene 30 in the temple. At the beginning of this three-section scene, the indication is simply PIÙ MODERATO with no change in time signature. Once again, I am on my own as to how much to moderate the speed. Here, I simply go with my judgment of what PIÙ MODERATO, a comparative statement, must mean following an ALLEGRO, at this tempo, and in consideration of a complete dramatic break. (Some scores indicate a change to $\frac{2}{2}$ which does not change our tempo analysis and should be conducted alla breve.)

In a sense however, Scene 30 is two scenes: Monostatos, the Queen of the Night, and her Ladies emerge and sing the first section. The loudest moment in this finale—and arguably in the opera—should come when they are being driven away (at about m. 807, p. 351 [vocal 168]).

Then after they disappear, there are 2 measures of recitative and two marked MAESTOSO, meaning that there is little connection or relationship between the PIÙ MODERATO section and the rest of the finale. In fact, the recitative may or may not even follow directly in real time.

On the other hand, the final two sections of the opera have no rest or recitative between them. As Table 2.2 indicates, the ANDANTE followed by ALLEGRO should be connected with a constant pulse for the chorus's final exclamation.

My favorite things

The Act I quintet, especially the simple, yet magical, descending staccato scales in the oboes, bassoons, and violins at "Silberglökchen, Zauberflöten" (No. 5, from m. 185, p. 105 [vocal 42]).

Chapter 3

Bel Canto Opera

Music historians call Italian opera from about 1810 to 1840 the school of *bel canto*—literally, beautiful singing. The three composers most often associated with the bel canto school are Gioachino Rossini, Gaetano Donizetti, and Vincenzo Bellini. Some of Giuseppe Verdi's early- and middle-period operas (through *Il trovatore* in 1853) qualify as bel canto operas as well.

The works of the bel canto school suffer from misguided tradition and the kind of bad cuts, indifferent execution, and corner cutting that all too often can be expected to result from over-performance. It is said that Arturo Toscanini eschewed conducting some of the most beloved of these operas (*Il barbiere di Siviglia* and *Lucia di Lammermoor*, in particular) because they had become so extremely laden with bad ideas that had become tradition.

Even when they are badly abused, however, the bel canto operas are still audience pleasers. Some attention to detail and tender loving care will make a world of difference for both our audiences and ourselves. In this regard, I am reminded of Mark Twain's dictum: "Always do right. This will gratify some people and astonish the rest."[1]

Each bel canto composer has his own strengths: Bellini was a master melodist. As with Franz Schubert, or even Anton Bruckner, one could say that melody, along with the somewhat more adventurous harmonic architecture on which his melodies rest, was his forte more than development and elaboration of themes or rhythmic structure. Rossini, on the other hand, demonstrates a greater talent for development. Donizetti combines a bit of each.

The three also have their own idiosyncrasies. All things being equal, an ALLEGRO in Bellini is not as fast as in Donizetti, which is not as fast as a Rossinian ALLEGRO. In addition, the comic works of Rossini tend to be quicker than the dramas like *Semiramide* or, especially, *Guillaume Tell.* Rossini is always a high-energy composer, however.

Vocalism

Common to the music of all of these composers is, of course, embellishment. The Italian style of "beautiful singing" is about more than such variations in the vocal line, and embellishment was practiced beyond Italy and for longer than a few decades. However, Italian composers treated singers as collaborators long after composers elsewhere were writing down their intentions with the expectation that performers would reproduce their notation faithfully.[2] Later in this period, we begin to see more decoration written out. Verdi even felt compelled to add a caution against improvising to his score at times (for example, in *Rigoletto*, Act III, No. 13, m. 13 [vocal No. 17, m. 20], and *Otello*, Act IV, m. 6 before GG).

The informed singer should know what the bel canto composers generally expected with respect to grace notes and appoggiaturas. All of the caveats mentioned in Chapter 2 apply here, however, and then some. This is in part because there is proportionately less scholarship available to us with respect to the music of the bel canto composers than with respect to Mozart's. With these composers, we simply have more history and more stylistic variety over several decades between Rossini's first operas and Verdi's early works.

As fewer scholars hoe a much bigger and more diverse field, we workaday performers lean in part on tradition handed down to us by our elders, including guidance about taste.

Elders? I guess that's my cue.

First, acciaccaturas—those shortest possible notes sung before the beat—are a bit more common in bel canto music than in Mozart's. We also encounter the more melodic appoggiaturas appropriate in Mozart's music (sung on the beat, in rhythm) in bel canto music. For instance, an appoggiatura would be appropriate in Cenerentola's heartfelt pleading in "Signor . . . in casa, in casa di quel Principe" (Act I of *La Cenerentola*, No. 5, p. 230 [vocal 93]). But more grace notes should be acciaccaturas. An example is in Ernesto's self-pitying farewell in Act II, Scene 1, of *Don Pasquale* (No. 5, from m. 6 of [3]).

Although appoggiaturas indicated by grace notes are less common in bel canto music than in Mozart's, the unwritten appoggiatura is called for even more frequently. That is, the pitch is changed when two notes of the same pitch occur, usually at the end of a phrase. This choice is based, in part, on the pattern of stresses in the syllables of the poetry. We traditionally hear such an appoggiatura when Count Almaviva first enters in Rossini's *Il barbiere di Siviglia*, for example, with "Ebben! gli amici" (p. 27 [vocal 13]). But as in Mozartean style, while this is a common and stylistically appropriate device, we cannot assume that every pair of identical notes must be changed.

Sometimes variations and embellishments are subtle, an occasional appoggiatura perhaps; but many longer passages are decorated more extensively. From Mozart's time through Verdi's middle period, one or more of an opera's principal characters would have been expected to deliver an extra jolt of excitement in a cabaletta, specifically in its repeat, which might also be followed by a coda. It is here that we encounter the interpolated pyrotechnics of legend.[3]

While some scores may contain the composer's own ideas about varying the vocal line, when we come across a repeat in a bel canto cabaletta and find it to be identical to the music as first stated, we may safely assume that variations were expected and are appropriate.

On the podium, there is a basic range of tempo that works very well for the majority of cabalettas. Just as dances like waltzes or minuets are taken at somewhat consistent speeds, most cabalettas fall within a range of roughly 104 to 116 quarter notes per minute. Naturally, it is impossible to prescribe a tempo that works for every cabaletta in every circumstance, but a sampling that illustrates this principle is listed below. All of these work well somewhere within this range:

Donna Anna in Act II of Mozart's *Don Giovanni*
Almaviva in Act I of Rossini's *Il barbiere di Siviglia*
Cenerentola at the end of Rossini's *La Cenerentola*
Romeo in Act I of Bellini's *I Capuleti e i Montecchi*
Norma, in Act I of Bellini's *Norma*
Amina at the end of Bellini's *La sonnambula*
Lucia in Act I of Donizetti's *Lucia di Lammermoor*
Ernesto in Act II of Donizetti's *Don Pasquale*
Abigaille in Act II of Verdi's *Nabucco*
Leonora in Act I of Verdi's *Il trovatore*

Speeding through these cabalettas drains them of their romantic flavor and limits what a singer might do with them. The desire to drag a tempo much slower is equally misguided. Doing so is sometimes described as romantic when it is really just exaggerated and self-indulgent.

Rather than wallowing in obvious distortions of what is on the printed page, it is better to look for opportunities for subtle rubato and varied articulation in this music. Without a bit of both—at any tempo—we risk devolving into mechanical singing on the stage or an oom-pah band in the pit. Executing these subtler strategies appropriately depends on deep contemplation of the notation and the text as well as an appreciation of performing conditions and conventions in the first half of the nineteen century. It also makes for memorable performances.

Once we have our apt dramatic interpretation along with our tasteful and stylistically appropriate vocal fireworks ready to go, we must sometimes consider an issue that hangs over many of the bel canto operas in a manner that we do not encounter in other corners of the repertory. It arises at the intersection of our much-prized high notes and the limits of the human vocal cords and eardrums. We face pitch issues because some numbers were originally in higher keys that were lowered a long time ago, probably to allow for interpolated high notes. Recent fashion requires more faithful productions. So, there is a trend toward restoring the original key of some numbers.

There are trade-offs in raising pitch, however, because we may safely assume that today's orchestra is tuning a semitone or even a whole tone higher than the orchestras did when the bel canto works were first performed. Pitch is something that creeps up gradually and reflects a bias toward brighter sound among instrumentalists, until singers and their producers have to draw a line in the sand. The Baroque specialists of our time finally chose to simply tune the orchestra down.[4]

Today, most orchestras in North America tune to an A that equals 440 Hz, and in music from Mozart on, we probably will not see tuning down any time soon. So certain interpolated high notes, taken into the original, higher key, are simply ill advised. A sustained E-flat when well sung is thrilling, and it is already higher than it was in the first half of the nineteenth century. But if we restore the original key of *Lucia's* mad scene, for example, and follow tradition, that E-flat becomes a loud high F sustained for several measures. Even if well produced, in today's tuning this is almost painful to most of the music-loving public in this kind of music. Note that this is a matter of context. Such stratospheric high notes in a jazz trumpet may be exciting, but would be harsh and wrong in bel canto.

So the decision to restore the original key is not a simple one. Let it be said, however, that if planned embellishments require transposing down, they may be prime candidates for modification anyway. In a work like *Lucia*, we often hear the same variations from the 1940s and 1950s. While there is nothing intrinsically wrong with these variations, they can seem old fashioned, so there is good reason to reconsider them. Many performers forget that the embellishments were highly individual. For me, it is always a joy to fashion cadenzas and variations to suit a singer's strengths. Such strengths might be breath versus agility, higher high notes versus better low notes, and so on. They all suggest different variations and embellishments.

Alas, the popularity and familiarity of some of these operas makes the decision to present new embellishments less than simple. When the audience expects certain variations or high notes and they are eliminated, the conductor can perhaps let any grumbling roll off his back. While I do sympathize with the singer considering such trade-offs, my own recommendation will always be to concern ourselves, above all, with delivering the best performance possible.

The Orchestra

It should be noted that musical instruments were still evolving during the period when much of our standard repertory was written and even continued evolving into the twentieth century. This means that instruments in bel canto scores may have had sonorities and capabilities different from those of instruments going by the same names in today's orchestras. Bel canto trombones, especially, were often valve instruments that produced a lighter sound than the slide instruments now being used.

When faced with a lot of brass in these scores, I often find it advisable to ask the players to lighten the sound relative to the dynamics indicated. The need to adjust the dynamics in the brass is rare in Rossini, occasional in Donizetti, but fairly common in Bellini.

There is also a tuning problem in the timpani in bel canto scores. At the time, the only way to change pitch was retuning by hand. With modern pedal timpani, the instrument can modulate to a new note immediately. In Bellini and early Verdi especially, the composers sometimes left the timpani playing in one key after the orchestra had modulated to another. If the key is closely related, as in a modulation from C to G or C to A minor, the result is usually not noticeable. However, in some works, like *Norma*, a bit too much dissonance can result.

Admittedly, Bellini is known for adventurous harmony, but was he *that* adventurous? The problem also crops up in the music of the younger Verdi, who represents the next generation. On the other hand, the problem is rare in the music of Rossini, who used the timpani less than Bellini did, and Donizetti, whose music has fewer modulations than Bellini's.

In any case, today's audience hears something wrong, and so do the players. Under such circumstances, adjustments are needed in some of the works of this era to take advantage of the capabilities of today's instruments. In the biggest companies, the timpani parts have been rewritten. But the conductor faced with rented parts needs to be alert to this problem.

Instrument evolution can also be a reason for substituting one instrument for another. For example, in Rossini's *La Cenerentola*, where the composer calls for a single trombone playing softly and quickly, a smaller slide instrument or even the valved bass trumpet may be substituted successfully. There are similar possibilities in some of Donizetti's works, as discussed below. (It is always an extra treat for me when a musician shows up to rehearsals with an older instrument based on his or her knowledge of the relevant history.)

As suggested earlier and as in Mozart's music, bel canto music can sometimes seem a little oom-pah if the conductor does not employ a bit of rubato and look for the line that lies at the heart of any given section and should be set in relief. On the other hand, the scores under discussion in this chapter are more specific about phrasing and articulation in the orchestra, so any adjustments should be subtle and follow whatever model the composer has already set. Now and then, I find an opportunity to add some expression from the podium. The first violins might imitate a donkey's braying, for example, in *La Cenerentola*. The opportunity is there after Magnifico sings "Ma quel asino son io" in his first aria, which appears in Act I, No. 2. Specifically, they might play harmonics up an octave on their first and third eighth notes beginning at m. 7 before 29 (p. 142 [vocal 53]). I find it entirely in keeping with Rossini's style of orchestration.

In an altogether different spirit, the violas may introduce a subtle whine by playing near (but not at) the bridge as the onlookers react with horror to the heroine's breakdown in the final act of *Lucia di Lammermoor* (No. 14, 31, p. 438 [vocal 196]). But "subtle" is the key word; we are not looking for horror film sound effects here.

My assertion that these scores come with additional—and welcome—specificity comes with caveats, however. Problems arise out of multiple versions written for different theaters, copyists' errors, and editorial indiscretion. Since this book cannot begin to list all errata and disputed passages, I will point to three by way of example. First there is a very significant tempo question in the score of *Il barbiere di Siviglia*, discussed at length below.

Second, there is what must be a copyist's error at the beginning of *Lucia's* Act I cavatina "Regnava nel silenzio," in which measures marked

ARCO and LEGATO in the manuscript (sixtieth page of music) turn up as PIZZICATO (No. 3, m. 3 of the LARGHETTO [m. 2 before [25]], p. 82 [vocal 32]).

Third, there is an anomaly in the Adalgisa-Pollione duet of Act I, Scene 6, in *Norma*. At PIÙ MODERATO ASSAI, the strings have an indication of PIZZICATO under Pollione's "Vieni in Roma, ah vieni o cara" (p. 185 [vocal 104]). But the parallel music about 67 measures later (p. 191 [vocal 107]) with the words "Qui, domani all'ora istessa," marked PRIMO TEMPO) has no such indication. Tradition has the strings playing pizz, which makes some musical sense. There is room to question, however. Did Bellini mean for this to sound different? More like the accented arco playing at PIÙ MOSSO a couple of dozen measures earlier? Happily, manuscripts indicate a repeat quite clearly, so the absence of a pizz indication is "just" an omission in the scores we have all been using for many years. (The Garland autograph has the repeat on leaf 98 recto; the Florence manuscript available for download has the repeat written out with pizz beginning on physical p. 331.)

The bottom line is that we can never stop thinking critically and asking questions about what is in these pages and what is not.

Structure

A good performance depends on an understanding that there is, indeed, a structure and a set of interrelationships among the tempos, notwithstanding the flexibility that is also required in bel canto music. Through this period, maintaining a constant pulse should be the default approach between adjacent sections of music. In addition, there is one specific relationship that we may expect to see when we look at virtually any of the bel canto operas and, in particular, in their grand and exciting finales: It is a doubling of the tempo at a stretto.

The word *stretto* comes from the Italian word for tight or narrow, and both "stretto" and "stretta" are correct as the past participle of *stringere*. It may be used in three different ways in music. Most musicians learn early on that it refers to a part of some fugues in which the music appears to accelerate because the voices begin to follow each other and overlap more quickly than previously established. In later nineteenth century music, STRETTO can mean the same as STRINGENDO, a squeezing or gradual quickening of the pace. But in Mozart through middle Verdi, it is a direction to roughly double the speed. Often, an exact doubling as measured by the metronome works, but the right speed is always at least close to double in this music.

It may help to remember that much of this music was often performed without a conductor. The conducting profession was just emerging in Italy during Verdi's career and emerging at different rates in different venues. A simple doubling of the tempo makes a lot of sense in an orchestra that is following a violinist or keyboardist who is trying to provide some kind of leadership while also being occupied with playing an instrument. A very simple shift like doubling the tempo cannot guarantee perfect ensemble, but it can help. In any event, the kind of flexibility and continuous, fine adjustments so essential in the music of Giacomo Puccini or Richard Wagner would be unimaginable without the modern conductor.

Some hold that there is another Italian tradition of doubling the tempo in the last couple of measures of a musical number. Those who endorse it describe it as often done. This is at least dubious, and I am confident that whatever its origin, it has not been often done in at least the past hundred years or so. It is something that can work from time to time (in my experience, for example, at the end of the overture to Bellini's *I Capuleti e i Montecchi*). That said, I would urge any conductor to use this technique sparingly and only when it seems extremely compelling based on how effectively the music is working in any given instance, rather than adopting it as a routine practice because of some presumed imprimatur—or prescription—of tradition.

The Act II finale of Mozart's *Don Giovanni* contains a section marked PIÙ STRETTO and, as a rule, we hear the tempo doubled at that point (No. 24, m. 521 [vocal p. 278, m. 1]). In this chapter, we will examine three passages in the bel canto literature in which the same doubling of the tempo works spectacularly: One is at LA STRETTA in the Act I finale of Rossini's *Il barbiere di Siviglia*. Another is after Romeo's aria and cabaletta in Act I of Bellini's *I Capuleti e i Montecchi*. And the third is at VIVACE in the Act II finale of *Lucia di Lammermoor*.

The simple explanation for why this tradition is so often not observed is that a conductor starts the preceding section too fast and really cannot go twice as fast at the STRETTO. We may hear an abrupt slow-down shortly before the STRETTO in order to be able to speed up again at the STRETTO itself. In a less ad hoc manner, some will make small but meaningful adjustments ahead of time in order to get through a STRETTO section at a chosen speed. Doing this may present something less shapeless to the audience, but it is also less interesting. In any case, it is something other than what is in the score.

This begs the question of why the dilemma arises in the first place, however. It is difficult to come up with an explanation other than a belief that flexibility is more important in bel canto music than structure, that there are no relationships to analyze and execute and that, therefore, anything goes. The animating belief then becomes a self-fulfilling prophecy: What the audience hears is something disjointed, something with no apparent structure and stripped of its forward thrust.

Rossini: *Il Barbiere di Siviglia*

> Therefore meter, the essential part of music, without which melody is incomprehensible and harmony falls into disorder, is ignored and violated by singers. They astound rather than move the public . . .
>
> —Gioachino Rossini[5]

Gioachino Rossini wrote a lot of great music in a career of relatively short duration (by his own choosing). He also wrote in diverse styles. For a long time he was known only for his admittedly great comedies, at least in North America. His serious and heroic works have gotten a bit more play in recent years, although he still holds the distinction of having written the work of the bel canto school most deserving of greater attention. This is his last opera, *Guillaume Tell.*

His *Il barbiere di Siviglia* (1816) is probably the most popular and often-performed comedy in opera. The industrious Figaro enters singing one of the most famous arias in the repertory, his "Largo al factotum." And Rosina—almost universally referred to as the "spunky" Rosina—has another in "Una voce poco fa." The purely musical issues in this opera are similar to those we encounter in Mozart's work. Everything has to sound crystalline and easy. The music is not tremendously tricky, as in Richard Strauss's works, but virtually every note is exposed. It has been said that comedy is hard. Actually, it is fragile; bad execution will shatter the mood in a heartbeat, and timing is everything.

Barbiere is usually performed with cuts, and most of the standard cuts occur in the recitatives. Cuts in recitative make sense in comedies being performed in a foreign language, even if a work is not very long. Otherwise, the most substantial musical cut that is virtually always made is the tenor's final aria. In fact, I have performed it in only one production. There is good reason to cut this aria. It was written for an opera originally named *Almaviva* when Rossini felt he could not use the current title, which belonged to Giovanni Paisiello's earlier and very successful opera. The story is effectively over when Count Almaviva launches into this very long three-part piece: introduction-aria-cabaletta. It also became *La Cenerentola's* final showpiece, "Non più mesta." Therefore, this is not music that is unjustly neglected or hidden from the opera-loving public; Rossini himself recycled it relatively quickly.

Great as *Barbiere* is, its very popularity, ubiquity, and rich humor in both the stage action and the music present their own set of problems. When the audience does not speak the language, comedy tends to broaden to the point of burlesque over time, complete with both vocal and dramatic exaggeration. With performances of a work scheduled regularly, year-in and year-out for about two centuries, performers may be driven to try too hard to come up with something new and different (always wonderful, except when it is not).

Bartolo's Act I aria is a case in point (beginning at ANDANTE MAESTOSO, p. 155 [vocal 108]). It is not unusual for a bass to want to change the tempo repeatedly. This is self-indulgent to the point of distracting and too clownish to accompany Bartolo's display of self-importance. It also blunts the impact of doubling the tempo at the ALLEGRO VIVACE after about 50 measures. A steady beat works beautifully and moves the story forward.

Similarly, certain "traditional" excesses in Figaro's "Largo al factotum" and Basilio's "La calunnia" should be forgotten. For example, Figaro's falsetto singing in the "Largo" is too buffoonish and not at all consonant with the style of the period. At best, the whine without any dramatic context that we are treated to in many a "Largo" adds nothing. There is a place for exaggeration in comic music, and a parlando line may be justified at times. But this is still opera, and bel canto opera at that.

Demand for Rosinas has always been high. But, for a time, supply was lower than it is today because relatively few mezzo-sopranos claimed the part that was written for them. Prior to Ricordi's 1969 critical edition of the opera, scores even supplied two different Rosina lines. One caveat for those casting this part is that Berta should be sung by the contrasting voice type; i.e., with a mezzo Rosina, a soprano Berta will serve best in the ensembles.

While any coloratura with the vocal agility and stage presence for Rosina will be a delight, the traditional variations that date back to singers such as Lily Pons are all wrong for the mezzo-sopranos who now dominate the world's stages in this role. Happily, as more and more mezzo-sopranos aspire to the coloratura repertory, new traditions are evolving. This is one role in which audiences get treated to a range of variations relatively routinely.

I would ask Rosinas of all kinds to forget one tradition: that of interpolating a virtuoso showpiece into the Act II lesson scene (at MAESTOSO p. 294 [vocal 212]). Adding external virtuoso music can make plenty of sense in other works, notably those with party scenes. But in replacing what Rossini wrote for this lesson scene, we toss out some of the composer's wit. First, the song he wrote is a parody of *opera seria* of his own time or a little earlier. Second, it is rather incongruously lugubrious for the spirited and attractive Rosina (MAESTOSO!). Also, a great showpiece contradicts Bartolo's complaint that this is tiresome music, far inferior to the even earlier music of his time. Last, Rossini has Rosina alternate between her pseudo-Baroque lesson song and SOTTO VOCE patter with Almaviva-Lindoro whenever Bartolo appears to doze. Back and forth she goes between the two styles to great comic effect. The tedious lesson song makes sense and sets up this contrast as well.

Tired musical jokes are also commonplace in often-heard comedies. Cadences lead easily to unrelated music. Thus, in their "Largo" cadenzas, baritones have even made reference to the 1930s popular song "Granada." But, without a doubt, one person's tired is another person's hilarious, so every interpolation of unrelated music cannot be ruled out in a comedy. In judging such a quote, we need to consider its subtlety and potential for distraction. Moreover, such references should strike our audience as clever, original, and apropos.

In fact, in operas of this type, there is a long tradition of including short quotes of famous music, often an homage to an earlier composer, at the end of the harpsichord's phrases in "dry" recitative. These are subtle because they are played by the harpsichord and they go by very quickly. If there is a need to interpolate anything at all in *Barbiere*, this longstanding tradition can produce many intellectually satisfying jokes that fill the bill. Even when listeners know they have heard such a completely unpredictable quote but cannot quite identify it, it brings enjoyment and serves as a great conversation-starter.

In my youth, I was quite doctrinaire about not introducing anachronisms. This limits the field to choose from, but not unduly. For example, an opportunity arises near the end of *Barbiere*, when Bartolo complains that Basilio has betrayed him by signing as a witness to the wedding of the young lovers. After the word "testimonio" (p. 420 [vocal 309]), a quote from the Queen of the Night's big vengeance aria from Mozart's *Die Zauberflöte* is apropos. However, I have also mellowed on the subject of anachronisms in comedy. Therefore, I find that a snippet from Carmen's "Habañera" fits nicely into Act I of *Barbiere*. Remember that Figaro and Almaviva have met unexpectedly on a street in Seville. The moment for the quote occurs after Figaro asks Almaviva what he is doing there and Almaviva says he will explain (after the word "spiego," that is, p. 75 [vocal 44]).

Rossini needs little help in making us laugh, however. He achieves truly buffo music that matches and mirrors the farcical events onstage. He shares pride of place with Jacques Offenbach when it comes to writing opera music that is, in itself, witty and sometimes hilarious. Giuseppe Verdi has moments like this in *Falstaff*, and Joseph Haydn and Igor Stravinsky at times match this kind of musical humor in their instrumental compositions.

In *Barbiere*, for example, Basilio's "La calunnia" (from ALLEGRO, p. 128 [vocal 87]) is marked by comic touches such as having the cellos play near the bridge of their instruments to produce a buzzing sound. In the quintet of Act II, we have repeated attempts to get rid of Basilio only to have him reenter in true burlesque fashion, and the dynamics and accents effectively mirror the stage action and the frustration of those who cannot get rid of him (from ANDANTINO, p. 314 [vocal 228]). This is followed by the shaving scene where the first violins also make a whirring or buzzing sound; and the scene ends with all of the strings playing at a speed that is just about as fast as one can play the notes. The tipsy quality in the orchestra of Act I's finale, while Almaviva staggers around the stage pretending to be a drunken soldier, is achieved with a double dotted rhythm followed by trills, alternating with loud triplets (MARZIALE, p. 176 [vocal 124, ALLEGRO]).

With *Barbiere's* storm, the "Temporale," we have a tempest in a teacup (p. 372, ALLEGRO [vocal 270]). The orchestra is very sparse without any timpani or percussion—although there is a bass drum at other places in the score. (There is a tradition of using bass drum and cymbals together. But I have always believed that *gran cassa* in the score means the bass drum alone throughout this opera. That is, no cymbals.)

The storm feels like a child composed it—a child of incredible musical sophistication, that is. Some wish to soup up the sound, but too much noise contradicts its gentle charm. (The score's loudest moments should occur in the Act I finale.)

Step into My Study . . .

Souping up the sound is not new, however; it is old fashioned. In the late nineteenth and early twentieth centuries, performances of *Barbiere* were padded with timpani and trombones where Rossini never wrote for them. Newer editions of the orchestra score contain fewer ***f***'s and ***ff***'s than we see in the Dover reprint available for download, which is consistent with modern scholarship regarding Rossini's comedies in general.

(This was even truer and more problematic in less-often performed Rossini operas since more of these would-be improvements made their way into the scores. As recently as the 1970s, the commonly used scores for *La Cenerentola* contained extra bassoons, trombones, and thicker orchestration in general in much of the opera.)

With lighter orchestration all around, individual musicians now play this music somewhat differently than they did forty or fifty years ago.

For example, many quick string passages are now played with a dry spiccato bowing as opposed to the slurred phrasing of years gone by.

Scholars have changed the way conductors perform Rossini comedies as well over the past forty-plus years. For example, when we have a sixteenth-note pickup in a slow tempo, like the one at the beginning of the introduction to Almaviva's cavatina, the sixteenth note should be treated as an acciaccatura (at LARGO, p. 30 [vocal 15]). At quicker speeds, such as 100 quarter notes per minute, a sixteenth pickup can be played as such. But at slower speeds, a sixteenth note can sound a little ponderous. In some recordings of the overture to *Barbiere* from the 1940s and 1950s, we can hear this heavier-sounding sixteenth note where informed performers would now use an acciaccatura.

The thinking is that this opening note should not sound like the sixteenth note that serves as a pickup to the overture of *Die Zauberflöte*. It also may be noted that some are questioning whether Mozart really meant the opening to *Die Zauberflöte* to sound so solemn or whether we should be performing that pickup, too, as an acciaccatura. I am inclined to agree with those who do, so I try to keep that lighter than I heard as I was growing up.

There are two issues that require some analysis in the Act I finale, and they are related. The first is an exaggeration in speed. Speed is an indispensable comic tool but not justified when we have to start changing the notes to accommodate the speed we have chosen. The second issue is a question of how the finale is structured.

The finale begins with Count Almaviva disguised as a tipsy soldier and gaining entry to Bartolo's house (MARZIALE, p. 176 [vocal 124, ALLEGRO]). The sextet starts after he eludes arrest to the astonishment of all (from ANDANTE, p. 222 [vocal 158]). It continues to the end of the act, comprising a bit more than half of the finale. Near the end of the sextet, some of the singers begin executing triplets (p. 265 [vocal 189]). But if we are moving too fast at this point, the triplets cannot be sung. For example, Berta, who starts the section with a triplet of G–A–G, has to sing G–G instead. These duple eighth notes that we often hear substituted for the triplets fit in a faster tempo, but the music is altogether different. We have cut a lot of notes.

My guiding principle is that any tempo decision that forces a change in the music in order to make it singable or playable cannot be correct. Further, as the singers squeeze twelve notes into the same time as they previously had to sing eight notes, the listener should feel a bump-up in speed even with no change in the conductor's pacing. There are, after all, more notes per minute once the triplets begin. Bear in mind, too, that these triplets go on for many pages as other characters join in, in either ascending or descending lines, reinforcing the giddiness and dizziness in the text. If we enter so fast that these triplets cannot be sung, however, we do not get that added intricacy and excitement and sense of acceleration that they can supply. So faster arm waving and eliminating triplets is a simplistic and ineffective strategy for making this finale sparkle as it should. I, for one, am unwilling to assume that Rossini just did not know what he was asking for when he wrote triplets or left us with a score that is not singable as written.

The second problem in this sextet also concerns pacing. Some editions divide the sextet into two segments and some into three (beginning on p. 222 [vocal 158]). They may be labeled in different ways but they are broadly described in Figure 3.1.

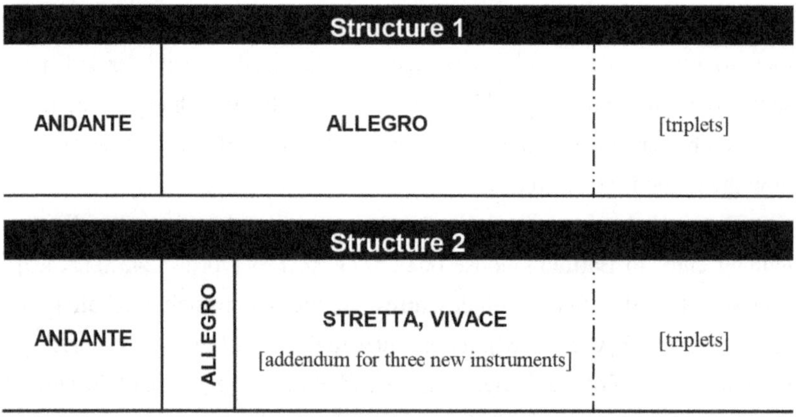

Figure 3.1 Act I finale, *Il barbiere di Siviglia*: two structures for the sextet (beginning on p. 222 [vocal 158]). The broken lines identify a *perceived* change in tempo when the triplets are introduced.

The vocabulary is less important than the number of tempo changes. The older scores, like the one available for download, clearly title the STRETTA and mark it VIVACE (p. 230 [vocal 166]). With the 1969 Alberto Zedda edition, both the title and indication disappeared for a generation. Now two critical editions published in recent years restore the title and indication (Bärenreiter) or restore the title and footnote different indications from two sources (Fondazione Rossini-Ricordi).

Happily, the manuscript of *Barbiere* sheds light on the situation. "The" manuscript is a bit of a misnomer, of course. The long list of autograph and printed sources in the preliminaries to the 2009 critical edition is a lesson in itself. A facsimile of one of the more important autographs (from Bologna) was published in 1993 with an invaluable introduction by Philip Gossett, and it gives us enough background to make some informed decisions.

Rossini, like others, drafted an original manuscript—there were no sketches—and scores were being fine tuned right up until opening night. In his introduction to the published facsimile, Gossett also reminds us that the paper had only a finite number of staves. If the composer needed more staves, he created an addendum (a *spartitino*). For this finale, Rossini wrote on sixteen-staff paper but needed nineteen staves when he got to the sextet. He created such an addendum for the sistro, bass drum, and reentering bassoon.

There are two important differences between the sixteen original staves and the three additional staves: First, the three additional staves are explicitly labeled LA STRETTA, which Rossini's contemporaries would have interpreted as an instruction to roughly double the speed. Second, they have a time signature of ¢ whereas the main score has a time signature of c. While ¢ does not automatically mean "go fast," we are more likely to see it—and especially a switch such as this one between c and ¢—when music gets faster.

There is further support for the three-section structure diagrammed in Figure 3.1: First, the STRETTA (where the addendum became necessary) marks the beginning of music that is different from what went before as well as the entrance of additional instruments. The passage is written in a kind of modified sonata form, with an exposition of a single theme, a short development section, and a rousing recapitulation and coda. A tempo change at the point where new music begins and new instruments enter seems quite compelling or, in any case, it is hard to argue *against* a tempo change.

Second, the very long stretch of ALLEGRO in the two-section alternative is intrinsically less interesting than a two-step increase in speed in a three-section structure (ending in a perceived additional bump-up in speed when the triplets are properly sung). It is easy for me to accept that Rossini created something more interesting, whether at first or on second thought. Observing the traditional doubling of tempo at LA STRETTA makes for a sense of great pep and exhilaration.

Given this structure, the question becomes how to pace the last scene to avoid obliterating the triplets. Even being careful to move the speed up in two steps, a strictly-by-the-books, formulaic approach can still result in a tempo too fast for most singers to execute this music. Note that this is a matter of context. It is not that the tempo is impossible for all singers, only that squeezing these triplets in at this tempo is going to be a hit-or-miss affair for most singers. So I start a little slower than I otherwise might and compromise on the math as follows:

$\frac{12}{8}$ ANDANTE, p. 222 (vocal 158), ♩. = 56
$\frac{4}{4}$ ALLEGRO, p. 227 (vocal 163), ♩ = 120
$\frac{4}{4}$ STRETTA, VIVACE, p. 230 (vocal 166), 𝅗𝅥 = 100

Based on what immediately precedes it, I would normally move into the ANDANTE at about 58 dotted quarter notes per minute, but tapping the brakes very slightly down to about 56 is safer. My first increase in speed, to about 120 quarter notes per minute, is then fairly extreme in percentage terms for a shift from ANDANTE to ALLEGRO and quite dramatic. But my second, into LA STRETTA at about 100 half notes per minute, is a somewhat gentler increase than a strict doubling. These numbers remain close enough to proportional to provide a sensation of smoothness, connectedness, and propulsion for both singers and audience without depriving the audience of some of the score's greatest delights.

My favorite things

The last part of the Almaviva-Figaro duet in Act I (from ALLEGRO, p. 97 [vocal 64]). While Almaviva rhapsodizes on winning Rosina, his melody is accompanied with a patter song in which Figaro looks forward to lining his pockets with Almaviva's payment. Soon the two are singing in delightful counterpoint and progress to an exhilarating conclusion with each singing the same words, "di me stesso maggior mi fa." There is an added moment of spice when the two voices come together dissonantly, which further contrasts the characters' nobler and more mundane goals.

Bellini: *I Capuleti e i Montecchi* and *Norma*

> In order to have effect, poetry and music require unaffected naturalness and nothing more. When we depart from this, we are lost.
>
> —Vincenzo Bellini[6]

The first observation to be made about Vincenzo Bellini is that he is, above all, a melodist. Giuseppe Verdi wrote of Bellini's "long, long, long melodies, like nobody wrote before him."[7] Donizetti and Rossini, as well as Verdi himself, wrote beautiful melodies of course, but there is something more fragile and often haunting about Bellini's.

Another feature of Bellini's writing for singers is that there is less speech-like declamation than in the rest of bel canto music. We hear arias emerge somewhat unexpectedly from more songlike introductory passages, rather than experiencing a sharp distinction between recitative and aria. The line is a bit blurred, a trend that would continue through the several stages of the Romantic era. In *Norma*, we hear such an *arioso* introduction at Adalgisa's entrance and in the entire scene before the duet with Pollione (Act I, Scene 5, from p. 156 [vocal 86]). The measures marked RECITATIVE are not quite the same recit as we would expect of Bellini's contemporaries or predecessors.

Another characteristic of Bellini's work is that there are fewer passages with incisive rhythm than Donizetti or Rossini might have supplied. And the accompaniment is remarkably minimal. His melodies seem to float on a magic carpet, with less visible machinery or support than we expect. Both Adalgisa's entrance and Norma's "Casta diva" are characterized by such relatively sparse accompaniment. Still, the score does not invite the conductor to add his or her own phrasing or articulation. Beyond paying attention to the balance issues as in all music, I adopt a "first do no harm" policy, much as singers need to be especially judicious when ornamenting this music.

Finally, Bellini has been widely recognized for his harmonies and frequent modulation, both adventurous for his day. We get a taste of this in “Casta diva,” and it lies at the heart of the grand finale to this opera, to which I will return.

The upshot of this—gorgeous and often sad melodies over atmospheric harmonies—is that, on average, Bellini should be performed at a more leisurely and caressing tempo than most of Donizetti and certainly Rossini. While it would be dangerous to drag or get lost in rubato, we cannot convey the spirit of this music if we have in mind a rollicking Rossini comedy or the generally faster music of the Baroque and Classical periods.

Similarly, the variations and decorations appropriate to Bellini are not the same as those appropriate to Mozart, Handel, Donizetti, and Rossini. Bellini’s are purely melodic variations and less about ornamentation. Whereas virtuosity can sometimes be a goal in itself in Rossini, in Bellini’s music it is inappropriate to place decoration that calls attention to itself ahead of vocal coloring or dramatic involvement. Coming up with just the right embellishments is, in the final analysis, a question of evolving scholarship, personal and collective taste and, naturally, the talents of the performer at hand.

Some details in the score may tell us about the composer’s taste and expectations, however. In his *I Capuleti e i Montecchi* for example, he wrote his own variant on Giulietta’s aria “O quante volte” (No. 4 from m. 8 of 38, p. 187 [vocal 43]). It appears on the phrase “Raggio del tuo sembiante” (39, m. 4, p. 191 [vocal 44]).

If we use his own work as our guide when we look to create variations, we will avoid some of the filigree and fireworks that may work well in Handel and are just all wrong in Bellini. For example, Tebaldo’s cabaletta repeats without variation, which a singer of the time would have read as an invitation to improvise. Example 3.1 suggests a variation that works stylistically. (Although this example takes a few suggestions from the critical edition, it does not conform entirely. My principal disagreement with those editors concerns their addition of “ah!” after the first “L’amo” in both the first statement and the repeat. In my opinion, this makes the line harder to sing and less intelligible to even an Italian-speaking audience.)

Example 3.1 Tebaldo's cabaletta in *I Capuleti e I Montecchi* (Act I, No. 2): The first statement begins at m. 9 of [18], p. 103 (vocal 20). The suggested variation would begin at the pickup to [20], p. 112 (vocal 23).

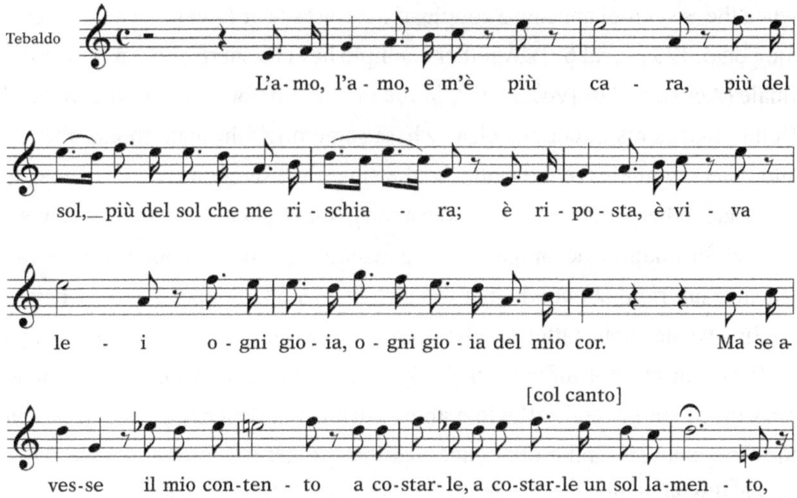

At the same time, Bellini was moving toward notation that gives more direction about ornamentation. For example, in the first measure that Norma sings in "Casta Diva," there is a turn that I would suggest following closely when the ∾ symbol appears a couple of measures later (Act I, Scene 4, beginning on p. 123 [vocal 62]). Another example lies in a sharp under a turn in the finale (Act II, p. 416 [vocal 262], in the measure before MAGGIORE). With it, Bellini makes his intentions clear where some might hesitate to use a sharp and others might leave the matter to the singer's discretion.

Like other ornaments and variations, turns should be executed with respect for tradition accompanied by a healthy dose of common sense. Some teachers are rigid about whether the turn begins on the note above or below the first written note. Others argue strenuously against introducing any sharps or flats that are not already in the key or among accidentals in the same measure. I am generally flexible about such rules, depending on my ears in the final analysis, and more concerned that we get the form and style right, especially when the composer has given us such clear models.

Bellini also indicated a desired pitch for what we have called the "unwritten appoggiatura" by adding what look like grace notes before pairs of identical notes. And he wrote out most of them in *Norma*.[8] These are the small notes in Adalgisa's first scene (Example 3.2). They may look like acciaccaturas or appoggiaturas depending on where any given edition places slashes, and some editors have even added slurs. That is, interpreting Bellini's idiosyncratic indications is complicated by scores that vary wildly. I find the proposition that they are indications rather than additional short notes persuasive. As to the slashes, I would offer that when they are there, their purpose is to indicate a somewhat shorter duration and ultimately, the difference should be quite subtle.

Example 3.2 Decoration in Adalgisa's first scene in *Norma* (Act I, Scene 5, p. 160 [vocal 88]). The vocal and orchestra scores are inconsistent about slashes on the small notes. We are omitting them entirely based on the Garland autograph.

Musicologist Philip Gossett once told me that a musician has to "react musically" to the situations with which Bellini presents us. In an e-mail, he commiserated about Bellini's inconsistencies and cautioned against editors who may try to regularize what cannot be regularized.

Step into My Study . . .

There are two orchestral issues that the conductor must confront in Bellini's music. They concern the brass and the timpani. I pretty routinely make adjustments in the dynamics for the brass instruments in Bellini's music. Even when we substitute instruments that we know to be closer to the originals of the early 1830s, the brass can sound like a marching band if we are not careful to keep them playing softer than the score seems to indicate. I find this to be true, for example, in *Norma's* opening chorus and the cavatina for Oroveso that follows. At one place in the score, the trombones are simply too loud, especially with modern instruments (from p. 42, m. 4 [vocal 14, m. 4]). Just a little while later, Bellini uses them only for punctuation, making the dynamics manageable. In addition, the need to adjust timpani parts, as discussed earlier, is fairly common in Bellini's music.

Tempo presents a different set of challenges. In a sense Bellini is the hardest of our three composers for the conductor. It is simply more treacherous to try to shape something that is inherently very flexible. So Bellini requires that the conductor look for relationships that hold the piece together and provide the scaffolding for his melodies. Being too rigid or aggressive destroys things utterly. Yet it is extremely easy to get too dreamy, too flaccid, and to seem self-indulgent. Happily, it is also true that wrestling with this issue yields big rewards. Handled correctly, this music can be transporting.

We discuss both of these issues in connection with *Capuleti* and *Norma* in the pages that follow.

Capuleti

I Capuleti e i Montecchi (1830) met with great success, fell out of favor, and has regained popularity in recent years. Looking to Shakespeare for guidance is a mistake, however. Shakespeare's great *Romeo and Juliet* and the Gounod opera based on it emphasize young love and tell us nothing about the reasons for the family feud. On the other hand, this opera is about the destruction of two young lovers in the context of a specific war that enveloped Italy for centuries, the war between the Guelphs and Ghibellines. There is as much about battles and duty as about love, and there are no party scenes.

Happily, the impulse to modernize by giving the part of Romeo to a tenor has fallen out of fashion, and we are able to hear the exquisite blending of soprano and mezzo-soprano as Bellini intended. Romeo and Giulietta live on a higher plane than the feud that will destroy them. The restoration of Bellini's sweet, sad final scene—after many decades of substituting the corresponding scene from an opera on the same story by Nicola Vaccaj—is also a boon. The Vaccaj ending better met the expectations of much, but not all, of Bellini's audience. Nowadays, many of us experience it as old-fashioned and dramatically incongruous in the extreme, no matter how well sung.

For the conductor, understanding the traditions of operas from this era can pay dividends in *Capuleti*. Most notably, executing a traditional stretto at the end of No. 3 in Act I will result in a rousing conclusion. This is the scene that contains Romeo's "Se Romeo t'uccise un figlio," followed by its cabaletta "La tremenda ultrice spada." We will anchor a discussion that will reference three different scores in the rehearsal numbers of the Kalmus score.

The aria begins at LARGHETTO CANTABILE (25, p. 141 [vocal 31]). We increase the tempo at the ALLEGRO MODERATO (27). This is followed by the cabaletta, which is a bit slower (ALLEGRO MARZIALE SOSTENUTO, 28). Then a new idea is introduced at PIÙ VIVO (29). This is followed by a reprise of the cabaletta with variations, from PRIMO TEMPO (30). Then the music from PIÙ VIVO comes back with the same indication (31). Only 6 measures later however, a coda begins with the introduction of a new melody and a shift in the accompanying figures (STRINGENDO SEMPRE at 32, marked STRETTO in vocal score p. 38). The eighth-note-plus-two-sixteenths figure that dominates the accompaniment in both PIÙ VIVO sections changes at STRINGENDO SEMPRE to a simpler pattern of higher strings and lower strings alternating eighth notes.

Looking ahead, the melody of the PIÙ VIVO sections will return in the final section, with orchestra only, but it will return in notes of twice the duration (34 [vocal p. 40]). At first glance, this repeat can seem like getting stuck in the mud. But the truth is that if the notes of twice the duration are coming at about twice the speed, they serve as the foundation of an exciting orchestral conclusion to end the scene in a supremely satisfying manner.

There is an interesting difference among scores, and it is worth examining: At 32, the older Ricordi score says STRINGENDO SEMPRE and the critical edition supplies the first of four STRINGENDO indications that lie between 4 and 6 measures apart. Then the editors supply a STRETTO indication 4 measures after the last STRINGENDO (which is m. 11 of 33 in the older score). In the notes, the editors of the critical edition explain that they consider the STRETTO to be implicit based upon the doubled note values and to be a natural consequence of progressive STRINGENDO indications.

This is reasonable as far as it goes. But I find myself returning to practical performing issues. I cannot argue with any conductor who accelerates twice or four times in those approximately 20 measures. But without a conductor, as this would have been performed in the era of its composition, this could not have been pulled off cleanly. (Bellini himself led the first three performances *from the keyboard*, as was common. Estimates vary since it did not happen overnight, but it would be at least another twenty years before professional conductors began to establish themselves in Italian opera houses.[9])

Furthermore, in my experience, the tradition of approximately doubling the speed abruptly at 32, where the Belwin Mills vocal score indicates STRETTO, also supplies a tremendous surge of energy. In fact, the gradual increase in speed suggested in the critical edition results in this coda's beginning in quite a plodding manner—rather inconsistent with the simplified accompanying figures hammering out the beat more insistently as well as men in arms singing about blood and country.

We should also remember that *stringendo* refers to more than just speed (more than *accelerando*), and that the repetition of the indication may not necessarily call for moving faster but, rather, maintaining tension and excitement in multiple ways. The repetition of such an indication—unusual in this era—could, in fact, mean "don't slacken." If that is the case, it reminds me a bit of the occasional ***fffff*** we see in music. (Tchaikovsky comes to mind.) It is not measurable in decibels but, rather, expresses something about intensity.

The bottom line is that those notes of twice the duration at the end of the scene (from [34]) should supply the lively reprise that was intended, and that will mean getting to about double-speed either gradually or abruptly. That is, either conductorial choice is justifiable.

My favorite things

Arguably, the dynamic high point of the opera is the conclusion of the Act II duet between Romeo and Tebaldo (which begins ALLEGRO at [133] of No. 9, p. 461 [vocal 111]). Without doubt however, the emotional high point—and my favorite moment—is the final scene. Both Romeo's part and his duet with Giulietta after she wakes capture the lyrical essence of this love story (No. 10 from ANDANTE MOSSO at [175], p. 551 [vocal 131]).

Norma

Norma (1831), the tale of a Druid priestess and her forbidden and fatal love, received a chilly reception at first but became Bellini's best known, most influential, and most performed work. Richard Wagner openly admired this opera and its finale in particular, and we can readily see how it inspired his own music. We can also see that it heralds the direction in which composers would take the operatic genre later in the Romantic era, and the somewhat different challenges in store for conductors.

The final 55 measures of the opera contain a statement, a repeat, and a coda (beginning at MAGGIORE, p. 417 [vocal 262 at the key change]). They are justly admired for both the nobility of the melody and the early use of sequential chromaticism. As in the climax of the sextet of Donizetti's *Lucia di Lammermoor*, careful control of both volume and pacing not only helps convey the spirit of this section but also illuminates the work's architecture. Although the coda serves as a stretto and its ALLEGRO AGITATO ASSAI (*ff*) calls for doubling the speed, none of it ever gets very fast.

This finale also contains particularly nuanced indications: The indications meant primarily for volume are about more than decibels, and the indications for speed speak to something more than milliseconds. For volume, we have the familiar crescendo, but we do not have a decrescendo. We have CALANDO. *Calando* means to wane or descend and it is sometimes considered to refer to tempo in addition to volume. In this finale, it influences both. Notably, the word for speeding up is not accelerando, the most common such indication. It is INCALZANDO. The root of this word is the verb *incalzare*, to pursue and, by extension, to press or threaten. So there is a certain tension implied, quite different from the light-hearted accelerando in, say, a Rossini comedy.

Bellini writes MAGGIORE at the start of these final pages, as he does elsewhere in *Norma*, indicating a change from minor to major harmony. Most composers do not indicate this relatively common device, so it is fair to assume that, for Bellini, the change of mood and character that the listener feels when harmonies shift in this manner—from brooding or somber to something more positive and affirmative—must have been particularly salient. The music is grand and serious, as Norma and Pollione submit themselves to the death penalty together. But it is also uplifting and, in the final analysis, cathartic. It is only in the coda, taken at double speed, that we are again plunged into a minor key as the lovers are burned at the stake. (As much as the melodic beauty of the work and the chromatic harmony, perhaps it was this pairing of love and death that so attracted Wagner to this opera.)

Back in the pit, we have a fairly long passage that is quite slow and soft, with some swelling and accelerating, then falling back, swelling a little more and falling back, until we reach the dramatic coda. So these final measures require some forethought to arrive at a plan. I suggest:

Statement:

mm. 1–8: MAGGIORE. Slow and soft, approximately ♩ = 60.

mm. 9–12: INCALZANDO E CRES. Gradually speed up to about ♩ = 72. Build volume to *ff*, quite loud but not the loudest and not as loud as in the corresponding passage in the repeat. About two and a half times as loud as we began.

m. 13: Hold the volume at *ff* but abruptly reduce the speed to the starting tempo.

m. 14: CALANDO. Fade the volume away to the level at which we began.
m. 15: The repeat begins in the second half of this measure.

Repeat:

mm. 15–22: Again, slow and soft as in the first rendition.
mm. 23–25: INCALZANDO E CRES. Begin building to a somewhat faster pace (♩ = 80). Build volume to something about three times as loud as we began with. This may still be something short of what we think of as *fff*, however.
mm. 26–28: Decelerate and stretch the climactic measure by momentarily dipping below the starting tempo. But return to the original tempo preparatory to doubling it for the coda. Again, the volume wanes in the fourteenth measure of this repeat (m. 28, CALANDO).
m. 29: Coda: ALLEGRO AGITATO ASSAI. Double tempo.

I always strive to maintain tension and forward propulsion, reserving the loudest moments and the greatest accelerations for the repeat and coda. For me, these are the loudest moments of the opera as well.

My favorite things

The final section. One can almost hear the end of *Tristan und Isolde* coming.

Donizetti: *Lucia di Lammermoor*

> Others have ceded their places to us and we must cede ours to still others. I am more than happy to give mine to people of talent like Verdi.
>
> —Gaetano Donizetti[10]

By any accounting, Gaetano Donizetti was a prolific composer. In the final years of his composing career, he became the lion of Italian opera for a time, at least in part because Rossini had retired and Bellini had died prematurely. Admittedly, Giuseppe Verdi was coming up fast. But it is also fair to say that Donizetti, with his mastery over the Classical forms combined with gifts for dramatic tension and melting lyricism, makes an apt subject for the end of a chapter on bel canto or an introduction to a chapter on Verdi.

He wrote many dozens of operas with additional versions of some while spending a great deal of time in Paris. The bel canto composers were all greatly admired and appreciated in Paris and, in point of fact, the world of Italian opera may be said to have included Paris. Rossini famously lived and dined in Paris and, yes, wrote some wonderful music in and for Paris. But Donizetti wrote even more music for a variety of Parisian theaters and composed more operas to original French librettos than the other Italians who were so fêted in Paris.

Théâtre-Italien produced some of his operas in Italian; among them was *Don Pasquale*, which might be said to be Italian with a slight French accent and reminiscent of Molière. He also composed to French dialogue for Opéra-Comique (*La Fille du régiment*); and he contributed several grand operas with French librettos to l'Opéra de Paris (e.g., *La Favorite*). He rewrote sections and composed entirely new music for *Lucie de Lammermoor* for Théâtre de la Renaissance, and some of the story line even changed. When composing to French librettos, he seems to have taken into account the rhythm and cadence of the French language in addition to the tastes of Parisian audiences. (However, we cannot always tell the extent of a composer's involvement in a translation or adaptation. Each opera has its own history.[11])

In addition to accommodating audience tastes, we can sometimes see that the score reflects the performing talent that he could expect to be available in Paris as opposed to, say, Naples. So in the orchestra pit, stylistic choices can be made to give the work a more French or Italian sound. For example, Donizetti's writing for the trumpets is high and soft at the end of the overture to *La Fille du régiment* and in the trumpet solo before Ernesto's aria at the beginning of Act II of *Don Pasquale*. This reflects the fact that the playing of the evolving trumpet and its sibling, the cornet, was at a very high level in Paris at the time. Moreover, the piston valve cornet was extremely popular and favored over the trumpet in some musical circles. So the cornet can fill in for the trumpet in *Don Pasquale*, depending on the comfort of the individual trumpet player with this instrument. This results in a lighter, more early-nineteenth century French sound.

Perhaps most impressive is Donizetti's gift for producing both comedies and dramas that are still regularly performed. It seems that Donizetti's captivating comedies get more attention nowadays than his dramas, with the notable exception of *Lucia di Lammermoor* (1835). But *Maria* Stuarda, *Anna* Bolena, and *Roberto Devereux*—to name but three of his other fine dramas—remain in the repertory and we do get treated to productions from time to time. The public never tires of *Lucia* however, and rightly so. For me, this opera, based on *The Bride of Lammermoor* by Sir Walter Scott, epitomizes Romanticism.

Unfortunately, much damage has been inflicted on *Lucia* over the years. It has been the victim of excessive cutting as well as a blind adherence to bad traditions built up over the years. A knowledge of tradition in a work like this is essential, but so too is some scholarship that goes beyond popular recordings. We need to be willing to bring some fresh thinking to a performance.

The lead role has been sung by a fairly wide range of sopranos. Some have been very light coloraturas, but in recent years, sopranos with larger voices and greater richness of tone have been favored. If they possess the requisite agility, they can be more dramatically compelling than the extreme soubrettes of the 1930s and 1940s. In addition, the standard embellishments can sound old fashioned to some of us. Given this diverse crop of sopranos, one would think that some new ideas would be heard in the embellishments. All too often however, one would be wrong.

There are traditions and interpolations that will probably always be with us. *Lucia's* mad-scene cadenza for example, has been performed almost invariably for more than a century. But it was never written by Donizetti and does not sound much like it was (although we may safely assume that some cadenza has always been inserted in No. 14 at the end of [31] [vocal p. 199, before ALLEGRO]). Once for a student performance, I found that we needed something shorter than the cadenza written for Nellie Melba fifty years after *Lucia* premiered. This may sound like an unfortunate problem to be overcome, but it was more like a gift, and I proceeded to write a soprano-flute-harp cadenza that incorporated two love themes from the opera. The audience heard something different, in a style closer to Donizetti's *Lucia*, and could enjoy the reappearance of two important themes. Lucia's Act I cabaletta offers another opportunity to replace embellishments much of the audience has heard and heard again. (This is "Quando rapito in estasi" from 30 in No. 3 [vocal p. 36] with the repeat appearing at 33 [vocal p. 39].)

One of Donizetti's more romantic touches was the use of the glass harmonica. In the original orchestration, it is featured in the mad scene of Act III. Ben Franklin's invention has an otherworldly sound, and it was firmly associated in the public's mind with young women and madness, as well as mesmerism. Unfortunately, by the time the opera opened, the composer had already replaced it, evidently for strictly non-musical reasons.[12] Or perhaps that was fortunate, since finding both the instrument and someone who can play it is beyond the capabilities of most opera companies nowadays. So we might be grateful that we have Donizetti's second thoughts, and they are more than satisfactory. That said though, every opera lover should at least once experience the eerie effect that Donizetti originally imagined in these passages.

Step into My Study . . .

While raucous brass is less of a problem in Donizetti's music than in Bellini's, the conductor may still encounter some balance problems. It happens, for example, in *L'elisir d'amore* where Adina's cabaletta near the end of the opera is accompanied by excessive brass.

The biggest problems in *Lucia* are found in the first scene. Both Normanno, and occasionally even some of the male chorus, can be obliterated by the orchestra, which has much brass with the indication to play loud. The first solution to the heavy brass writing is to ask the brass to play more softly than the score indicates. This is usually sufficient to obtain the right balance with the tenor if he has been cast with the right *spinto* voice.[13] If his part is still difficult or impossible to hear, the elimination of the brass in a few measures, where other instruments play the same line, may be necessary.

Within the *Lucia* orchestra itself, there is one passage in Act I where an ascending low scale in the cellos seems weak against the chorus and brass. This happens in No. 1 at 3, m. 9 (vocal p. 2, m. 22 of ALLEGRO GIUSTO) and again at m. 4 before 5 (vocal p. 3, last measure). To give these measures more punch, the scale may be doubled in the basses. In Donizetti's era, this might have been a problematic passage for the basses, though less so than some passages in Mozart's or Beethoven's works. Today, the level of difficulty is standard for any professional orchestra bass player.

Finally, cuts are a major issue in *Lucia.* No opera in the standard repertory has been so mangled. Uncut, the work should take about three hours and fifteen minutes, assuming a set that permits little or no waiting (a minute or two) between scenes and two intermissions of twenty minutes each. Many theaters cut the opera down to two and a half hours, given the same set and length of intermissions, out of a misguided concern for the audience's attention span.

Often two sections are omitted entirely: the Act II scene between Raimondo and Lucia just before the finale and the opening scene of Act III, a confrontation between Edgardo and Enrico. In addition, there is a very substantial cut in the final pages of the Act II finale, the confrontation between Edgardo and everyone at the wedding.

In the Raimondo-Lucia scene of Act II, Raimondo convinces Lucia to marry Arturo by appealing to her sense of duty (No. 7). So, when she does marry him in the next scene, it makes more sense than it does without this conversation. The scene can benefit from some modest cutting that should be obvious to any conductor familiar with the style and the language. But restoring it really improves the storytelling.

In the Act III confrontation between Edgardo and Enrico, both characters are further developed (No. 11, the so-called "Wolf Crag's" scene). From a musical standpoint, the scene puts added demands on the tenor and makes him equal in importance to the soprano. The main reason given for cutting the scene is the need to construct a different set. However, contemporary efforts to be more cinematic, moving from scene to scene in more abstract sets without pauses for changing sets, should help justify restoring this scene.

In opening the third cut, the gain is mostly musical. This final STRETTO of Act II is actually in sonata form (No. 10, beginning at **50**, vocal p. 130). The standard cut excises the development, recapitulation, and the beginning of the coda, dismembering the form completely. We are left with a statement of two themes and part of the coda. One measure of how exciting the STRETTO is uncut is how exciting it *remains* in spite of the loss of about half of its measures. (Some recent recordings restore this music.)

Yet the violence so often done to this magnificent finale gains us only about two minutes. So why is it cut? The reason usually given is a lack of stage action. Remember that this music plays after both the sextet, which really does have to be sung by singers standing still, and a little filler moving the story forward. Many feel that so much music without action asks too much of the audience, but this STRETTO is so lively that one could imagine a great deal of action to drive Edgardo from the scene. And the judicious control of steadily accelerating tempos across so many pages of music magnifies the drama and excitement and makes the reappearance of a musical idea in a repeat the very opposite of boring.

The STRETTO begins as the chorus pounces on Edgardo (vocally), and soon everyone is singing "Esci, fuggi," with the indication VIVACE. Along with the strongest of the faster indications, it has the indication TUTTA FORZA over the vocal lines and the beginning of music different from what went before. Thereafter, we have only two indications nudging us a little faster in each case. But roughly doubling the tempo at VIVACE is key to driving this act to a breathless conclusion. I reserve the orchestra's loudest playing for this stretto as well. Specifically, the STRETTO develops as follows:

Exposition:

Theme 1, "Esci, fuggi" ([50] VIVACE [vocal p. 130]).
Theme 2, at Lucia's "Dio, lo salva" ([51], m. 2 [vocal p. 132]).

Development:

Rhythmic and harmonic development of Theme 1 on "Infelice, t'invola" ([52] PIÙ MOSSO [vocal p. 139]).

Recapitulation:

Contrapuntal and intense reprise of Theme 1 on "Esci, fuggi" ([54] [vocal p. 144]).

Coda:

Like the Development in exploring harmonies and keys, but longer.
New idea 1, at Lucia's " . . . si, e l'estrema domanda del core" ([55] PIÙ ALLEGRO [vocal p. 148]).

New idea 2, at Lucia's "core che morendo sul labbro" (m. 4 before [56] [vocal p. 150]). New idea 2 explored sequentially.

Orchestra alone, restatement of Theme 2 for 7 measures, followed by 9 measures of emphasis (final 16 measures of the act).

Now in sonata form, we normally expect to hear the second theme come back in the recapitulation section, and possibly in the development section. Notably however, Donizetti bends the rules a little in order to surprise us. After a series of cadences that could easily end the act, he brings back Theme 2 in something of a short coda to the coda that has great dramatic impact. We really owe it to our audiences to deliver this stretto intact rather than in fragmentary form.

My favorite things

Act III's "Al fin' son tua, al fin sei mio" (No. 14, from m. 8 before [31] [vocal p. 195]). This quiet phrase in the middle of the vocal virtuosity of the mad scene captures Lucia's fragility. For me, this is the opera's emotional high point. In an era in which mad scenes were common, *Lucia's* stands out for its sincerity and effectiveness.

Chapter 4

Verdi

Keep well in mind, my dear Giulio, that the success of our operas rests most of the time in the hands of the conductor. This person is as necessary as a tenor or a prima donna . . .

—Giuseppe Verdi[1]

Giuseppe Verdi dominates Italian music of the Romantic period. His earliest efforts are grounded in the bel canto style, but if there is one quality that marks him from his early works through his final period, it is his refusal to stay put and repeat his own past successes or the formulas of the previous generation. He built upon bel canto traditions, and he stretched them. The extended solos for violin in *I Lombardi* and the clarinet in *La forza del destino* take a trend of the bel canto school (particularly in the music of Bellini) to ever greater heights. *Rigoletto* sounds conventional to our ears more than a century and a half after it opened, but the complaints of some of its critics were rooted in its through-composition, which was fairly extensive for its time in Italy.

The originality of *Macbeth*, even in its first incarnation of 1847, is startling in many ways. The plot is more modern relative to those of many of the great Romantic-era operas. Its psychological insight and emotions are set to music to a degree rarely encountered in opera since Mozart. In addition, the plot is revealed in a new and more realistic kind of operatic drama. We may reasonably compare Lady Macbeth's sleepwalking scene and aria with corresponding "mad scenes" from the bel canto masters. Lady Macbeth's sleepwalking scene, while difficult to sing, does not put as much emphasis on obvious virtuosity and it ends relatively quietly. In addition, during this aria, a doctor and lady-in-waiting comment on her behavior, rather than a big chorus like the one that watches the heroine's descent into madness in Donizetti's *Lucia di Lammermoor* or Bellini's *I puritani*. In short, in *Macbeth*, the composer's emphasis has shifted toward more realistic theater—both in the absence of virtuosic singing and in the privacy of the scene.

To those who love lyric theater, Verdi's use of the orchestra is simply theatrically perfect. The Requiem Mass achieves tremendous drama through orchestral color, and *Falstaff* achieves something magical. Conductors do not run into great dilemmas resulting from his choice of instruments or the instruments' evolution, with one possible exception: the cimbasso. Most of the time the tuba substitutes for the cimbasso. The tuba lacks one important talent, however. It cannot play staccato as well or as easily as the cimbasso. Of the operas discussed in this chapter, *Rigoletto* and *Traviata* in particular are ill served by this substitution. If I cannot get a cimbasso and its player for these operas, I omit the part or use a bass trombone where possible.

The Two Verdis

Very broadly, a conductor might place Verdi's operas in two categories: those that come with trunks full of sometimes dubious tradition and those that are performed with greater attention to and respect for the score.

Those in the first category come from Verdi's early and middle period, although not all early and middle works carry this burden. It is in the most-performed and most-beloved works, such as *Rigoletto* and *La traviata*, where we find the greatest accretion of tradition, some valid and some not. Serving as the conscience of a production requires distinguishing the rules and conventions by which the composer likely expected everyone—pit and stage—to operate, requiring little if any discussion, from specific performance ideas contributed by later generations.

We do not run into difficult structural questions in these operas, however. Tempo relationships are generally quite clear and metronome indications are frequent enough. Rather, the conductor needs to know the importance of such musical conventions as the constant pulse and the stretto, on the one hand, and needs to seize upon opportunities for imaginative phrasing and articulation on the other. This is because, in this period, it is still true that at least some of the scores are more sketchy about execution than those we see later in the nineteenth century.

The second category contains works that come with less baggage, and he wrote the greatest of these later in his career. In these masterpieces of the late nineteenth century, the conductor's job is affected by two trends at work in the wider music world. One is that Verdi becomes more specific in his scores, leaving less to performers' improvisational talent and taste and even sometimes cautioning against specific traditional practices. For the conductor, this clarity and specificity are an asset. The other trend is that of ever greater fusion of music and drama. For the conductor, this means that the scores contain greater through-composition with intersections to be navigated, then-unconventional rhythms and tempo relationships, increasingly elaborate counterpoint, and ever larger and better orchestras expressing ever more intense feelings through music. Richard Wagner took these compositional methods further, and it is fair to give him credit for leading the way. However, Verdi began testing boundaries and conventions in his characteristically Italian manner more and earlier than is sometimes acknowledged.

That is, this composer participated in making the modern-day conductor increasingly indispensable inasmuch as he demanded more from the orchestra pit and continuous fine adjustments from the leader of the performance. Verdi himself, while conducting at least the first few performances of his earlier works, began turning leadership over to these new conducting specialists entirely as scores became increasingly complex.[2]

Otello and *Falstaff*, his two last operas, share a symphonic character and are both entirely through-composed. They are virtually always treated with complete respect. *Aida* lies somewhere in the middle, as perhaps befits the opera that marks the end of the composer's "middle period" by many reckonings. It is relatively less laden with tradition that needs to be reconsidered and reined in than some of his earlier operas, and the score contains many examples of what were modern techniques in 1871.

Singing

Before we can conclude an introduction to any discussion of Verdi, the much-lamented dearth of Verdian singers must be addressed. It is *relatively* easy to cast a soprano for *Rigoletto's* Gilda. But an Aida is harder to find. Otello may not be as hard to cast as either Tristan or Isolde, but as a nearly heldentenor part, it is a challenge nonetheless. It is also becoming increasingly difficult to find spinto sopranos and spinto tenors capable of operas like *Il trovatore, La forza del destino*, and *Don Carlo* (in any of its versions).

No single explanation satisfies besides the operation of fashion. The genes responsible for human vocal cords have not changed during my lifetime. But there are demonstrably fewer Verdians and far more coloratura mezzo-sopranos than on the day I was born. The growing interest in Baroque and earlier music has resulted in far more excellent countertenors than I could possibly have anticipated during my conservatory days.

In recent years, Eastern Europeans increasingly have picked up some of the slack and supplied the voices of greater heft that are needed for Verdi's operas. Singers have probably sung roles outside their native languages since the first aria was written. The good ones learn the language, and the best of them learn the style well enough to sing idiomatically.

A Caution for Singers

Verdi does something intriguing in several of his works: he appears to misplace accents. That is, the natural accent of the music falls on an unexpected syllable. Some want to correct this by rewriting the rhythms. But the problem crops up often enough to rule out copyist error. Since I have yet to be persuaded that Verdi made this kind of mistake in his mother tongue, I resist efforts to help the composer out, and I look for a rationale for the odd accents.

He does this when a character is excited, confused, or even laughing or crying. For example, in the Requiem Mass, the chorus alternates *libera* accented on the first syllable with the same word accented on the second syllable and does the same with *Domine*, in both cases conveying desperation (the climax of No. 7, from m. 382 [vocal p. 226]).

Similarly, in Act I of *La traviata*, we should not conform "Turbata anima mia" with spoken Italian, accenting *anima* on the first syllable (m. 10 of No. 3 [vocal p. 65]). Violetta is at least flustered at this point, and maybe even shaken.

A question arises early in Act I of *Rigoletto* however, when the Duke speaks of Ceprano's wife. The two scores available for download disagree on how the words fit with the notes in ". . . Cepran[o] la . . ." (Act I, No. 2, m. 40 of [1] [vocal p. 4, last measure]). I have always thought that the Duke is deliberately mispronouncing Ceprano's name with the emphasis on the first syllable. This is, of course, contemptuous, a put-down. If this is so, he would also be subtly playing on the word *ceppo*, which translates as a log, stump or, perhaps, blockhead. There are some early sources and older scores that justify the vocal score's three syllables, which makes the emphasis on the first syllable quite obvious. The orchestra score's notation, and the elision of the final syllable in the name makes emphasis on the first syllable arguable or at least less obvious. Full disclosure: the editors of the critical edition have come down closer to the orchestra score (though they omit the slur [m. 96 in the critical edition]).

Rigoletto

By one recounting, when asked about his favorite, Verdi replied that as a professional he preferred *Rigoletto*, but as an amateur *La traviata*.[3]

Rigoletto (1851) continues to enthrall audiences after well over a century. It has a flawed character's sympathetic story, exquisite melody, and enough opportunity for virtuosity. That it continues to elicit enthusiasm from artists who have performed it many times fuels the excitement, and that enthusiasm follows directly from its beauty and its solid construction. This begins with the simple but effective use of a single motive (a repeated single note in dotted rhythm), greater through-composition than his audiences were used to at the time, and relatively straightforward relationships and transitions to keep it all moving.

The title role is one of the most difficult baritone parts in Verdi's operas, which means that it is one of the hardest in the standard repertory. Ideally, the baritone has a dark voice but can sing fairly high; the part is also quite long. The Duke should be a lyric tenor, something like Alfredo in *La traviata*. The part requires a voice that is lighter and more flexible than the spinto tenors like Radames in *Aida* or Manrico in *Il trovatore*.

Gilda has been increasingly cast as a very light soprano, which makes some dramatic sense for the cloistered ingénue. While flexibility is important in this role, however, it also requires a voice of power and endurance roughly equivalent to Violetta in *La traviata* and Leonora in *Il trovatore*. With too light a voice, there will be difficulties in the duets.

Varying the vocal line is acceptable at times, but there is not room for a lot of embellishment in this opera. For example, the Duke's "Questa o quella" in Act I is very short, and is written to lead directly into the next section without a break ("Ballata," No. 2, m. 51 of [1] [vocal p. 5]). For today's audience, variations at its end come off as old fashioned, and it should not be ornamented. On the other hand, embellishing his Act II "Parmi veder le lagrime" is stylistically correct (from ADAGIO, No. 8, m. 10 before [23] [vocal p. 116]). And "La donna è mobile" in Act III (No. 11, from m. 37, ALLEGRETTO [vocal p. 173]) may reasonably conclude with the famous Enrico Caruso cadenza with the high B-flat. A very small adjustment in the sparing accompaniment (delaying the final chord) may then be made to allow his high note to ring out alone to maximum effect.

Some variation is customary and acceptable for the cadenza at the end of Gilda's "Caro nome" in Act I—although one runs the risk of making it too flashy (No. 6, with the cadenza at m. 1 before [18] [vocal p. 97]). Gilda should not sound like *La traviata's* Violetta. Hers is an innocent vivacity, and she is only just awakening to erotic feelings. I like to ask the soprano to try this aria as written, just fading away at the end and *acting* the part of the ingénue. This leads quite naturally to the dreaminess in her repetition of her new lover's name as she exits.

There is also a tradition of altering a phrase earlier in "Caro nome"; and this may be because a breath is needed more than being a matter of interpretation or artistic choice. Example 4.1 illustrates the phrase and two approaches.

In the common execution, Gilda injects "ah" and adds two staccato articulations, grabs a breath, and places a fermata on two subsequent notes. It is far preferable to move the second syllable in order to make room for an acceptable breath and maintain the legato phrasing, in tempo, that works to reinforce both innocence and sensuality.

Example 4.1 Variations for Gilda's "Caro nome" in *Rigoletto* (Act I, No. 6, from m. 3 of 17 [vocal p. 96]).

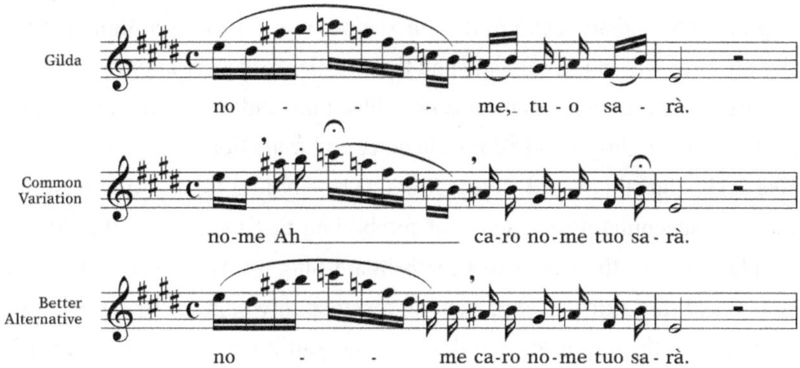

With or without excess fireworks, sometimes sopranos want to drag this aria down from the indicated ALLEGRO MODERATO, at 76 quarter notes per minute, to ADAGIO. Even disregarding the metronome marking, ALLEGRO MODERATO reflects a mood very different from that of ADAGIO. The entire aria is about infatuation and awakening desire. A tempo much slower than ALLEGRO MODERATO makes the quickened-heartbeat effect impossible.

After "Caro nome," *Rigoletto's* "curse motive" is echoed when Gilda exits from the stage singing "Gualtier Maldé" twice in a dotted rhythm (18, from m. 3 [vocal p. 97]). Instead of the B–B–B–E figure we see in the older scores, however, the critical edition has Gilda singing B–B–B–B, making this reference to the motive even more salient and potent. But the second time the figure is sung, we have a short crescendo and then her next "Caro nome" beginning with E. It seems likely that that crescendo toward E is the reason that the B–B–B–E tradition took hold. It is understandable. I am inclined to hammer home the B–B–B–B when she first sings her lover's name, but accept the B–B–B–E the second time for better transition to the next E. It softens the impact of the motive a bit, but it sounds better. It is also to be noted that with that E, Gilda begins a repeat of the first lines of her aria followed by "Gualtier Maldé" twice again, in a similar dotted rhythm, but this time on E–E–E–E. These two repetitions of "Gualtier Maldé" overlap the astonished courtiers' singing about her beauty.

In years gone by, we often heard trills ascending an octave in steps to high E across her final 3 measures. This ascent is best omitted since the trills tend to sound too loud with most sopranos who have voices big enough to sing the part, and any echo of the curse motive is hidden even more than it already is by her being offstage and the courtiers' onstage activity advancing the plot. A subtler variation is possible at the end of "Caro nome": start the trill with slightly longer duration notes and transition to shorter duration notes. This has the added virtue of better resembling the motivic material and thus accentuating the sense of foreboding that hangs over this opera. People come to the opera to hear brilliant singing of course, but "Caro nome" and this exit music present an instance in which we would do well to remember the importance of dramatic verisimilitude in holding the audience spellbound.

At the end of *Rigoletto's* second act (the "Vendetta"), when Gilda climbs through a passing note to take her last two notes up an octave and Rigoletto bumps his last note up an octave, the result is thrilling and enhances the cathartic moment as long as the notes are well executed (No. 10, at m. 13 before the end of the act). But a traditional high note that is redundant and dramatically unsatisfying is in the last act, when Rigoletto is about to throw what he thinks is the Duke's body into the water. Many baritones replace the written D-sharp with a grandstanding F-sharp on the syllable "l'on" in "All' onda" before we hear the Duke's voice offstage singing "La donna è mobile" (No. 14, [48], m. 54 [vocal p. 222]). If we consider what Rigoletto is about to do, we might conclude that some dispatch in finishing the deed would be advisable dramatically. A high note, which always at least feels like it entails a pause and an increase in volume, is anticlimactic and antirealistic. In addition, for me, the substitution is musically repetitive with Rigoletto's line a few measures earlier on "gioia!" since both are dominant-tonic cadences in a short space of time.

In the pit, some of *Rigoletto's* interesting instrumentation includes the way the solo cello takes the lead during the title character's Act II "Cortigiani," in which he pleads with the courtiers to have pity on him and release his daughter (No. 9, from [27] [vocal p. 150 at the key change]). Another example is the passing of the Duke's "La donna è mobile" melody to the sinister-sounding bassoon in the last act, just before Sparafucile says "È là il vostro'uomo" (No. 11 at [33], m. 17 [vocal p. 176, system 5]). The Act III storm has an offstage chorus in addition to the orchestra's portrayal of the rain and wind, an unusual choice and quite evocative (intermittently in No. 13 [vocal Nos. 17 and 18]). I would add that this storm is more dramatically important than at least some operatic storms, accompanying as it does the murder of Gilda. Making that murder the loudest moment of the performance therefore makes sense to me.

The eerie atmosphere of the Act I duet between Rigoletto and the assassin Sparafucile is quite original (No. 3 [vocal No. 6]). There are none of the higher instruments such as flutes, oboes, or violins; it is scored for clarinets, bassoons, bass drum, violas, cellos, and basses. But most remarkable is Verdi's giving the main melody to solo cello and solo bass, both played with mutes (beginning at m. 13), while the singers are assigned something a bit more melodic than recitative but not quite arioso and definitely not the main melody.

It may be necessary to defend the use of the mutes though. I am used to the fact that singers fear not being heard, but it always amazes me when an instrumentalist resists the use of an indicated mute on similar grounds. Yet I have heard cellists and bassists express just that fear. So, of course, I do my best to reassure them that I will not have the nonmuted instruments playing too loudly, and I emphasize that they, the muted instruments, *have the melody*. It is important to recognize that the mutes change the timbre of the instrument and do a lot to create the aforementioned eerie atmosphere—at least as much as suppressing some, but by no means all, volume. With this modest reduction in volume, it is possible for the singers to deliver a true pianissimo. The mutes really cannot be dispensed with and there is no good reason to do so. This issue can also come up in Act I of *Otello* where only a quartet of muted cellos play. And similarly, dropping the mutes undermines the intended mood (from [RR], m. 11).

Step into My Study . . .

Rigoletto is relatively short, and while less cutting is done today, some cuts live on. As is true elsewhere, one reason to cut is redundancy. For example, a case can be made for cutting the repeat of the Duke's cabaletta "Possente amor mi chiama" in Act II, since the words and the music are identical (No. 8, [24], m. 50 [vocal p. 130], with the repeat about 40 measures later at PRIMO TEMPO). Tenors rarely arrive at rehearsal with the kind of embellishments that would justify singing the repeat.

But in other instances, the apparent redundancy is superficial and something subtle but of genuine musical and dramatic interest is excised. A large cut of some significance comes in Act I, where Rigoletto sings the section beginning "Ah veglia o donna" (No. 4, [12], m. 15 [vocal p. 71, last measure]). This is repeated by Gilda and followed by a Gilda-Rigoletto duet, in which she sings a counter-melody. The traditional cut has Rigoletto singing just 4 measures of the first section and then jumping to the corresponding spot in the duet. It therefore makes a hash of the form: statement followed by restatement and then variation (a contrapuntal variation in this case).

One of the (happy) problems with an opera like *Rigoletto* is its abundance of beauty. It may seem that we can dispense with some of it and little is lost. But the impact of an opera is cumulative, and there is a different frisson when a composer as skillful as Verdi brings back a melody and then brings it back with a counter-melody woven around it. The pleasure we feel is multiplied when we recognize the melody the second time. And it increases exponentially when the counterpoint comes in. That is, yes, this counterpoint can seem even more thrilling than it usually does with the traditional cut. The audience may not know what is missing—the generosity of a great composer—but that is an unsatisfying justification for a cut like this, to say the least. While this passage admittedly makes a big role even more taxing, a baritone who can sing the part can sing it with this music.

There is also a longstanding tradition of making one very small but unfortunate cut in the Gilda-Duke duet of Act I, a cadenza that cannot remotely be considered redundant (No. 5, from [14], m. 29 [vocal p. 87]). When heard complete, the light, rapid intertwining of the unaccompanied voices comes about as near to titillation as music can take us. It is usually shortened because the tenor lacks the coloratura technique it calls for. It must be executed with a light and virtuosic touch to be effective. I always ask the singers to give it a try, but if they cannot make it sound both ecstatic and easy, the traditional cut is preferable.

There is one tradition that stands out in terms of the violence it does to a score, however. It occurs at the start of *Rigoletto's* Vendetta at the end of Act II: Rigoletto substitutes an E-flat for the written C on "Un vindice avrai" and eliminates a rest, swooping down to the next note (No. 10, m. 58 of [30], which is one measure before ALLEGRO VIVO [vocal p. 165, last measure]). The loss of the dramatic silence that the rest supplies, combined with the changed pitch, links together what Verdi wrote as two distinct sections. There are at least five musical reasons that this dubious practice is the epitome of bad tradition.

The Vendetta is sung in four subsections. The melody is sung first by Rigoletto, then Gilda, and then Rigoletto again, followed by a coda where father and daughter sing together. Verdi starts us off quite soft (***pp***), and given that Gilda is often cast with a lighter-than-ideal voice, some instruments may need to dip down to ***ppp*** when she sings alone. We are working at cross-purposes if Rigoletto starts his line singing too loudly. Moreover, with a melody repeated three times, beginning quite softly and becoming quite loud (***ff***) when the passage becomes a duet, we build intensity through each repetition.

In addition to volume, there are both tempos and harmonies to be considered. Specifically, the pivotal rest in m. 58 concludes a MODERATO section that begins at a speed of about 100 quarter notes per minute when Monterone first appears (m. 37 [vocal p. 164)]). Then after Rigoletto swears that Monterone will be avenged, the scene has a new mood, ALLEGRO VIVO and a metronome indication that is abruptly faster at 138 quarters. The instruction to Rigoletto at ALLEGRO VIVO is CON IMPETO, or impulsively, and *impeto* can have connotations of transport, rush, and rage.

Now whatever the singer does while the orchestra is silent for more than 2 measures—with the addition of a fermata—the conductor can then strictly observe the tempo change. However, the fact that the new tempo is unrelated to the previous tempo can be somewhat hidden from the audience's ears when the baritone holds his note for the entire measure and swoops into the Vendetta. The singer creates continuity where abrupt discontinuity is intended. Is tossing out the rest a good idea in order to thwart any applause? No. The composer dramatized a kind of mental break in the title character and injected suspense. Everything else about the scene conspires against applause, and a good actor (and actress) can hold the audience still, making clear that Rigoletto's rage is only getting started.

With the interpolated high note (an E-flat), we also hear a change in the harmonic structure. There is nothing musically wrong in the interpolation. Indeed, Verdi and others employ this kind of enharmonic transition all the time; i.e., pivoting on a note that is in both keys. Its effect can be exciting, but the fact is that the composer did not write such a relationship here. He gives us the tonic note of C minor and then begins a new musical idea in the key of A-flat major, after the rest, on the words "Sì, vendetta tremenda."[4]

Moreover, what concludes the music in C-minor is a variation of the curse motive. Bringing out themes and motives—without lapsing into exaggeration, of course—serves to enhance the pleasure an audience experiences in these complex, multi-layered works of art. It is one of the reasons these masterpieces "wear well." And I would offer that little is gained and something is lost when such an important, unifying motive is omitted, even once.

In summary, our five reasons *not* to do this—and notice that this has *nothing to do with taste or unwritten rules*—are: a ***pp*** indication, silence with a fermata for both singer and orchestra, an abrupt change to an unrelated tempo, the tonic of the prevailing key, and an echo of the single motive of the opera. All of this screams full stop and signals a dramatic turning point. Rigoletto is a suddenly changed man, with an emphasis on suddenly.

Beginning the long Vendetta relatively softly—and with the discontinuity in the harmony and tempo made obvious by observing the rest—permits a good singing actor all the space he needs to demonstrate the depth of his rage and his murderous intentions. It also gives Gilda all the more to work with as she sees her father snap before her eyes. Yet, at this point in musical history, performers are often afraid to do what is written, afraid to deprive the audience of what it has been led to expect. This is unfortunate.

By today's standards, the tempos in the score may seem slow: from a MODERATO section (100 quarter notes per minute), to ALLEGRO VIVO (138 quarters), to POCO PIÙ at the coda (144 quarters at [31], m. 36 [vocal p. 170]). At a faster speed however, the relative proportions between the sections should be respected. Therefore, if I want to get to about 160 quarter notes per minute at the coda, I need to plan ahead, and conduct the MODERATO at about 116 quarter notes in order to achieve the intended dramatic effect.

It is also stylistically acceptable—and a time-honored tradition—to bump the tempo up a little for each of the three statements in the ALLEGRO VIVO section. This of course requires more planning to ensure that we land where we want to land, with a coda at least 50 percent faster than the MODERATO section.

However, like anything else, the tempo must work with the singers involved. I have also done this Vendetta with Gilda's restatement a little slower than Rigoletto's statement followed by a much faster restatement by Rigoletto. This works for some singers and it works dramatically since Gilda is pleading between Rigoletto's bursts of rage. What works least well is performing the entire ALLEGRO VIVO section at a single tempo. It is difficult to overstate the importance of making this entire conclusion to Act II as exciting as it can be.

My favorite things

The final duet, especially the flute arpeggios on Gilda's "Lassù in cielo vicina alla madre" and then those of the violins on the repeat (No. 14, at [51] and at [52] [vocal p. 228–229]). A lesser composer would have used the harp perhaps, or repeated the flute effect. These arpeggios can be magical, especially with a Gilda who has good breath control and can sing long lines, which allows me to slow slightly on the repeat. This, the emotional high point of the opera for me, could not be more perfectly scored.

La Traviata

La traviata (1853) got off to a rocky start but, after a bit more than a year, and with some revisions, its remounting was a success. It has been characterized as a bel canto opera, probably largely because of some spectacular vocalism. While some people may disagree as to whether the opera is forward looking enough to be called the first verismo opera, it is most definitely not a bel canto opera. First, the plot is modern. Indeed, its heroine's lifestyle was considered too racy for a contemporary setting, and initially it was set in the 1700s. The other modern aspect of the opera is its extensive through-composition. There are fewer set pieces with the kind of clear dividing lines that typically provoke applause than we find in the bel canto literature.

The role of Violetta requires acting ability with a voice of some size, beauty, endurance, and flexibility. Alfredo's part is on the lyric side for a Verdi tenor. But the part also lies a bit low for this type of tenor, so it is relished by some but is a problematic role for other, equally good tenors. The baritone Germont has a relatively short role, but the part still requires a noble timbre and the combination of dramatic power and lyricism that is the hallmark of all Verdi baritones.

Decorating the vocal line in this opera is simply unwarranted. Its demands for vocal virtuosity are mapped out in the score. At the same time, many of the traditional interpolated high notes work beautifully. At the end of Act I's "Sempre libera," for example, Violetta's replacing her last E-flat (on the first syllable of "pensier") with a rest, a G, and an E-flat an octave above what is written is acceptable. This is in m. 8 before the end of the act (No. 3, p.106 [vocal p. 76]). However, while this variation is brilliant and exciting, substituting a B-flat for the interpolated high E-flat is anticlimactic. If the soprano does not want to chance the E-flat, it is much better to put a slight hold on the high C that begins the preceding measure and perform the end of the aria as written. This serves the drama without risking a bad note or an anticlimax.

Similarly, moving the final C up an octave at the end of Alfredo's Act II cabaletta is in keeping with Verdian style. It may be risky, however, given how low the part lies. Since the high C is an embellishment, many fine tenors have sung the cabaletta without it, and it should not be performed if risky. By the same token, the lack of a high C is no reason to cut the cabaletta. (The cabaletta in No. 4 begins on p. 118 [vocal 84].)

In both of these cases, it is common and reasonable for the singer to omit a few notes just before the bravura ending in order to capture sufficient breath.

There are a few passages that would benefit from reconsideration of the tempos we traditionally hear. Act III's "Addio del passato" is one of two lovely melodies that express Violetta's grief (No. 8, from p. 353 [vocal 213]). The mood of the last-act aria is previewed in Act II with her "Dite alla giovina" (No. 5, from p. 158 [vocal 105]). Their similarity in melody, rhythm, and accompaniment is unmistakable, and the score indicates a similar speed for both. This tells us that the echo of Act II in Act III is no accident; it also tells us that dragging down the tempo of "Addio del passato" too much is wrong. As a rule, it is hard to maintain an interesting and beautiful line when we slow down too much, and a good singing actress does not need to handicap herself with a too-slow tempo. The score's 50 dotted quarter notes a minute may seem a bit fast to our ears—perhaps because we have grown so accustomed to hearing both of these passages played much more slowly. Nonetheless, a tempo much slower than 40 dotted quarter notes a minute makes either section quite saccharine and indulgent.

Another moment that is often distorted by a wrong-headed tempo is Violetta's cry of "Amami Alfredo" in Act II (No. 6, p. 190 [vocal 123]). Despite there being no indication to slow the tempo, it is inevitably heard at a much slower tempo. The word *amami* has its accent on the first syllable. When taken too slowly, the accent inevitably shifts to the second syllable. More important, we lose the sense of desperation inherent in the phrase when it is stretched more than just a little.

The opposite tempo issue arises in the short Act I duet between Violetta and Alfredo. Violetta has a figure with an exacting rhythm that is often approached faster than indicated (No. 2, from 1 measure before BRILLANTE, p. 57 [vocal 45]). The rhythm will be repeated several times and will reappear when the couple sings together in the cadenza. It is difficult enough even at the indicated tempo, and poorly calibrated tempo traditionally has resulted in a variety of alterations in the music.

The cause of its becoming virtually unsingable lies embedded about 20 measures earlier. At that point, Alfredo has a line with the indication CON ESPANSIONE. Naturally, after our romantic hero pours his heart out "expansively," I will return to the previous tempo. However, I must not over-shoot and get faster than the indicated ANDANTINO of about 96 eighth notes per minute.

I have heard it moved up close to 108 eighth notes per minute or so, and this is bound to render Violetta's lines at BRILLANTE impossible.

I like to relax the speed a very little for Violetta's coquettish reply to Alfredo's ardor but quickly reestablish the indicated tempo. Such rubato is altogether fitting in Italian music of this period, as long as we do not get carried away and let Violetta's line drag too much. This kind of fine and fleeting adjustment honors the tempo for the longer passage, honors this exacting rhythm as written, and honors a tradition that holds the singing actor at the center of our attention.

There is an additional consideration in the pit: These notes are doubled by flute and clarinet players who, depending on the theater, may or may not be able to hear the soprano. A carefully controlled tempo—not too slow, not too fast, but just right—also allows the precise ensemble between the pit and the stage that can lift a performance from very good to truly *brillante*.

Step into My Study . . .

With *La traviata*, we have a relatively short opera with excessive traditional cuts and traditional inattention to clear tempo indications.

Cuts

Again, when the music and the words are identical, cutting may be reasonable. For example, a case may be made for cutting the repeat of the tenor's cabaletta: "Oh mio rimorso! oh infamia!" The cabaletta, in No. 4 of Act II, begins at ALLEGRO (p. 118 [vocal 84]), and the repeat 36 measures later is identical.

There are instances where cuts are ill advised and unnecessary, however. The reprise of Violetta's Act I "Ah, fors' è lui" could be included for both dramatic and musical reasons (No. 3 at DOLCISSIMO p. 85 [vocal 67]). Dramatically, the text is different and deepens our understanding of Violetta's situation at the moment. Musically, since the cabaletta "Sempre libera" is almost always repeated, repeating the aria gives the scene a symmetry and balance and respects a form dating back to Mozart: the aria and cabaletta each sung twice.

Another example is the cabaletta of Germont's Act II "Di provenza" (No. 6 from ASSAI MODERATO, p. 209 [vocal 132]). I have generally included this cabaletta since the 1980s and my request is usually met with surprise. There are prominent theaters where it is rarely, if ever, performed. The reasoning for restoring it runs as follows: If Germont is so upset by Alfredo's response that he turns on his son—in many stagings even striking him—the stark change of mood going into the cabaletta makes perfect dramatic sense. Germont catches himself and proceeds more cautiously. As to the redundancy: that is Germont's character. Throughout the previous duet with Violetta, he has made the same basic argument to her in various ways until he has broken her down. He is insistent. He never stops pleading his case or, less kindly, he never stops nagging. On the other hand, part of the cabaletta is repeated and the repeat is identical. Cutting the repeat is far more reasonable than eliminating the cabaletta in its entirety.

The second verse of Violetta's last aria, beginning "Le gioie, i dolori," also deserves inclusion (No. 8 from p. 356 [vocal 215, last measure]). The text is so poignant that a good singing actress—certainly a requirement for Violetta—can supply the most intense emotion of the performance. Although the music in both instances is identical, as in Mozart's and the bel canto operas, there is an opportunity to vary the accompaniment. The strings may begin by playing three notes in one bow direction for a relatively legato sound. Then, on the repeat, they might produce a much shorter, drier sound or even tap the string with the bow. There are many such choices that can be made, some representing greater license than others.

Traditionally, the final lines of Alfredo, Germont, Annina, and the Doctor have been cut at the end of *La traviata*. While this is a musically acceptable approach, it robs the work of one of its verismo moments. It is unlikely that no one in the room would say a word upon Violetta's death. On the other hand, even if I restrain the orchestra—and there is a limit to how much the sound can be reduced—there can be difficulty hearing at least some of the cast in some productions. So it is also possible to make the final measures purely symphonic. Or in more colloquial terms, it is possible (and great fun) to let the orchestra rip. Either way, I impose a little rubato on the final beats—the briefest possible hesitation—to continue Violetta's struggle, if you will, as well as to forestall applause for just a moment. Violetta's death deserves nothing less than all that a full symphony orchestra can deliver.

Tempos and Tempo Relationships

As noted earlier, there are instances when singers would benefit from a more disciplined approach to tempo in this opera. For the conductor, identifying tempo relationships and keeping transitions smooth is not very difficult. But there is one passage that, far from requiring careful calculation of tempo changes, demands the opposite. The LARGO of the Act II finale has acquired all kinds of tempo changes that Verdi never wrote, along with corresponding conducting adjustments (continuation of No. 7, p. 320 [vocal 185, m. 1]). But this long sequence from the entrance of Germont with "Di sprezzo degno," is marked LARGO, all the way to the end of the act. There are no changes indicated through Alfredo's remorse, "Ah si che feci?" or Violetta's aside, "Alfredo, Alfredo, di questo core" or the onlookers' comments.

It requires a lot of discipline to portray contrasting emotions for about six and a half minutes at an unwavering tempo. If we trust Verdi, however, that discipline will lend a unity to the whole and produce a tremendous cumulative impact, ending with the opera's loudest moment. It will not, however, if we treat this as three or four distinct pieces, each with its own tempo. My personal experience is that 42 to 46 quarter notes per minute works for the entire section, with only the modest flexibility typical of nineteenth-century music. There should be no need to alter the beat pattern throughout.

Throughout this section, Alfredo and Germont have a lot of staccato and accent marks, and this contrasts nicely with the more legato line of Violetta. Furthermore, Alfredo often has many more syllables than his father (or anyone else) and correspondingly shorter notes, resulting in a more tearful impression. The three principals' lines will come through best if Alfredo keeps his notes fairly short, Germont's are just a bit longer, and Violetta lets her notes sail over everything else in as long a line as possible. Devoting a little extra time in rehearsal to getting these lines crystal clear is well worth it.

In the Orchestra

With respect to the use of the orchestra, *La traviata* includes one of the more complicated bandas to try to move into the pit. This is because Act III's "Baccanale" includes a chorus (No. 9 from p. 360 [vocal 218]). If there are not enough musicians to place the banda backstage, then some can "travel" backstage (or into the wings) and return to the pit to finish the opera if the distance permits. Alternatively, if it can be worked out with the union, the musicians can record this small amount of music to be played during the performance. Once, in a very small theater, I was able to position the chorus in a box in the auditorium so that the chorus and instruments sounded close together even though the instruments were played from the pit. But this was a very special case. Some have performed this music with the chorus singing unaccompanied. For me, this is the worst choice.

A different kind of problem arises in Alfredo's Act II aria, at least for some of us. At "De' miei bollenti spiriti," the violin and viola parts are marked PIZZICATO while the cellos and basses are directed to play ARCO (No. 4 at ANDANTE, p. 111 [vocal 79]). A tradition dictates that we switch those articulations, having the lower strings play pizz and the higher strings arco (spiccato). Arturo Toscanini adopted this change and it was an old idea when he did it. As a rule, I try to find a rationale to remain with what is written; that is, to figure out what I am missing. But as this score has it, the sound seems all wrong to many of us. Full disclosure: I have yet to find any support for this tradition among scholars who have pored over the sources and done their best to resolve questions and address ambiguities, as is clear in the critical edition. Understandably, then, there are those who will not make this switch.

One issue preoccupies me more than any other in a performance of *La traviata*, however: maintaining its spirit of beauty and delicacy. Even though it uses the same-sized orchestra as *Rigoletto*, it has a lightness that is special. In addition, relative to *Rigoletto* and other Verdi operas, this score is a little on the sketchy side, so thoughtful consideration of dynamics and articulation is called for, particularly when we see music repeated but unvarying.[5]

The prelude begins ADAGIO and ends ALLARGANDO, DIMINUENDO, MORENDO, which anticipates the entire story. But taking the concluding ALLARGANDO too broadly, as we often hear, will give the moment ponderousness that ill suits it. This is because as Act I opens, we find ourselves at quite a festive party in an opulent setting.

In addition, the curtain goes up to ALLEGRO BRILLANTISSIMO E MOLTO VIVACE. So those final 2 measures of the prelude should not drag us down too far in speed. I use the waning volume as effectively as I can. It is also to be noted that after the entire orchestra bubbles with the Champagne-like music immediately after the prelude, Verdi reduces the string section to just a few players. In fact, depending on the size and acoustics of the theater, this passage can sound exquisite with just a string quintet, which reasonably could be playing at the kind of party we see onstage.

An aspect of the score that can throw us off track a bit if we are not attentive is its repeated rhythmic figures in the accompaniments. These are just chords used percussively. They were unusual for the time and anticipate the work of today's composers of every kind: i.e., concert and opera composers but also rock musicians and jazz combos. In the confrontation between Alfredo and Violetta of the Act II finale, we can sustain the drama but avoid excess by having the violins, and at times violas, play these *ostinati* using one of the light, bouncing bowing techniques like ricochet in No. 7 from p. 303 [vocal 174]). Other choices that may create short and long effects are *spiccato*, *battuto*, or *molto tenuto* alla *corda*. Any of these may be used when Germont sings of his daughter in Act II (No. 5, from ALLEGRO MODERATO, p. 139 [vocal 94]), and through much of the last scene of the opera including the heroine's final aria.

Thoughtful choices about articulation—as well as tempo and dynamics—can also paint different pictures in *La traviata's* two preludes, which look very similar on the page. While the first prelude has delicate lines, it has some subordinate lines (in the cello in particular) that can be accented a bit to inject some tension, perhaps embedding the idea of a struggle in the listener's mind. This has to be very subtle in light of the act's opening scene, but it is consistent with the spirit of Violetta's aria "Sempre libera," which closes the act. It is fair to say that sopranos will each supply us with a different mix of emotion in this aria, but some desperation or rebelliousness is part of that mix. In the last act prelude, on the other hand, very similar music played a bit more slowly, softly, and even gently can preview her acceptance of death as inevitable. It may also be noted that the first act prelude is in B minor, and the prelude to the last act is in C minor, the key commonly associated with funerals.

These effects depend on having the proper number of strings, however. A reduced section will not create the same effect and may require different choices.

My favorite things

The LARGO of the Act II finale, discussed above. It paints all of the characters and the Parisian atmosphere in one great ensemble.

Aida

In a way, some of the greatest challenges in *Aida* (1871) belong to management. It is expensive to produce, and cutting corners in *Aida* is self-defeating to say the least. I refer both to the quality of the physical production in every respect and trying to trim ten or fifteen minutes off the running time.

In addition, *Aida* is one of those works that come to mind when the dearth of Verdian singers is lamented. The five leads are all spinto singers; they have to cut through a lot of orchestra. They are hard to find and expensive. Aida and Amneris must have great control over an extended range. Radames is a long part and a little higher than some other spinto tenor parts. Unlike Manrico, however, he does not require a high C (neither a written C nor a traditionally interpolated note). Amonasro, the Ethiopian king, is not easy but it is relatively short. Still, he needs volume yet some lyricism in the duet with his daughter. Lastly, the part of Ramfis requires a deep resonant bass with a bit more range than average. In Act I, Scene 2, he has an a cappella high F and other, optional notes that lie more in the baritone range than in that of the bass. In the beginning of Act III, however, he descends to the low F-sharp almost two octaves below that high F.

Aida contains considerable through-composition, some unconventional tempo relationships, and a big, passionate orchestra. It also contains Verdi's most extensive and sophisticated use of motives; it is sophisticated in that he brings motives and themes back in subtler ways than he and his fellow

Italians had before. Near the close of Act II, Scene 2, for example, we hear four themes played simultaneously (from SOSTENUTO COME PRIMA, m. 9 before W [vocal p. 191]). On the other hand, when the melodies and themes reappear in *Aida*, they tend to do so in much the same form; i.e., with the same rhythms and at approximately the same tempo, if with different instrumentation. It would take the next generation to follow Wagner into reprising the motives in more varied and disguised forms.

One of the composer's more striking novelties in *Aida* is the way he joins each pair of scenes in the first, second, and fourth acts. We should note that, in each case, the end of the first scene is marked not by an ending bar line but with a double bar line, suggesting that we are bridging from one section to another of the same piece. The manner in which the harmonies and themes link the two scenes was quite modern and unconventional for Verdi's audiences but yields benefits for modern audiences: fewer breaks, more flowing drama. The music can support a relatively cinematic transition from the first to the second scene in each case, assuming the physical production permits this.

In Act I, an E-flat handed-off from the cello to the harp in the last measure of Scene 1 serves as a pivot in a transition from A-flat major to E-flat major. Several modulations form a bridge between the two scenes of Act II. And in Act IV, the theme that ends the "Judgment Scene" at a high dynamic level opens Scene 2 quite softly (with another shift between related keys). Then the music previously written in quarter notes is varied a little both melodically and rhythmically and written in eighth notes. So the audience hears, effectively, the same melody at the same speed, yet subtly transformed and hushed. Moving seamlessly between these scenes befits the relentless progression to the awful denouement.

The end of the Judgment Scene, in fact, is the emotional high point of the opera for me and nearly the dynamic high point. The end of the "Triumphal Scene"—the Act II finale—will be louder because of the sheer number of forces assembled, but there I must exercise some caution to maintain clarity and avoid a downright raucous sound. At the end of the Judgment Scene on the other hand, I am egging the musicians on to play very loud (or, as loud as they can without getting raucous there either).

No matter how expert the through-composition, however, no matter how much the composer wanted to obscure any seams, in some places in some operas we have to make room for applause. In *Aida*, one example comes immediately after the heroine's "O patria mia" in Act III. Here we have a very few orchestral measures before Aida's a cappella line, "Ciel! mio padre!" This seems to indicate that the section after "O patria mia" should be performed immediately, without any pause for applause. Much as, musically, we might like to barrel ahead at the end of the aria, however, it is not possible to step on the inevitable applause for Aida's aria or compel Amonasro to enter awkwardly during that applause. I find that it is reasonable to pause for applause after the final note Aida sings ([G], m. 5 [vocal p. 215]), delaying the few bars of orchestral music that follow. Then after applause, I start that short orchestral passage as Amonasro enters and slide directly into the next musical section as the father-daughter conversation takes place.

Verdi continues to vary his orchestral palette in *Aida*. The oboe moves up and down a Middle Eastern-sounding scale to give an oriental flavor to the heroine's Act III aria "O patria mia" (from [C], ANDANTE MOSSO [vocal p. 210]). The opera also has a bass clarinet, a relatively new instrument at the time. It has a warm and mellow sound and adds a certain gravity to the scene between Amneris and Radames prior to the judgment of the priests in Act IV, Scene 1 (from m. 4 before [B] [vocal p. 262, m. 3]). Had Verdi used the more obvious bassoon in that range, the color could be construed as either somewhat comic or even a bit macabre.

One of the more notable orchestral passages is the barcarole-like opening of Act III (the Nile Scene), which gives a sense of the movement of a great river. As the violins play staccato Gs cycling through four different octaves, I like to ask them for one of the bouncing bowing techniques such as *saltando*, which helps set the melody in the flute in relief.

In addition to a conventional banda that plays throughout Act II, we hear the onstage Egyptian trumpets (two parts) at the most thrilling points of that act's finale. (See especially Scene 2, from m. 5 before [E], "Ballabile" [vocal p. 122], where both groups of Egyptian trumpets onstage play against an offstage banda and the orchestra in the pit.) Special trumpets were fashioned with fixed pitches for the initial production of *Aida* and, since then, other instruments of varying reliability have served. Today, the best results are obtained with an instrument that is, in fact, a modern trumpet built with an elongated body, strictly "for show" if you will. Once we have obtained the right instruments, the trumpet players ascend to the stage in costume. In the best case, the set permits the trumpet players to play at the top of the proscenium; otherwise, they may play at the extreme opposite sides of the stage's apron. Whatever the arrangement, the greater the separation between the Egyptian trumpets and the pit, the more soaring will be the counterpoint, particularly where the two Egyptian trumpet parts come together and play antiphonally while the more quotidian banda and pit accompany.

Step into My Study . . .

In *Aida*, tempo relationships are fairly straightforward and metronome indications are abundant. Like some other works however, *Aida* can inspire exaggeration. One example occurs before the final orchestral coda of Act II, Scene 2. The music is moving at about 132 quarter notes a minute, and soon the melody heard earlier in the Egyptian trumpets will return at TEMPO PRIMO (m. 9 before the end). This is 100 quarter notes a minute, established at the top of the scene. Some are tempted to slow about 4 measures before the TEMPO PRIMO indication, preparatory to that reprise. But this is something akin to the unwelcome elbow in the ribs, urging "Hey, listen up, something great is about to happen." The truth is that nobody is going to miss the excitement when that melody returns at an abruptly slower tempo. And the dramatic difference is that the disciplined observation of the tempos as written will capture the energetic cheering followed by elation of the celebrating crowd. There is a release, a climax, when the melody returns; and signaling it early blunts its impact.

Another interpolated ritard that similarly blunts the impact of what Verdi wrote occurs in one of the other thrilling crowd scenes of the opera. It is worth pausing to analyze because the scene contains one of those moments when we can go astray as a result of inattention. It occurs in the large ensemble in Act I, Scene 1, after the King and Ramfis cry "Guerra!" and Amneris sings "Ritorna vincitor!"

The tempo is ALLEGRO MAESTOSO at 88 quarter notes per minute for 48 measures from R to U (vocal p. 36–45). Then the score indicates PIÙ MOSSO at 116 quarter notes a minute when the King and Ramfis start cheerleading with cries of "Guerra!" (U). Soon thereafter, the score indicates gradually increasing speed over 13 measures (INCALZANDO from U, m. 5 [vocal p. 46]). A swing into beating twice per measure and accelerating to about 66 half notes a minute is reasonable. Then Amneris sings "Ritorna vincitor" directly to Radames (A PIACERE at U, m. 18 [vocal p. 50]). And 5 measures later, the orchestra alone returns to PRIMO TEMPO (at V [vocal p. 51]).

Amneris generally, and rightly, slows down and milks this command to her hero, but this should not slow down the subsequent music. It is to be noted that A PIACERE is always a very short-term indication to give a soloist room for expression, and this scene has well in excess of a dozen specific metronome indications. If Verdi wanted us all to slow down until further orders, he would have had something more specific to say at this point. So immediately after Amneris's short line, when the crowd echoes her command for just a few measures, I snap back to the brisk tempo resulting from INCALZANDO.

(Unfortunately, the editors of some vocal scores have misled their readers by repeating a COL CANTO indication for the chorus's repetition of her line beginning in the following measure. This indication is not in the orchestra score when the chorus repeats these words, however. So this is one of many instances where editors trying to be helpful ensure that a tradition is practically set in stone and difficult to eradicate.)

Only 3 measures after Amneris's A PIACERE line, the indication is PRIMO TEMPO for the grand march out of the scene. That is, ALLEGRO MAESTOSO, 88 quarter notes a minute. The grandeur of the march that leaves Aida alone on the stage is all the greater with a quick reminder of the faster tempo we were in before the brief interruption of Amneris's line. And Verdi's vision of a battle-hungry crowd for just these few measures is much more exciting and dramatically authentic than dragging the whole company slowly and grandly into the march. The crowd shouting "Guerra!" is anything but majestic, even though its members are priests and dignitaries.

When we return to the tempo of ALLEGRO MAESTOSO, we are also returning to the melody first stated at the earlier ALLEGRO MAESTOSO. So, PRIMO

TEMPO means that even though we may not feel the tempo change as seamless, there is a largely unconscious recognition of approximately the "right" tempo because we are returning to a musical idea heard earlier. Thus, this indication requires planning of a somewhat different kind than we have discussed heretofore.

Before concluding a discussion of *Aida*, there is an interesting question to consider in Act I, Scene 2. The scene opens with the priestesses singing offstage, followed by a faster ballet. Soon, Radames and Ramfis sing onstage at a noticeably slower tempo, GRAVE (at C [vocal p. 69]), and they are joined by priests onstage. After that, the priestesses offstage return for 2 measures, marked PIÙ MOSSO, COME PRIMA (at D [vocal p. 73]). Then the priests' and priestesses' lines alternate for several measures.

So should each of the choruses continue in its own tempo (come prima)? Or should both continue at the somewhat faster tempo of the priestesses from this PIÙ MOSSO forward? I believe the former approach is what is intended. Different conductors might reach a different conclusion about whether the tempos should shift for a single measure at a time but, to me, it is intrinsically more interesting, more realistic, and more dramatic for the two choruses to continue on separate paths. Such drama in music was something Verdi spent a lifetime striving for, and *Aida* is an opera that is adventurous and innovative in a number of ways. Simply shifting both choruses to one tempo seems quite pedestrian.

It would be reasonable to ask whether Verdi would not have specified the alternating tempos. But as specific as he was becoming, this is still nineteenth-century Italian opera. Given the conventions of his time, I would hardly expect a new tempo expression every measure or two. I might see something like that in a twenty-first-century score, but not in a nineteenth-century or earlier score. Only general guidance about the pattern desired would be needed among those who shared the same performing conventions.

Two additional observations are appropriate: At times, the priestesses drop out or briefly reinforce the pattern of the men on stage. The onstage priests and soloists sing more measures without the priestesses than vice versa. In addition, sometimes both of the choruses and the soloists are singing the same tempo. All of this means that there are more measures with the priests' tempo, and it is that tempo that will dominate the scene and end the act rather than the faster tempo of the priestesses. This, too, strikes me as more apt dramatically.

It is also worth noting that the voices from offstage will generally sound a little slower because of the distance the sound must travel. So however much faster the women sing, it will not be quite as different when it reaches the last row in the top balcony.

My favorite things

The opening of Act III, discussed above. One can practically feel the Nile's current.

Otello

Some consider *Otello* (1887) to be Verdi's finest work. It is without doubt one of the most successful adaptations of Shakespeare in opera. Continuing on the path he had been on, Verdi combined music and drama with a great deal of intense emotion and what is arguably his most Wagnerian score. Composer Arrigo Boito as librettist has always received a great deal of credit for the success of *Otello* and *Falstaff*, including credit from Verdi himself. He skillfully compressed very large works and supplied words that allowed Verdi to create melody throughout but rarely stop the action for an aria.

The lead is Verdi's most dramatic tenor role. The part is more than spinto; it is virtually a heldentenor part. It is also long and requires an extended range. Act II, in particular, requires considerable stamina. He has a quartet, a scene with Iago (Jago in the score), an aria, and a duet with Iago. In some measure, this explains why most tenors simply cannot sing the aria "Ora e per sempre addio sante memorie" at or near the indicated 88 quarter notes per minute (at the second [C]). However, the (admittedly understandable) tendency to go extremely quickly can equally handicap the tenor because there is a traditional PIÙ MOSSO—which I endorse—at the second [E]. I have found that beginning the aria at about 104 quarter notes per minute, or just a little faster if necessary, permits a move to 116 quarter notes, or possibly even 120 quarter notes at the fastest, right after the aria (at the second [E]).

Within these limits, it is imperative that a conductor keep the orchestra from getting too loud. If Otello feels he has to push to be heard in this aria, and especially in the two pages that follow the aria, he will almost certainly exhaust his vocal resources. This does nobody any good and the conductor really has a duty to avoid being the cause of a breakdown.

Desdemona is a classic Verdian soprano like Leonora of *Il trovatore*, Luisa Miller, or Alice Ford of *Falstaff.* She must not be cast with too light a voice. In Act III, she sings over a full orchestra with a dramatic tenor in a mighty duet. Iago is a bass baritone closer to Macbeth than to Germont. However, what is paramount in this role is for the singer to be a fine actor with a complete command of nuanced Italian and impeccable diction.

Verdi's fully developed orchestration skill, and the public's growing taste for hearing the orchestra featured, are evident from the opening scene. The opera begins with a wild storm that Otello's ship weathers to deliver him to Cyprus. This is one of the most exciting storms in music—of which there are many. One relatively unusual touch is an organ. It plays a pedal point (specifically, a cluster of C, C-sharp, and D) from the second measure through the entire storm. Personally, I like Arturo Toscanini's aggressive approach to this opening, beating four times per measure, then in two at "Dio Fulgor della bufera" (H, m. 7).

The storm has its potential difficulties, however. There is, for example, a passage where the trombones have a G-flat major arpeggio in sixteenth notes at a tempo of 152 quarter notes per minute. This would have been unplayable on slide trombones as recently as the late nineteenth century and may well have been written with piston instruments in mind. Indeed, in the mid-twentieth century, Arturo Toscanini gave those notes to the French horns who are not playing anything for that moment. There are a couple of other instances that look like they were probably written for piston instruments (for example, Act III, at m. 6 of the second J in the act). Today, the best trombone players in the best orchestras can play these passages; but they are greeted as the point of pride that they should be. Competent trombonists in good orchestras may find these passages a little beyond their abilities.

An equally difficult passage occurs for basses near the end of the Act IV (from POCO PIÙ MOSSO at U). After Desdemona's sad "Salce" and

"Ave Maria," the basses enter in an unrelated key. But Verdi also writes high above the normal range for the instrument, into the viola range in fact. The combination of the unrelated key and strange timbre that results from pushing the basses so high helps establish some tension and foreboding as Otello enters through a secret door and approaches Desdemona with murder on his mind.

In this wonderful score, we find additional orchestral color in the four solo cellos that begin the love duet at the close of Act I (from **RR**, m. 11) and the offstage mandolin and guitar that accompany the children's chorus in Act II (from the first **Q**).

Step into My Study . . .

Otello's sweep arises equally from its through-composition, its counterpoint, and its intriguing tempo relationships.

Especially in its first three acts, the opera was written to be played without interruption. Even though we have distinct sections, even arias and duets as well as choruses, they continue into what follows without any possibility of stopping for applause. In the last act, we generally stop to permit applause for Desdemona's twin arias "Salce" followed by "Ave Maria." Doing this, however, spoils the pungent effect of the entrance of the basses in an unrelated key (at **U**), as noted above. It seems that Verdi must have written this harmonic relationship knowing that it would be covered by applause, just as he earlier wrote the connection of scenes in three of *Aida's* acts knowing that applause, and probably a scene change, would break this connection for the listener. As in *Aida*, of course, we can experience this connection in recordings.

With *Otello*, Verdi also continues his exploration of counterpoint's possibilities in theater. It may not be as obvious as in the ensembles of *Falstaff*. But it is in fact abundant, sophisticated, and completely integrated with the drama. We see notable examples in the quartet in Act II and, above all, in the Act III ensemble.

The quartet in Act II of *Otello* may seem to resemble the *Rigoletto* quartet in that it pairs two male-female couples (from LARGO at m. 19 of **X**).

But *Otello's* is more complicated than the *Rigoletto* quartet, where Rigoletto and Gilda sing to each other while the Duke and Maddalena do likewise and all are relatively equal. In the *Otello* quartet, Iago and Emilia whisper to each other. While Desdemona sings to Otello, he voices his own thoughts rather than engaging in a conversation.

Correctly balancing all of this is quite difficult. At first, Desdemona should sound louder than the other three voices. Only at Emilia's "uomo crudel" and Iago's demand for the handkerchief does that couple begin to fully sing out (from m. 2 before [Y]). Otello also sings out 5 measures later when he laments that Desdemona is lost and he is mocked. Here, the entire orchestra moves from ***pp*** to ***f***. In addition, even within the orchestra there are times when some sections or players are playing softly and others more loudly. Observing these indications, too, is essential to properly balancing this quartet.

The great Act III ensemble includes counterpoint far more sophisticated than, say, the terrific finale that concludes Act II of *La traviata*. It has much in common with the Act III ensemble of Amilcare Ponchielli's *La Gioconda*, written eight years earlier. While *Otello* is surely the greater opera, Verdi seems to have been influenced by Ponchielli (or Ponchielli's success). Both ensembles have a soaring melody with a chorus and several characters singing music that fills out and supports this melody.

In *Otello*, the ensemble begins after Otello manhandles Desdemona before the Venetian delegation and nobles assembled at Cyprus (from LARGO at the second [J], m. 18, in Act III). But it is the exchange between the conspirators, Iago and Roderigo in this case, that is most striking. They conduct a private dialogue that is unrelated musically and therefore stands out in contrast. This makes the counterpoint more complex but also makes the scene more effective in theatrical terms; it helps tell the story and develop the characters. For the conductor, the goal in this ensemble should be controlling the tension to arrive at the climax only at the F major chord on Desdemona's "quel sol sereno e vivido" (at m. 7 of the second [P], marked RITENUTO). The climax of this scene is one of the two dynamic high points of this opera for me, the other coming in the storm that opens the opera.

When it comes to tempo, performances of *Otello* are generally very respectful of the score. There is one clear tempo relationship in Act I, however, that is rarely heard executed as written. Doing so takes some virtuosity on the part of Iago and, while it is not hard for the conductor, it takes some planning: Iago's toast to the marriage of Otello and Desdemona must have a pulse slow enough to permit doubling the tempo at PRESTO DOPPIO TEMPO. The effort is worthwhile because Iago's tongue-twisting patter can be very effective at generating excitement, portraying his diabolical nature, and showing off his command of the language and his diction.

As ever, I need to know where I want to end up and then plan the tempo shifts accordingly. Since the nearest prior tempo indication is many pages earlier in the score (m. 8 before X), some judgment is required. But in my opinion, based on all that comes between, Iago's toast may be considered the beginning of a separate section.

I aim to get to about 100 quarter notes per minute when the chorus stops singing and Iago begins goading Cassio to drink up (CC). Iago's toast (m. 4 before DD) and the brief repartee that follows allow me to broaden the tempo closer to 90. Then, doubling the tempo to 90 half notes per minute at PRESTO DOPPIO TEMPO results in a fast but singable speed (DD, m. 15).

Giving the Machiavellian Iago some of the tools of comedy and giving him total command of the stage at times is entirely consistent with Shakespeare's work. It is passages like this that makes Verdi, in the opinion of many, the most successful translator of Shakespeare into music. It is also worth pointing out that even audiences that do not speak the language get it when a singer's diction is crisp. That is, a rapid-fire passage like this conveys something about the story and the character even when the audience has to lean on the supertitles. (It might also be argued that Iago shares the emotional high point of this opera at the end of Act II where he begins his campaign to drive Otello mad.)

There are many instances like this where tempo relationships are expressly stated, but there are also some more complicated relationships, particularly in Act III as Otello descends into madness.

Act III, going mad in private

The tension begins when Otello confronts Desdemona over the handkerchief that she must produce to prove herself faithful. From here until the transition to the next scene, where the trumpets announce the arrival of the ambassador, we should steadily build drama and tension in a line that is *almost* straight.

The score indicates ALLEGRO AGITATO, 132 quarter notes a minute from m. 5 of the first [E] through m. 8 of the first [G]. When Desdemona takes the position that Otello must be kidding, the meter changes to $\frac{6}{8}$ (m. 9). Verdi indicates a constant pulse, now 132 eighth notes a minute, making it half the speed. That is, I continue beating at the same speed, and the eighth note takes twice as long as it did before. But because the stresses come less frequently in $\frac{6}{8}$ meter as opposed to $\frac{4}{4}$ meter, the listener perceives the beat, or pulse, as a bit slower than half the speed.

More technically however, this is a somewhat unusual use of a meter change with an indication of LO STESSO MOVIMENTO. More often, at a meter change, the perceived change in speed is subtle and driven by that shift in meter. In this case, we have an equivalence that results in a stark shift, magnified a bit by the change in meter. The result is a slight instability rather than the perfect seamlessness of shifting to exactly half-tempo.

Otello gets increasingly aggressive as Desdemona tries to defend herself through a series of four indications of unrelated tempos, until we work our way back to ALLEGRO AGITATO, 132 quarter notes a minute (at m. 8 of the first [J]). After she expresses wounded horror ("quella parola orrenda" at m. 1 before [L]), he changes tack. Contemptuous but detached, he escorts her out the door. At TEMPO PRIMO ([L], m. 6), we return to the music with which their conversation began (at [C]) and so reestablish 72 quarter notes a minute. A more proportional relationship would require ratcheting down to half-tempo (66 quarter notes a minute).

He then sings his aria "Dio! mi potevi scagliar," ADAGIO (from the first [N], 66 quarter notes per minute). The aria involves a gradual speeding up of the tempo and a simultaneous crescendo. But this slow buildup in speed is unsteady. Music that progresses from 66 to 60 to 126 quarters and then to 80 half notes per minute, of course, is perceived as getting faster. But the more we study it, the more we recognize that it is jerky, as the entire scene has been. Of course, this is an aria; each singer, and each performance by the same singer, will vary to some extent.

Still, the series of metronome indications gives us guidance: *Otello has lost it.* Any attempt to iron out the transitions in this scene—with a ritard here or an accelerando there—is misguided. The music should leave the listener with feelings of instability and even chaos.

Act III, going mad in public

After Otello's aria, Iago manages to stage manage events to convince Otello that there can be no doubt about Desdemona's guilt, and they plan her murder. Then, Otello, the ambassadors, and others assemble for the final scene of the act (from the second [C]).

In this scene, rather than subtle discontinuity, we have relatively abrupt tempo shifts, which reflect the greater violence onstage, the shock it engenders, and Otello's scene-closing seizure. For example, the scene opens by carrying the tempo forward from the end of the previous scene, where Iago takes his leave and Otello exits to receive the ambassadors (100 quarter notes a minute). There is one measure of recitative, and then the score indicates 126 quarter notes a minute (from the second [G]). Suddenly, Otello denounces Desdemona, angrily hurling her to the floor. This new section is marked PRESTO with 144 quarter notes a minute (at the second [J], m. 4). Verdi's desire for a sharp discontinuity here, reflecting rage, is clear and easy to implement. Each of the subsequent tempo indications in the scene is similarly unrelated to what went before.

Of course, the audience does not analyze tempo relationships or necessarily recognize them—any more than it analyzes iambic pentameter during a performance of the Shakespeare play. That extra drama that is present in some performances in what may seem to be some indefinable way, however, may well arise out of this subtle shattering of subconscious tempo expectations.

My favorite things

The Otello-Desdemona duet at the end of Act I (from POCO PIÙ, m. 15 before [SS]). In this ecstatic duet, the two singers never sing together until the last note, which is part of what makes this note so wonderful.

Falstaff

If in *Otello* Verdi was operating at the peak of his dramatic powers, *Falstaff* (1893) is his towering musical achievement. It is a wonder of contrapuntal invention of a kind rarely encountered on an opera stage, and it is the tightest and most concise of his operas. It is a loving homage to Rossini and earlier composers as well as to William Shakespeare, whom he revered. It has been noted by others but bears repeating: The composer within striking distance of his eightieth birthday also perfectly captured teenage love in what was his only successful comedy.

Constantin Stanislavski's observation that there are no small parts, just small actors, certainly applies to this, the ultimate ensemble opera. Each singer must be a first-rate musician with excellent rhythm. They must all act with both the body and the voice, and comic timing is important. Ideally, the parts of Falstaff and Quickly should have *voci grasse* (fat voices), a wonderful phrase I learned from Renato Capecchi, a distinguished Ford and Falstaff himself. It means voices of resonance that project throughout their ranges, especially in the low register.

For conductors, *Falstaff* is like a big puzzle that brings continuous pleasure as we work through it. Rather than peaks of excitement, we find a continuous music drama that can no more be broken up by applause than can a Wagnerian opera. Motives do not figure in *Falstaff* and, although it is melodically inventive, we do not come away with a lot of tuneful recollections. (A few times, Mistress Quickly sings a simple five-note figure to ridicule Falstaff. But this operates less as a motive than as a running gag, the punch line coming when Falstaff cuts her off by singing it himself in Act III, Scene 2 [at 47, m. 16].) The effect of the opera is cumulative, something like a Bach fugue—leavened with wit and affection.

The orchestration demands excellent and refined musicians, especially among the woodwinds. They have the effervescent opening of Act I, Scene 2, in Ford's garden to themselves. It is only fair then that the strings realize a similarly sparkling turn themselves at the opening of Act II, Scene 2, in Ford's house. In addition, the English horn has an important solo in Act I, Scene 2, when Meg and Alice read Falstaff's letter (at 21).

Three substantial orchestra-only passages contain what should be the orchestra's loudest moments. They occur after the singing stops on the last pages of Act I, Scene 1; Act II, Scene 2; and after the final fugue in Act III, Scene 2. The orchestra should never get heavy, however, even when a character is expressing anger.

(To my mind, *Falstaff* is not primarily a *buffo* opera and so, like the comedies of Gaetano Donizetti, it has emotional content that can be played straight to good effect. If it is, then Falstaff's dejection at the opening of Act III can reasonably be considered the opera's emotional high point.)

A couple of orchestra-only passages require the conductor to execute long crescendos. This is not difficult, but it does require recognizing the potential for the orchestra to become a distinct character in the comedy and taking the time in rehearsal to gauge the build-up and balances.

One such passage occurs at the top of Act III, Scene 1, in front of the inn. It begins with the basses alone, and additional instruments join in every few measures until the whole orchestra is laughing (at [4]). The indicated 112 quarter notes per minute is about as slow as this should be. Some conductors want to slow this section, possibly because there are a few measures that are pretty close to unplayable at the indicated tempo—even for very good orchestras. The problematic measures belong to the wind players, but going too slow will often result in difficulties for the strings. There is a better solution.

Specifically, the difficulty lies in a pattern of very short notes alternating with equally short rests and lasting for 8 measures (from [1], m. 5). It begins in the divisi clarinets who are joined by divisi oboes as well as the bassoons and horns. Cleanly executing these measures will take a disproportionate amount of rehearsal time if it can be pulled off at all. I have found two adjustments that work. The first is to reverse the notes and rests so that these short notes are played on the beat. The second is to have these winds repeat each of their sixteenth notes instead of observing the rests (the pattern they are given after the measures in question and the pattern in the strings throughout). For flawless ensemble, the passage will still require some extra focus during rehearsal, but even the best orchestras will appreciate some adjustment in these measures.

Later in Act III, Scene 1, the composer again expands the orchestra section by section beginning with trills in a solo flute (at [10]). The rest of the orchestra gradually joins in as Falstaff waxes poetic about the joys of alcohol consumption. Readers of a scholarly bent may delight in the grace notes in this passage. They harken back to the Baroque period, telling us to revert to an older tradition of starting trills from the note above. But in addition, doing this with the grace notes rather than just a verbal indication injects some brio. It gives us that jolt of spirit and excitement that comes when musicians play or sing slightly before the beat. (That is, very slightly and in a regular and disciplined—definitely not accelerating—pattern.) Another effect may be found in the violas' first measure in this passage (m. 5 of [10]). There we find that the upper note of the trill should be flatted. This divergence in the violas introduces an especially pungent dissonance on Falstaff's word "cor."

There is a small question for the conductor in this passage. The bass drum has both a trill and a tremolo indication (at m. 2 before [11]). These cannot be played at the same time. The bass drum's normal double-headed mallet will allow only for the slower tremolo. But the drummer can also use two timpani sticks, which would yield a faster alternation between notes that is more like a trill. The unpitched bass drum cannot perform a trill, of course, but the fast series of hits will give such an impression. Acoustics and the size of the orchestra will play a part in deciding which the percussionist should use.

For the most magical effects however, we have the final scene of the opera. This is the night-time scene in Windsor Park with a distant chorus invoking sundry deities from mythology. The harp, which is not common in Verdi's orchestration, plays only in this scene. In fact, though *Falstaff* is an homage to Rossini, much of the first part of this final scene takes inspiration from Berlioz and Liszt as well as Wagner (especially in the close of *Die Walküre*). Thus it also looks forward to the works of music's impressionists like Claude Debussy's *Nocturnes*.

Step into My Study . . .

Falstaff's magnificent contrapuntal sections are what set it apart and ensure that the conductor earns his keep. The final fugue is certainly the most talked-about section of the opera (Act III, Scene 2, from m. 4 of [55]). This is a single-subject fugue employing ten voices, a notable challenge for Verdi to have set for himself. Another contrapuntal gem is the music of Act II, Scene 2, where Falstaff is hiding in the laundry chest while Ford and his cronies think he is behind the screen where, instead, Nannetta and Fenton are hiding (between [59] and [66]). Here we have several unrelated but meshing lines coalescing.

However, the most complicated and treacherous part of the opera is a pair of ensembles, each with interlocking ideas, in Act I, Scene 2. First, the women discuss and laugh at Falstaff's letters. They alternate between $\frac{6}{8}$ and $\frac{4}{4}$ passages through most of this music. When the men enter, we have the first of two double ensembles. Their lyrics reflect their diverse reasons for plotting against Falstaff. They sing in duple meter ($\frac{2}{2}$) against the women's triple meter ($\frac{6}{8}$). Then, most of the cast leaves the stage, and there is an interlude with a love duet between Nannetta and Fenton. Third, the rest of the women and men return to the stage and the counterpoint becomes even more complicated.

Verdi's simultaneous duple and triple meter was a bit harder than anything Italy had seen up to this point. Mozart did a little of this in *Don Giovanni* with the three dances played simultaneously at Giovanni's dinner party at the end of Act I. In that number, however, a small amount of rhythmic raggedness in three distinct melodies, with some offstage, might pass unnoticed. Here, on the other hand, we are aiming for something as crystalline as a Bach fugue. For equivalents, we have to leap ahead to the music of Richard Strauss or look back to some of the more complex ensembles in Wagner's *Die Meistersinger* or Berlioz's *Benvenuto Cellini.*

In the need to have a plan that spans many pages of the score and maintains relationships between even nonadjacent sections of music, this scene tests a conductor. The difficulties of the long love duet of *Tristan und Isolde* are real, but this *Falstaff* scene is not for wimps either. The music of these double ensembles involves more actors than does that duet, and they are singing what ultimately become three ideas. They also sing considerably faster and often in conflicting rhythms, while they enter and leave the stage and execute a variety of stage business.

The scene is summarized in Table 4.1, with suggested tempos where the score lacks metronome markings. It is worth remembering that a difference of, say, ten beats per minute, at the speeds typical through most of this music, is imperceptible to all but those with a stopwatch in hand. The purpose of the table, then, is not to supply a recipe to be strictly observed, but to describe the long arc of music and how I personally plan the journey from the beginning to the end.

Table 4.1 *Falstaff's* double ensembles, Act I, Scene 2. Where the score lacks specific metronome indications, suggestions are enclosed in square brackets.

		First Double Ensemble
women alone at	$\boxed{21}$	$\frac{6}{8}$ ANDANTE SOSTENUTO ♪ = 126
	m. 5	Begin alternating $\frac{4}{4}$ ALLEGRO ♩ = 126, with $\frac{6}{8}$ ANDANTE ♪ = 126,
	$\boxed{22}$, m. 17	$\frac{12}{8}$ SEMPRE LO STESSO MOVIMENTO [♩. = 42]
	m. 20	Mid-measure meter change to $\frac{4}{4}$ [♩ = 46]
	3 measures before $\boxed{23}$	$\frac{4}{4}$ ALLEGRO PIÙ PRESTO 𝅗𝅥 = 92
	$\boxed{23}$	$\frac{2}{4}$ ALLEGRO ♩ = 120
	$\boxed{24}$	$\frac{6}{8}$ UN POCO MENO ♩. = 100
	$\boxed{25}$	$\frac{6}{8}$ PIÙ MODERATO ♩. = 88
men enter at	$\boxed{26}$ through $\boxed{29}$	Simultaneous $\frac{2}{2}$ and $\frac{6}{8}$ LO STESSO MOVIMENTO 𝅗𝅥 and ♩. = 88
		Love Duet, $\boxed{30}$ through $\boxed{36}$
		Second Double Ensemble
men alone at	$\boxed{37}$	$\frac{4}{4}$ ALLEGRO VIVO ♩ = 126
women enter scene at	$\boxed{38}$	$\frac{2}{2}$ ALLEGRO (COME PRIMA) 𝅗𝅥 = 88
women enter musically at	m. 7	Simultaneous $\frac{2}{2}$ and $\frac{6}{8}$ [𝅗𝅥 and ♩. = 88]
	$\boxed{39}$	$\frac{6}{8}$ PIÙ PRESTO ♩. = 126
	3 measures before $\boxed{40}$	$\frac{4}{4}$ LO STESSO MOVIMENTO ♩ = 126
	$\boxed{40}$	[beating twice per measure 𝅗𝅥 = 63]
orchestra alone at	$\boxed{40}$, m.14	$\frac{6}{8}$ VIVACE [♩. = 126, beating once per measure 𝅗𝅥. = 63]

In the first double ensemble, the only way this music can stay together and sound clean is if the women's six eighth notes last exactly as long as the men's eight eighth notes. This requirement—different meters played and sung perfectly in sync—is why it is imperative that the music not get too fast too early. One particularly tempting moment comes early in the scene. After a gorgeous melody worthy of Desdemona, the women mock the overly exuberant final sentence in Falstaff's letter and break into laughter (CON CARICATURA, from m. 20 of [22]).

If I do not hold the reins tightly, the ability to transition smoothly into the women's main theme in $\frac{6}{8}$ at [25] will be lost. Happily, dramatically, it makes sense to cast the women's laughter as ironic, and that beautifully supports maintaining the tempo and dovetailing with the men when they enter at [26]. The tempo can then remain singable for everyone and the ensemble clean.

Quickening the pulse a very little during [22], m. 20, to get to about 46 quarter notes per minute will allow a seamless transition at the next tempo change. It may also be helpful to subdivide the last beat (i.e., beat the eighth note) as we conclude m. 4 before [23]. My target is for the new half note to take as long as the previous eighth note—exact proportionality—at m. 3 before [23].

After the pep and complications of the ensemble, as we might expect, the music becomes simpler and the tempo more relaxed for our young lovers, Nannetta and Fenton (from [30]). They sing in $\frac{3}{4}$ time, alternating ALLEGRETTO and PIÙ LENTO, with the other women interrupting briefly mid-duet to move the story forward in $\frac{4}{4}$ time ([32]).

After the love duet, however, we are off to the races again. The men enter, and their tempo is the same as that which dominated the duet ([37]). But the duet ended with a short pullback in tempo, so the music here will naturally sound a little faster even though I re-establish 126 beats per minute.

Verdi will take us from that tempo to the fastest tempo of the scene in an ensemble that is a little easier for the conductor in technical terms. In the first, the tempo waxes and wanes as the conspirators hatch their plans and the plot thickens. In the second, shorter ensemble, there are fewer transitions with only one pullback in speed.

There is a great deal to pay attention to as the speed gets faster, however, and one intersection that requires planning. At the PIÙ PRESTO ($\boxed{39}$), there seems to be no exact proportionality with what has gone before, and the orchestra, which is playing alone for a couple of measures, is changing rhythms. The way to get the entire ensemble gliding into the new, faster tempo is to give the couple of measures just before the PIÙ PRESTO a very little extra propulsion. More specifically, I find that the best way to pull this off is to focus on the eighth note *sung by the men* before they leave (i.e., in the $\frac{2}{2}$ music that begins at $\boxed{38}$). If I drive the tempo from 88 beats per minute to roughly 92 in the couple of measures before PIÙ PRESTO—the difference being practically imperceptible at this speed—the eighth note both before and after the PIÙ PRESTO will be extremely close. This supplies the ensemble with both the drive and cohesion it needs. It would also be acceptable to take the PIÙ PRESTO just a little bit faster than indicated, preparatory to the VIVACE conclusion to the ensemble.

Then, at the VIVACE, the orchestra takes over, returning to the melody that opened the scene (at $\boxed{40}$, m. 14). The act may be brought to an energetic conclusion by maintaining the same pulse or even pushing it a little faster. Executing this transition into VIVACE presupposes that the 2 measures of laughter stay strictly in tempo (from $\boxed{40}$, m. 12).

Pushing the tempo at VIVACE might not be inevitable in other late Verdi operas. But the style of this opera is so lovingly old fashioned, so purposely anachronistic, that treating the conclusion of this ensemble as a Mozartean or bel canto stretto gives an immensely satisfying result. That is, a constant pulse, where the new dotted half note equals the previous half note, is appropriate. It is also to be noted that we are moving so fast by the end of the scene that conducting alla breve is appropriate; i.e., beating once per measure in the final $\frac{6}{8}$ VIVACE.

My favorite things

The final fugue, discussed above, an invigorating piece and one of the most thrilling conclusions to any opera. It also looks back to Bach after the highly romantic *Otello.* In some measure, we are reminded of the way in which Richard Strauss took inspiration from Mozart for his *Der Rosenkavalier.*

Chapter 5

Wagner

> The whole duty of a conductor is comprised in his ability always to indicate the right tempo. His choice of tempi will show whether he understands the piece or not. With good players, again, the true tempo induces correct phrasing and expression and conversely, with a conductor, the idea of appropriate phrasing and expression will induce the conception of the true tempo.
>
> —Richard Wagner[1]

Richard Wagner's operas require very good orchestras, imaginative stage directors and designers, and lots of preparation. Though his librettos have been subject to some criticism, the fact is that they fit his music well. Moreover, whatever challenges they may present to the stage director, many of these works also have the virtue of being timeless. Indeed, the three operas discussed in this chapter have all been moved in space and time with success.

For the conductor, particularly in his mature works, understanding the structure of these works—how they cohere—requires almost as much effort as one puts into learning the text and the music. In a sense, Wagner took the idea behind the great Mozartean operatic ensembles—constructing long passages of music out of discrete but interlocking parts—and imposed the same discipline over ever more pages of the score. His music is filled with short-lived tempo fluctuations for expressive purposes, as we might expect in some of the most romantic music ever written. But the joints between interrelated sections must be carefully considered if the intended sweep is to be realized. *Das Rheingold* runs at least two and a half hours with no intermission or a moment's break for applause.

One of the happy discoveries in Wagner's scores, however, is how well balanced they are. Balancing the volume between the stage and the pit always requires attention, of course. But balances within the orchestra can also be an issue, especially later in the Romantic era. Still, in performances of Wagner's scores, given a reasonable level of care, the orchestra sounds exactly as you would expect from perusing the score. This is not what makes Wagner great in and of itself, but it merits mention.

Wagner extended the capabilities and range of the instruments in the orchestra and pioneered the use of certain instruments, particularly the "Wagner tuba." Even orchestras used to opera will find Wagner more arduous. This is particularly true if they have not performed Bruckner's works. Wagner and Anton Bruckner wrote music that is difficult in the same way for the winds, and for the brass in particular. Their music requires a lot of long, sustained notes and, sometimes, difficult keys for particular instruments. In a good performance there is also a lot of soft playing over extended periods of time, which can be difficult to sustain.

A corollary is that trying to reduce the orchestra for these works is particularly problematic. As we proceed through the Romantic era with ever bigger orchestras, the subject of reducing the orchestra increasingly comes up. This is always unfortunate and some reasons for doing it are worse than others. However, there are cities where the pits will not even fit the players called for in the original score. So that settles that. (In fact, some of the reductions we may hear in the United States date from the days before so many regional opera companies existed and the Metropolitan Opera's touring company performed in those very same pits.) The absence of a lush string sound is unfortunate, of course, but it will have different effects in different theaters. If I have to make do with fewer strings than ideal, I may even be able to compensate sometimes with different bowings. Reducing eight horns to four, however, means that each horn is being asked to play difficult music for a longer period of time.

When it comes to voices, this composer also made new demands. The range for which Wagner wrote these parts and, in some cases, their exhausting length created the need for a special breed of singer. He required greater power and stamina. In addition, when planning and studying the operas composed for Bayreuth in particular, we should take into account the covered pit of that theater. Even a reduced orchestra placed in a pit in front of the proscenium will create more sound for the singers to overcome than a much bigger orchestra under the stage.

Finally, both singers and conductors need to recognize how lyrical much of this music is. In fact, I want lyricism to be the strongest impression that my audience walks away with after a performance of Wagner. This implies a control of dynamics: never having singers or orchestra push the volume beyond what they, individually, can achieve with a beautiful sound. In addition, whether the tempo is *sehr langsam* or *sehr schnell* the notes have to cohere into a recognizable musical idea. As in the case of dynamics, singers and instrumentalists vary in their ability to perform beautifully and hold the audience's interest at different speeds.

Keep in mind that Wagner admired Vincenzo Bellini, that most lyrical of Italian composers.[2] So whether performing the "Ride of the Valkyries" or the "Annunciation of Death," the message here is "Know thyself." Know the fastest and slowest, as well as the loudest and softest, you can sing, play, or conduct while maintaining beauty and conveying meaning.

Der fliegende Holländer

At its premiere in 1843, *Der fliegende Holländer* was performed in a single act, and it often still is. Later, Wagner adapted it to be performed in three acts. Some argue that we should revert to one act and some want to perform it in two acts. Since most companies will be renting orchestra parts for the three-act version, either of these choices means that some adjustments must be made to the score and parts.

For one act, we eliminate the breaks that Wagner added in his revisions and are contained in today's scores. Thus, we cut 12 measures from the end of Act I, 32 measures from the beginning of Act II, and 12 measures from the end of Act II. For two acts, we keep his revised ending to Act I and only make the 12-measure cut at the end of Act II to connect it to Act III.

Personally, I think taking a single intermission after Act I works dramatically and musically and gives both audience and performers the right break. I would never rule out a one-act production, however, since it can give the opera great sweep and line. Moreover, some opera houses have the resources to do it very well. But when asked about restoring the original orchestration, I demur. It is a bit crude and brass-heavy, and as early as three years after the premiere, Wagner began making changes. These changes reflect his ever-growing mastery of this art, and he continued to make changes as late as 1853.

Example 5.1 Romantic rests in *Der fliegende Holländer* (from m. 2 of No. 6).

For example, when Senta first sees the Dutchman (*Der Holländer*) in Act II, Wagner's original idea called for brass and timpani. He finally chose only woodwinds and pizzicato strings, however. They are followed by solo timpani playing softly, perhaps echoing Senta's heartbeat (Example 5.1). As he wrote to Franz Liszt weeks before the opera was performed in Weimar: "Herewith I send you another alteration; you will see where it belongs. The effect of the brass and the kettledrums was too coarse, too material; the spectator should be terror-struck by the cry of Senta on seeing the Dutchman, not by kettledrum and brass."[3] Instead, the loudest part of the opera, as well as its emotional high point, is at its end, Senta's suicide (p. 402 [vocal 253]).

Note the use of the rests at irregular intervals in Example 5.1. We see something similar but more complex and daring on the opening page of *Tristan und Isolde*. *Tristan* premiered twelve years after the last revisions to *Der fliegende Holländer* and more than twenty-two years after *Holländer* was heard in its original form.

In the revisions, as mentioned, Wagner also added music. In the rewrite, after Senta jumps to her death and the orchestra erupts, the added music is both gentler and more sophisticated, more in line with his later works. Wagner also embedded these additional musical ideas at the end of the overture, foreshadowing the end of the opera. This ending has been called "Senta's Apotheosis" and, in addition to being very beautiful, the revision gives us a window into the evolution of this artist's career-long attraction to stories where love brings redemption and transcendence but also death (the final 22 measures in both the overture and the last act).

So I am inclined to respect Wagner's own assessment that the original orchestration left room for meaningful improvement.

When it comes to casting, the oft-mentioned blending of Italian and German styles in this opera makes Erik's part in particular somewhat difficult. In his aria at least, Erik is unequivocally an Italianate lyric tenor, whereas for the rest of the opera he can have a more dramatic sound. So, he needs a bit more heft in the middle register than his Italian counterparts. I will admit that after hearing and even performing this opera multiple times, it was a particularly beautiful tenor voice that really drove home the lyric nature of this part for me. Management should make every effort to cast a big beautiful voice for Erik; the payoff is substantial.

The Dutchman is one of those parts that requires a big personality and great stage presence. He is a bass-baritone roughly equivalent to Scarpia in Puccini's *Tosca*, Escamillo in Bizet's *Carmen*, or Wotan in Wagner's own *Die Walküre*. Although much of the part lies in the bass range, a great deal of the duet with Senta lies in the baritone range, and the sound must have the power to cut through an orchestra that is rather heavy. On the other hand, Senta's father Daland is a classic bass role.

Senta is a lirico spinto soprano. She needs power on top but must have substance in the middle of her range. It is a higher part than Wagner's

Brünnhilde or Sieglinde in the Ring or Isolde of *Tristan und Isolde* or Kundry in *Parsifal*.

Step into My Study . . .

While revolutionary—really ushering in a new era—*Der fliegende Holländer* is wonderfully familiar. One of the reasons that it no longer sounds so surprising, of course, is that so much of what Wagner pioneered has become standard fare—the expanded use of motives and his adventurous harmonies, for instance.

But another reason that *Holländer* sounds familiar is Wagner's use of traditional forms. Besides giving the opera much of its lyric quality and rhythmic vitality, these standard forms help guide us with respect to tempo. For example, Senta's aria is marked as a ballade (Act II, No. 4, from p. 177 [vocal 110]). If we are familiar with Chopin or Brahms ballades, Wagner's metronome indication for this aria makes perfect sense; it also connects the tempo to the Dutchman's motive. There is no justification for making it excessively ominous. Even in dramatic terms, there is no contrast if Senta is singing a dirge from the beginning.[4]

Similarly, if we recognize the lively dance called the hornpipe, we will not push the speed much faster than humans can reasonably dance. The Norwegian sailors have two hornpipes, for example. There is one in Act I about fair sailing conditions (No. 3, from VIVACE MA NON TROPPO PRESTO, p. 132 [vocal 76]) which is reprised partially as part of the bridge music that opens Act II in the three-act version. The other is in Act III in which the same sailors address the Helmsman (No. 7). Both are very like the traditional Celtic "Sailor's Hornpipe."

These forms also serve to unite the work to the extent that they contain rhythmic patterns that keep reappearing. That is, *Holländer* has both melodic and rhythmic motives. The melodic motives for the Dutchman, Senta, "redemption through love," "eternal wandering," the Norwegian sailors, and so on, are all laid out in the overture.

In a motive that appears throughout the opera, Wagner uses seconds in a dotted rhythm. It appears in the hornpipes mentioned above, in the introduction to Act II (from m. 33), in the music of the Norwegian sailors in Act III (a bit more than half way through No. 7, p. 339 [vocal 214]), and in the Norwegian Maidens' "Spinning Chorus" (Act II, No. 4).

The Spinning Chorus, by the way, is a ländler, a dance a little slower than the hornpipe (No. 4). Although a speed slightly faster than the 66 quarter notes per minute indicated in the score may suit the tastes of today's audiences, this chorus should not be very fast. (I lean toward about 72.) It is a gentle piece suited to a group of young women who go about domestic chores such as spinning. So this is not Charlie Chaplin on the assembly line in *Modern Times*. Indeed, a footnote at the beginning of the scene cautions the conductor to hold back throughout so that the scene never becomes hurried.

My favorite things

The Dutchman's aria (Act I, No. 2). This mighty aria completely and thrillingly encapsulates the tormented title character's back story as well as his despair.

Die Walküre

At one time in North America, Wagner's works were rarely seen in opera houses other than New York's Metropolitan Opera. These are big works requiring a large orchestra, many rehearsals, and often complicated physical productions. That said, Wagner operas began to appear more frequently throughout North America beginning in the 1970s and, by the 1990s, many ever-improving regional companies were producing the occasional Wagner opera.

After *Der fliegende Holländer*, the Wagner opera most likely to be performed is probably *Die Walküre* (1870) since, despite its being part of the four-opera Ring Cycle, it can nonetheless stand on its own dramatically. *Das Rheingold* also has a self-contained story to some extent, but the complicated stagecraft and the large cast make it less likely to be produced. It is, however, sometimes performed in concert by symphony orchestras, usually as a special event. When we get to *Siegfried* and especially *Götterdämmerung*, the operas get increasingly difficult to mount outside the context of an entire Ring.

In addition, *Die Walküre* has generally proved to be popular with the ticket-buying audience. In part, its popularity may be attributed to its relatively greater abundance of melody. The opening of Act III, the Ride of the Valkyries, is perhaps the most familiar piece of German music aside from the first movement of Beethoven's Fifth Symphony. Act I can stand alone as a concert piece with some of the most ecstatic love music ever written, as can the finale of Act III, "Wotan's Farewell." Let it be said, however, that if the Act III finale is performed without singers, it is less effective than *Tristan und Isolde's* "Liebestod" or *Parsifal's* "Good Friday Spell" when they are performed as purely orchestral pieces.

In this opera, we encounter all of the classic Wagnerian voice types. The Wotan of *Die Walküre* is probably the most difficult of the three Wotan roles in the Ring. His opening lines in Act II and his final aria are clearly in the baritone range, but most of Act II is in the bass range. The only two similar roles in the Wagner canon are the very long role of Hans Sachs in *Die Meistersinger von Nürnberg* and the title character in *Der fliegende Holländer*.

Siegmund, along with Tristan (a longer and more taxing role) and Parsifal, are prime examples of the heldentenor, but some of Wagner's tenors are even harder to cast in some ways: Siegfried in the opera *Siegfried*, Lohengrin, and Tannhäuser sing higher, for example.

Brünnhilde is the quintessential Wagnerian dramatic soprano. The part requires a voice of rich power in the middle and lower ranges but she must also ascend to high C. Sieglinde is a dramatic soprano with a more lyric timbre, more like *Der fliegende Holländer's* Senta or Isolde. The role of Isolde is more strenuous because of its greater length, however.

Die Walküre's orchestra ranks among Wagner's largest. This opera employs four players per woodwind section, eight horn players (with four playing the Wagner tuba at times), three trumpeters, one bass trumpeter, three tenor trombonists, one bass trombonist, one bass tuba player, six harpists (three on each of two parts), and two pair of timpanists-percussionists. In addition, offstage, we have one stierhorn, for which a bass trombone is often substituted.

Step into My Study . . .

The prelude to Act I of *Die Walküre* plunges us into a wild storm that is composed using a surprising economy of means and a rather large amount of repetition that never gets repetitious. With the right control of tempo and dynamics, the excitement just keeps building. It begins with a driving rain established by 60 measures of sextuplets on a single note in the second violins and violas (the note of D). The second violins are directed to play this note simultaneously on two strings, giving the passage added weight and a certain roughness. For the next 20 measures, we hear this "storm motive" played against or alternating with either the "Donner motive" (from the final part of *Das Rheingold*) or a variation thereof.

On paper, when considering reducing the orchestra, the timpani look like they should be at the top of the list for reasons of both budget and space in the pit. When the two timpani enter (m. 80), there are 42 measures of a rolled A written for one or both of them, but the two parts are easily combined. If two timp are available however, I like to separate them. It is ideal to place one player in the pit and the other far upstage. This can be anywhere that the player and instrument will be unseen. Such placement will create a stereophonic effect when the two players overlap for the first 19 measures of the rolled A. If this is not possible but there is still space in the pit, then placing them on opposite sides of the pit will create some effect worth achieving. In a concert version, placing them on opposite sides of the stage is easy and effective, of course.

At the other end of Act I, we hear and see Siegmund pull the sword from the tree (from MÄSSIG SCHNELL, p. 144 [vocal 81]). The trumpets, supported in canon by the trombones and bass trumpet, blaze this melody with an indication to play quite loud. For me, this is the primary emotional climax of Act I. In a production of a stand-alone *Die Walküre*, no motive looms larger than the "sword motive." It appears continuously throughout the first act, but never more thrillingly than in this scene. If this music is strongly associated with Siegmund, we may also note that the arpeggios that begin softly in the harp and strings certainly coincide with Sieglinde's ecstatic reaction at this turn of events. For the record, however, the often-heard scream from Sieglinde is not in Wagner's score. Therefore, while some have performed it effectively, it should be omitted if the soprano is not able to effectively pull it off.

There is a secondary emotional climax as well, when Siegmund calls out for aid, "Wälse! Wälse! Wo ist dein Schwert?" in Act I, Scene 3 (p. 65 [vocal 44]).

Two other moments should be the loudest points in the opera, on the other hand. One should come when Wotan breaks Sigmund's sword in Act II, Scene 5 (from p. 398, m. 3 [vocal 197]). The second should be just before Wotan's appearance in Act III near the top of Scene 2, especially the 2 measures before he sings (p. 551 [vocal 259]). Ergo, wonderful as the Ride is and affecting as both the primal cry of Siegmund and the pulling of the sword from the tree should be, I believe in holding back the orchestra a little in those passages. Indeed, for Siegmund's cry, the orchestra is not playing very much at all. It is Siegmund who is pumping out enormous effort, and the last thing I want to do is drown him out.

On hearing the opera, one might easily think that the contrapuntal section before the eight Valkyries leave the stage in Act III would be the most difficult passage to conduct (Scene 2, from p. 573 [vocal 272]). But the more that one studies *Die Walküre*, the clearer it becomes that the most difficult conducting lies in the static scenes where one has to maintain intensity despite slow tempos: in the first scene, between Siegmund and Sieglinde, for example, and in the Annunciation of Death scene between Brünnhilde and Siegmund in Act II, Scene 4 (from p. 329 [vocal 165]).

The final scene—with Brünnhilde and Wotan alone together and the spectacular magic fire music—contains some of the most sublime musical passages ever conceived. Principally, Wagner uses expressive leaps to continuously ratchet up the intensity. He first uses a seventh and then an octave, in the English horn and oboe, to express great sorrow and emotion (from ETWAS BREIT, WIE IM ANFANG on p. 604 [vocal 292]). After Wotan sings, "der freier als ich, der Gott!" the orchestra plays this same glorious melody with leaps of sevenths and ninths in an orchestral interlude (beginning at p. 663, m. 5 [vocal 319]).

Inspired by Wagner's later composition in *Tristan und Isolde* (especially, in the Liebestod), I like to emphasize the implied crescendo just before the climax of this passage in order to throw it into sharper relief. I reduce the volume at A TEMPO (p. 666 [vocal 320]), asking the brass for ***p*** and the strings and winds for ***mp***, and then execute the crescendo for 4 measures. This allows the ***ff*** for all of the instruments written at the end of those 4 measures to serve more clearly as the climax.

"Wotan's Farewell" is a lot more than this short orchestral passage however, and there is a baritone to consider. This final scene requires planning to maintain tension and illuminate the emotional trajectory but also to ensure that the baritone can get through it singing his best. Wotan's gradual acquiescence and farewell to his daughter is written in three sections. He begins in the same tempo as Brünnhilde has sung, which is SEHR BEWEGT (p. 644 [vocal 311]), a fast tempo something like MOLTO AGITATO. For most of this scene both characters have had indications of passion and urgency and agitation. Each subsequent section gets slower, however.

The farewell begins with Wotan singing "Leb wohl du kühnes, herrliches Kind" (p. 653 [vocal 314]). It continues over the next 18 pages with two transitions to be executed: from SEHR BEWEGT to ETWAS LANGSAMER (p. 662 [vocal 319]) and then to LANGSAM (p. 668 [vocal 320]).

Slowing as Wotan's pain mounts and events take their course is essential to achieving the intended emotional climax. Going half-tempo at each transition can easily be justified since most of this opera works best adhering to tradition and keeping a constant pulse. However, as suggested, doing so also is likely to put a strain on the baritone at the end of a long opera.

There are two alternatives that will work. One is making the transition to the second section, ETWAS LANGSAMER, faster than half tempo (i.e., slowing down by about a quarter) and then going into the LANGSAM at half-tempo. However, I find it more effective to halve the tempo at the first transition, but execute some rubato to speed things beginning about 10 measures before LANGSAM (i.e., during the orchestral interlude). I might, for example, execute a ritenuto for about 2 measures followed by a più mosso for about 8 measures just before the transition into LANGSAM. Such rearing back momentarily and then pushing ahead briefly would bring us to the beginning of the LANGSAM section at a tempo that would permit halving it. Rubato in a dramatic scene should never be so extreme that it calls attention to itself, but some rubato here is idiomatically romantic and dramatically in keeping with this emotional farewell. (The score has a healthy sprinkling of POCO RITENUTO, POCO ACCELERANDO, POCO RALLANTANDO, and so on within this very scene.) It follows, however, that the POCO RALLENTANDO that is indicated near the end should be slight indeed. I base it largely on how the baritone is faring (p. 671 [vocal 322]).

Either alternative lets us observe a strict halving of the tempo between ETWAS LANGSAMER and LANGSAM. Why be rigid about going half-tempo at one transition but not the other? The answer is in the notes: The same melody played in quarter notes and dotted eighths in the ETWAS LANGSAMER section is continued in eighth notes and dotted sixteenth notes in the LANGSAM section. This means that a shift to half tempo is quite compelling: The melody continues to sound the same. The continuity, the seamlessness is perfect.

My favorite things

The melody in the orchestral interlude after Wotan's "der freier als ich, der Gott" in the final scene, discussed above. This is perhaps my favorite moment in all of music.

Tristan und Isolde

Tristan und Isolde is Wagner's most musically daring work. It is also among the hardest musical works in any category to realize. It must have seemed impossible in 1864 when Vienna gave up on it after over seventy rehearsals. Only the infusion of funds from King Ludwig II of Bavaria made a second try possible and successful the following year.

The challenges facing the conductor may be less obvious to the audience than those that the singers tackle, but they are no less real. *Der Rosenkavalier* is more complex and *Die Meistersinger von Nürnberg* is longer, but few works in music require as careful an analysis as *Tristan.* Few have the combination of difficult tempo relationships and constant, subtle rubato as this opera does, and these are coupled with balance issues and the need for loving support from pit to stage. Let it be said, however, that few works in music reward extensive preparation more than *Tristan und Isolde.* The long arcs of music that make *Tristan* so challenging at first also make for tremendous payoff—intellectually, psychologically, and emotionally.

In terms of vocal demands, the listener is struck by the sheer endurance required. The work is daunting for the two lead singers. At least one of them is onstage virtually all the time and, usually, they are together. Although many Wagnerian roles are hard to sing, none is more taxing than these because of their length. Only Hans Sachs of *Meistersinger* is longer.

However, unlike the operas of *Der Ring des Nibelungen*, where cuts are virtually impossible, either for musical or dramatic reasons, in *Tristan und Isolde* there are some that can prevent either Tristan or Isolde from expiring before they run out of words or notes in this punishing opera. While Wagner gave us no specific cuts, he himself wrote that, outside of Bayreuth, cuts should probably be considered in this particular work. I always prefer to look for judicious cuts rather than risk driving a singer past endurance. That is a disservice to the singer and the audience.

We cannot speak of standard cuts for a number of reasons. There are no repeats, for example. Nor is there a shared performing history in the industry that includes cuts that "everybody" expects. So there are no obvious choices. Broadly, however, Acts II and III provide opportunities to lighten the burden on the singers. Act II, Scene 2, is entirely devoted to the lovers' duet. With the confrontation with Melot and Mark and all of Act III yet to come, one can understand why cuts have been made here. The even longer Act III, Scene 1, after the Shepherd departs, becomes a dialogue between Tristan and Kurwenal. It is an especially demanding scene for the tenor, who needs to do considerable emoting as Tristan descends into delirium and then needs to weather the shorter scene in which Tristan dies. Some cutting in this marathon is also reasonable.

When it comes to dynamics, Isolde's Act I curse (from SEHR SCHNELL, m. 7 before [Q] [vocal p. 43]) supplies a big moment and the end of her final aria, a cathartic one. But this opera does not have the dynamic contrasts we normally think of in opera—not even contrasts comparable to those in the other two operas discussed in this chapter. Thus, my focus remains on the impact on the singers. The aim is to restrain the orchestra. A lot of the biggest moments of the opera occur with voices.

As with any Wagner opera, one can dig endlessly for *Tristan's* motives; scholars have identified dozens. But when we have so many motives in a single work, they lack the structural importance of the single theme in such works as Berlioz's *Symphonie fantastique*, Schumann's Second Symphony, Verdi's *Rigoletto* or *La forza del destino*, or Bizet's *Carmen*. In *Tristan*, the way half steps expand into whole steps or the expansion of the ascending sixth into the descending seventh, the delayed harmonic resolution, as well as the persistent chromaticism, are ultimately far more important for both the conductor—and even the serious student—in understanding the composition than are motives never identified as such by Wagner. Indeed, using the word "theme" in its broadest sense, the instability we feel through so much of this opera may be said to tell the story of *Tristan und Isolde*.

This feeling of instability is induced in the listener in three ways that are still mightily effective after all these years. The first is harmonic suspension. At the top of the opera, the orchestra wanders around the chromatic scale for 16 measures before we feel we are grounded in a key. Only then does the orchestra sing the "love potion motive"—the main element of the prelude—in a full-throated manner. We must wait for Isolde's final aria to hear the most complete resolution in the opera. For me, the emotional climax of the opera is at this resolution.

The second is the suspension of time. Notice how the rests between each phrase on the opening page decrease in duration: seven eighth rests, four eighths, an eighth plus eighth with a fermata or, effectively, three eighths (twice), and two eighths (twice again). This measured silence of the entire orchestra, on top of a slow pace, really gives us the impression that time stands still, in part because the silence is so unexpected. But this silence can speak. Wagner achieves a completely different kind of acceleration with these decreasing periods of silence. It is a hesitant speeding up. Very romantic, like the increasingly short breaths of a person growing more excited or aroused, a person in a decidedly unstable state. A conductor needs to trust these unexpected moments of silence and respect them. They can be very effective.

The third source of instability is found in Act III. The composer breaks the rules of rhythm employed from the Baroque period until his own time, writing both changing and conflicting meters. No one onstage or in the auditorium could ever mistake this for rock-solid stability. Scene 2 begins with almost 80 measures of rhythms that change constantly and in no immediately discernable pattern. What follows is a section of conflicting rhythms that conclude Tristan's delirium and give way to his death.

Wagner sets up these conflicting rhythms by dividing the orchestra roughly in half and writing some parts in large triplets (from **Bb** on p. 392 [vocal 294, last 2 measures]). This creates considerable dissonance and also prepares the orchestra to transition into two different time signatures at ZEHR ALLMÄCHLICH NACHLASSEND IM ZEITMASS (m. 9 of **Bb** [vocal p. 295]). The dissonance gets less extreme, however, as those with a $\frac{2}{2}$ time signature play longer lines and those in $\frac{3}{2}$ meter play a now-distinct, churning counter-rhythm. When the music reverts to a single time signature, the conflicts are gone and we transition to a reprise of the music of the prelude (at ZEHR LANGSAM, **Cc**, m. 9 [vocal p. 296]).

Step into My Study . . .

Wagner's scores are carefully constructed. There is considerable guidance about phrasing for example, which influences perceptions of mood and speed. Sometimes the same music appears in different parts of the opera with little change other than in time signature and the related difference in note durations.

In *Tristan*, we also encounter larger beat units more often than we expect. In particular, we see a $\frac{2}{2}$ time signature, with its half note pulse, relatively frequently. This tells the conductor to "think" alla breve. With Wagner's heavier orchestral palette, his $\frac{2}{2}$ time signature beaten twice per measure keeps relatively fast—but not really very fast—music flowing naturally and keeps the orchestra from crudely overwhelming the singer as it might if I were to beat four times per measure. On the other hand, in slower music, Wagner's time signatures call for beating more often per measure, usually thinking and phrasing in quarter notes.

Two passages illustrate the effect of changing the pulse or beat unit. The music in the Act III Liebestod is the same as in the Act II love duet

("Liebesnacht") where the interruption by Mark and Melot results in dissonance and an absence of resolution. But in addition, the two passages have different pulses. The music at "Wie sie fassen, wie sie lassen . . ." in Act II (from m. 14 before [Ff], p. 264 [vocal 201]) appears at the same speed in Act III beginning at ETWAS BEWEGTER (m. 17 before [Gg], p. 425 [vocal 314]). In Act II, in addition to thwarted resolution, it has a wild urgency quite different from the grandeur of Act III's version. The $\frac{2}{2}$ signature suggests intensity without excess weight in the Act II love duet; the $\frac{4}{4}$ at the end of the opera, serenity without bogging down.

Only one musical idea in *Tristan* is paced quite differently. That is the Love Potion music, first heard at the beginning of the prelude to the opera. It is reprised as discussed later in this section: in Act I, Scene 5 (after Tristan and Isolde drink the potion) and in Act III, Scene 2 (Tristan's death). All three statements are paced and phrased in eighth notes. This is a much shorter-duration pulse for the opera's slowest music.

In *Tristan*, Wagner also made his intentions clear with explicit tempo relationship indications—more than he did in the other two operas we are discussing.

Remember that this composer was himself a member of the then-emerging conducting profession. In addition to composing and conducting, writing librettos, and even ultimately designing his own theater, he wrote at some length about the art and craft of conducting. But while beginning conductors are drawn to the master's exhortations about freedom, his clarity about tempo relationships does not stick as readily. One look at the score of *Tristan und Isolde* should help to cure this defect. Without a lot of planning and analysis, this work with little stage action cannot hold together and carry the audience along through its running time. The conductor can also sabotage the singers very easily.

Act I, Scene 3

The first important set of related tempos begins about the middle of Act I, Scene 3, and continues into the beginning of Scene 4, from Brangäne's trying to encourage Isolde by telling her that every man she meets loves her, to Isolde's sending her greeting to Tristan. This part of the story spans eight musical sections, beginning very fast and ending at a dramatically slower tempo. If it is not started at the right tempo, the drama of the final subsection will be lost, at least to some extent. We cannot play and sing slowly enough to produce the contrast intended where the final indication calls for a dramatic slamming on the brakes. Beginning this sequence at about 96 half notes per minute works well. Other speeds may be possible, but only within limits; this one allows for the relationships and contrasts indicated in Table 5.1.

Table 5.1 Act I of *Tristan und Isolde*, tempos and relationships (from approximately the middle of Scene 3, p. 54 [vocal 43]).

At... *	Suggestion
m. 7 before Q (48), $\frac{2}{2}$ SEHR SCHNELL *Isolde: mir lacht das Abenteuer! Fluch dir, Verruchter!*	Very fast. Approximately 𝅗𝅥 = 96, but several rubato indications will slow it down (to about 𝅗𝅥 = 82).
T, m. 23 (49), $\frac{3}{4}$ 𝅗𝅥. = 𝅗𝅥 *Brangäne: Was wähnst du Arge? Ungeminnt?*	Faster: the new measure takes as long as a half measure in the previous section. Approximately 𝅗𝅥. = 82.
U, m. 29 (51), $\frac{6}{8}$ ♩. = 𝅗𝅥. *Brangäne: ... Macht. Kennst du der Mutter Künste nicht?*	The tempo is halved. Approximately ♩. = 82.
V, m. 7 (53), MOLTO RALLENTANDO *Brangäne: Gegengift.*	Start at about ♪ = 82 and slow down smoothly. Then we may decelerate to a pulse of perhaps 60 in a couple of measures. (NB: This brings us close to the tempo of the prelude to the opera, and the prelude's music is being quoted at this point.)

(*Continued*)

Table 5.1 (Continued)

m. 10, A TEMPO (MÄSSIG) *Brangäne: Den hehrsten Trank ich halt' ihn hier*	Speed up to a moderate tempo close to the one established at U, m. 29. Targeting about ♩. = 80 makes sense—close to the pulse at which we began but not quite there.
m. 25 (54), $\frac{2}{2}$ SCHNELL *Brangäne: Der Todestrank!*	Speed up markedly. Making the new half note faster than the previous dotted quarter note will work well. Thus, we can reestablish our beginning pulse of 𝅗𝅥 = 96.
	Scene 4
top of the scene (55), $\frac{6}{8}$ LEBHAFT ♩. = 𝅗𝅥 *Isolde: Land!* *Kuwenal: Auf! Auf! Ihr Frauen!*	Slow down to where the new dotted quarter note takes as long as the previous half note. But a slight acceleration to roughly ♩. = 108 at about W, m. 11 (m. 8 before the upcoming MASSIG) will support Isolde's transition into the next section.
W, m. 19 (57), $\frac{4}{4}$ MÄSSIG ♩ = 𝅗𝅥. *Isolde: Herrn Tristan bringe meinen Gruss...*	Dramatically slower: One beat equals the entire previous measure of six eighth notes. If we were traveling at ♩. = 108, we are now at ♩ = 54. This remains singable whereas reestablishing the pulse of 96 (♩ = 48) could put too much strain on most singers. (This tempo indication is incorrect in the vocal score.)

* Vocal score page in parentheses.

Act I, Scene 5

Act I, Scene 5, on the other hand, supplies a test of rubato management skills, beginning right after Tristan sings "Tristans Ehre höchste Treu!" (at Kk, p. 104 [vocal 87]). Within a mere 17 measures, beginning at m. 5,

Wagner writes GEDEHNT (stretched), RASCH (rapid), ZÖGERND (hesitant), LANGSAM (slow), GESTEIGERT (more intense), ETWAS BREIT (somewhat broad), LEBHAFTER (more lively), and SEHR LEBHAFT (very lively). SEHR LEBHAFT lasts for a whole 9 measures until another LANGSAM appears with a shift from $\frac{2}{2}$ meter to $\frac{6}{8}$. This occurs right after Isolde sings "Ich trink' sie dir!" Then after 17 measures, we see indications of ETWAS BEWEGT (somewhat agitated) with a $\frac{3}{4}$ time signature, followed by RALLENTANDO and then LANGSAM (back to $\frac{6}{8}$) in the course of just 8 measures.

Notice however, that most of these indications are written over the vocal lines. Clearly my job is to support the singing actor on the stage; and some of these indications speak to more than speed. But at the meter changes, some decisions are called for. Making smooth connections with what went before follows the model the composer set through most of the preceding music. If we are traveling at about 60 half notes per minute when we encounter the $\frac{6}{8}$ LANGSAM at $\boxed{\text{Kk}}$, m. 32, a transition to 60 eighth notes per minute is musically smooth and works with the drama onstage.

I find validation for this choice in two ways: First, at 60 eighth notes per minute, we are reprising the music at the beginning of the opera's prelude at the approximate speed of that prelude. Second, 40 measures later, after both have drunk the potion, the time signature returns to $\frac{2}{2}$ with LEBHAFT MIT STEIGERUNG (at m. 11 before $\boxed{\text{Ll}}$ [vocal p. 90]). Here, where the stage directions call for a passionate embrace, the new half note can work beautifully at the same pulse as the previous eighth note.

Act II, Scene 2

In Act II, Scene 2, there is more music with fewer of these mathematical relationships. This sounds simpler but, in fact, requires greater attention to detail in studying and greater discipline on the podium because the critical guideposts are hundreds of measures apart.

The sequence begins after Tristan and Isolde have sung praises to the potion and expressed their yearning for the night. The next indication will be a few measures before Tristan sings "O sink hernieder, Nacht der Liebe." It is marked MÄSSIG LANGSAM at a change to $\frac{3}{4}$ meter ($\boxed{\text{U}}$, m. 69 [vocal p. 173]).

If this section is started too slow, it will be impossible for Tristan to sing his music as written. Breathing in the middle of this short phrase should not be necessary, but it is sometimes heard because the tempo has just gotten too slow at this point. Moreover, if Wagner is being consistent—and there can be little doubt of it—his shift from a $\frac{2}{2}$ time signature to $\frac{3}{4}$ is telling the conductor to pace with a quarter note pulse and not let the tempo drag.

If Tristan hits a wall at "O sink hernieder," the seeds of the problem probably lie 25 measures earlier at his "Liebeswonne ihm lacht!" There, the indication is LANGSAMER, UND ALLMÄHLICH IMMER LANGSAMER. But this follows a very fast tempo, and LANGSAMER is a relative term, meaning *more* slowly. So I keep the tempo up enough that the singers do not expire 25 measures later at "O sink hernieder." That is, my goal is to exercise enough control to arrive at the MÄSSIG LANGSAM at a moderate tempo and hold it there so that the singers can get through their duet elegantly.

Also, since I need to slow gradually (*allmählich*), I avoid stark tempo changes, even when they can be executed smoothly. To look for a mathematical relationship like going half-tempo at MÄSSIG LANGSAM is misguided, in my opinion. I find it best to decelerate over the preceding 19 measures so slowly that the listener cannot detect a change from measure to measure and we can slide into the new section without an apparent change in tempo.

I find a clue to the right tempos in the cello part in the orchestral passage between these two indications. While others play long, legato lines, Wagner writes a repeated and syncopated figure in the cellos. If I target a singable 80 or so quarter notes per minute for "O sink hernieder," then the cellos can begin at about 106, evoking an elevated human heartbeat. And that leaves room to slow in two stages to what amounts to a speed closer to a resting human heartbeat. It is singable, and it seems apt. Here is a series of tempos leading up to "O sink hernieder" that work (beginning on p. 221 [vocal 172]):

U, m. 50: $\frac{2}{2}$ LANGSAMER, UND ALLMÄHLICH IMMER LANGSAMER, as Tristan sings "Liebeswonne ...," 𝅗𝅥 = 72

m. 59: Cello "heartbeat" figure begins, ♩ = 106

m. 64: ♩ = 96

m. 69: $\frac{3}{4}$ MÄSSIG LANGSAM, as the cellos hand off the "heartbeat" figure to violas, ♩ = 80

Pickup to m. 75: Tristan sings "O sink hernieder . . ."

Looking forward about 200 measures through a series of rubato indications, that MÄSSIG LANGSAM tempo ([U], m. 69, p. 223 [vocal 173]) must be reestablished at m. 22 before [Aa], p. 246 [vocal 188]) as indicated in the first row of Table 5.2. If the tempo is not fast enough, Tristan will have a difficult or impossible task at "So starben wir," about 50 measures later (at [Aa], m. 33, p. 249 [vocal 191]). To get him through that passage, the only solution will be to maintain a constant pulse, rather than the constant eighth note indicated. This is making the best of a bad situation since it maintains continuity, a smooth transition from one section to another. It is not what the composer indicated, however. Instead, the time signature and indication at the new $\frac{6}{8}$ require holding the eighth note constant and continuing to resist any tendency to slow too much.

Table 5.2 Act II, Scene 2, of *Tristan und Isolde*, tempos and relationships (from p. 246 [vocal 188]).

At... *	Suggestion
m. 22 before [Aa] (188), $\frac{3}{4}$ LANGSAM (WIE ZUVOR) ♩ = ♩ *Tristan: Doch, stürbe nie seine Liebe...*	Slow, as before; i.e., at MÄSSIG LANGSAM, ([U], m. 69, p. 223 [vocal 173]). Here we are beating quarters.
[Aa], m. 13 (190), $\frac{4}{4}$ SEHR RUHIG *Tristan: Was sturbe dem Tod...*	Very calm, still beating quarters. The pulse is unchanged.
m. 27 (190), LANGSAM *Isolde: Tristan der Tod gegeben?*	Rubato for not much more than one measure.
m. 28 (191), NICHT SCHLEPPEND!	Don't drag!

(*Continued*)

Table 5.2 (Continued)

Tristan embraces Isolde.	
m. 33 (191), $\frac{6}{8}$ the six ♪ = six ♪ in the earlier $\frac{3}{4}$ *Tristan: So starben wir um ungetrennt ewig einig...*	♪ = ♪ The eighth note is equal to the eighth note established at m. 22 before Aa. We are now beating dotted quarters. The pulse slows relative to the pulse in both preceding sections.
Bb, m. 21 (194), $\frac{3}{4}$ *Tristan and Isolde: Liebe nur zu leben!*	Meter begins changing in violins and others will switch three measures later. The eighth note remains constant, so the pulse is quicker (beating quarter notes).
m. 16 before Dd (198), $\frac{2}{2}$ LEBHAFT, MIT STEIGERUNG *Orchestral passage leading up to Tristan and Isolde: O ew'ge Nacht, süsse Nacht!*	Lively with increasing emotional intensity. Making the new half note equal to the previous quarter note (constant pulse) creates a seamless transition.

* Vocal score page in parentheses.

From "So starben wir" to the climax of this long and intense duet, I continue with a fairly steady pulse resulting in proportional relationships at the two major transitions listed in the last two rows of Table 5.2.

The sequence leading up to and out of "So starben wir" is complex because it involves some transitions maintaining a constant pulse and others where the pulse will vary. It also involves relationships between nonadjacent sections. That is, the girders that hold this duet together and allow the singers to climb to a justly famous climax are spaced nearly 400 measures apart. But with these supports in place, we can relish a great deal of rubato, both indicated and implied. While it is always a mistake to go too far, it is entirely in keeping with Wagner's own essays and correspondence to linger or accelerate at appropriate emotional moments.

Act III, Scene 1

In the very long first scene of the last act, it makes sense to me to maintain tempos that reinforce the contrast between Kurwenal's positive nurturing of the sick Tristan, on the one hand, and Tristan's gradual descent into delirium and death, on the other. One decision point is after Tristan sings "Wo bin ich?" Here the tempo shifts from LANGSAM to LEBHAFT ([A], m. 46, p. 307 [vocal 233]), without a meter change or explicit relationship given. But a solid equivalence between the quarter note in the LANGSAM and the half note in the LEBHAFT section (i.e., doubling the tempo) works beautifully.

Soon, though, Tristan raises himself, asking weakly (MATT) "Kurwenal—du? Wo war ich? Wo bin ich?" with the indication ETWAS LANGSAM ([B], m. 8). Going a little faster than half tempo makes dramatic sense; it works well to portray the disconnection in Tristan's text. It is also consistent with the cumulative effect of the rubato indications. As important, it will carry the performers satisfactorily through the explicit quarter = quarter at a change in time signature where the indication is VORHERIGES ZEITMASS (m. 14), which is the previous tempo. This transition aptly represents the calming effect of the stalwart Kurwenal.

Act III, Scene 2

It is in the second scene of this act that Wagner writes his groundbreaking meter changes followed by conflicting rhythms. Getting the tempo relationships right can only increase in importance.

The orchestra splits into two groups with different time signatures at SEHR ALLMÄHLICH NACHLASSEND IM ZEITMASS ([Bb], m. 9, p. 393 [vocal 295]). I like to take the 16 measures that follow to gradually slow down by almost half, beating in two and then in four. Then at 6/8 SEHR LANGSAM, I halve the tempo with an eighth note equaling the quarter note of the previous section ([Cc], m. 9, p. 395 [vocal 296]). This is a reprise of the music of the opera's prelude at a tempo that is likely to be just a trifle slower than in the prelude. Anyway, that is a reasonable goal that is perfectly fitting for Tristan's death.

My favorite things

The opening of Act III. The opening motive in the violins becomes the ascent in thirds over 4 measures. It captures loneliness and longing better than almost anything in music. Then, the long English horn solo depicts hopelessness and yearning perfectly.

On a lighter note, I do admit to feeling tickled by the hint of Wotan's Farewell that begins 15 measures from the end of this long and so-serious opera (in the flute, oboe, and English horn). It reminds us that Wagner interrupted his work on the Ring to compose *Tristan* and needed to get back to that.

Chapter 6

French Romantic Opera

Faust (1859), *Carmen* (1875), and *Samson et Dalila* (1877), still popular to this day, represent the three styles vying for supremacy in France in their time: Romanticism, Realism, and Wagnerianism (the Modernism of the day). Impressionism was on the horizon and would soon become a major force in music but, with the exception of Debussy's *Pelléas et Mélisande*, it manifested itself more in instrumental music than in lyric theater.

Something else was going on in nineteenth-century France, however. More than any other country in Europe, France was simultaneously creating two distinct kinds of lyric theater that would enter the standard operatic repertory and even the ranks of the "war horses": grand opera and operetta. *Samson* et *Dalila* was grand opera—almost entirely through-composed, *à la* Wagner. *Carmen* and *Faust* had their origins in nineteenth-century French music theater. In contrast, by the mid-nineteenth century, German opera was virtually all music, notwithstanding the example of Beethoven's *Fidelio*. Meanwhile, the Italians never had much dialogue with music.

So France has contributed handsomely to the standard operatic repertory. Since the mid-twentieth century, however, its operas have unquestionably suffered a decline in popularity, with the notable exception of Georges Bizet's *Carmen*. Jules Massenet's *Manon* has perhaps suffered the greatest decline in frequency of performance relative to its earlier popularity. But the cost of producing *Manon* may be as much the reason for a fall-off in productions as its box office appeal. Other works that have receded are Massenet's *Werther* and *Thaïs*, Bizet's *Les pêcheurs de perles*, Ambroise Thomas's *Hamlet* and *Mignon*, and Léo Delibes's *Lakmé*.

If French operas experience poor box office, the reason may lie in the esthetic in some measure. Many French operas of the Romantic period have something in common with French academic painting of the time—works by artists like William-Adolphe Bouguereau, Gustave Doré, Théodore Géricault, and Jean-Léon Gérôme. This means a love of allegory and idealization, a preference for historical and mythological subjects, and the reinforcement of conventional morality. To its detractors, it is bourgeois, sentimental, clichéd, or merely decorative. A decline because of esthetic is unfortunate. Many works that can provoke giggles can also be very moving when taken on their own terms and performed with sincerity and care.

Gounod: *Faust*

> Can [*Faust*] be said to be my best work? Positively I do not know. . . . Success is rather the result of a certain combination of fortuitous circumstances and favorable conditions, than a proof or measure of the intrinsic value of the work itself. It is by the surface that the favor of the public is first gained; it is by the depth that it is maintained and strengthened.
>
> —Charles Gounod[1]

Charles Gounod's *Faust* was first heard as an operetta with spoken dialogue in 1859. The fully sung version that we hear nowadays did not reach l'Opéra de Paris until 1869. The story is taken from Johann Wolfgang von Goethe's touchstone retelling of the legend. But Gounod's version focuses on one slice of Goethe's story, the romance between Faust and Marguerite. Faust enters into his pact with the devil primarily for restored youth and carnal pleasure.

In Gounod's telling, then, the story becomes a cautionary tale about Marguerite's fall as much as it is about anything else. One consequence of this is that we need to try to see *Faust* through the eyes of its earliest audiences. To treat *Faust* as a kitschy or ludicrous period piece is to assure a less than satisfactory outcome. The universality is there to be mined, and an imaginative director can still shock an audience. Satan is not a joke or a cartoon in this work. The church scene should be terrifying, and the death of Valentin should convey Marguerite's anguish at being cursed by her dying brother.

On the other hand, an overly dark, somber reading can be tedious and is not entirely authentic, either. The message of the final scene, after all, is redemption. And that finale should be catnip to directors with any talent and some budget. I have seen it staged very effectively with just a blinding white light while the angels sing.

By today's musical standards, *Faust* is a fairly straightforward opera. It can be difficult for today's audiences to understand how radical it seemed when it was new. But the "clear, simple, and yet delightfully coloured orchestral music" that now seems virtually to define French lyric style were, in fact, novel for audiences of the day.[2] Still, *Faust* is characterized by much less chromaticism than we find, for example, in the works of Liszt or Wagner (even the earlier Wagner works).

While not as avant-garde as some protested at the time, the stepwise ascent from the key of G to A to B in the final trio achieves an exciting effect with fairly simple means. Marguerite begins the main melody in G major with "Anges purs, anges radieux" at MODERATO MAESTOSO (m. 31 in No. 31, p. 443 [vocal 291]). She then moves up to A major as counter-lines are sung by Faust and Méphistophélès. Faust urges her to follow him while there still is time to get away, and Méphistophélès urges her to follow and urges both to hurry. Finally, all three move up one more time to B major.

This music, like the bel canto operas, requires singers with refined vocal technique and voices of real beauty. We should be able to execute exquisitely soft playing or singing, for example, at the right moments. As recently as the 1960s, singers brought their own variations and ornaments to this music but this practice has fallen out of favor. The composer supplied ample trills, runs, and other decorations.

Singers from different musical traditions have, at times, brought a welcome jolt of intensity to *Faust*. Feodor Chaliapin and later Boris Christoff as Méphistophélès come to mind. Cesare Siepi, who also sang Méphistophélès, was something of a model of masculine elegance, or elegant masculinity if you will. Combinations of elegance and fire like Siepi's can thrill an audience.

Méphistophélès is one of the harder parts to cast in this opera. While a certain roughness and huskiness can work well enough in other bass parts—villains and some elders—that is not the case here. Méphistophélès must be a classic French *basse chantante*, a lyric bass. He should be seductive, which requires the beauty of tone and elegant phrasing that such a bass can deliver. He needs stage presence, too. Only a singer with a big personality and charm will be credible.

Faust himself is a lyric tenor, lighter than most of Verdi's tenors. And Marguerite must be a lyric soprano capable of some coloratura. But it is important not to cast too light a soprano because of the church scene and the last scene. The part is roughly like Verdi's Violetta in *La traviata*, a bit heavier than Gounod's own Juliette.

Some of the star turns for the three leads include: Faust's Act III cavatina at seeing the modest dwelling of Marguerite, "Salut! demeure chaste et pure" (No. 12, p. 166 [vocal 114]), Marguerite's Act III "Jewel Song" (No. 14b, p. 184 [vocal 127]), and Méphistophélès's Act IV "Serenade" (No. 24, p. 325 [vocal 226, from ALLEGRETTO]). These are all good melodies and opportunities for a gifted singer to thrill an audience.

Méphistophélès also has a lively and entertaining rondo in "Le veau d'or," which ironically quotes the traditional French Christmas carol "Les anges dans nos campagnes" ("Angels We Have Heard on High" in the English version). This is in Act II on "Autour de son pédestal" (No. 7, from m. 32, p. 98 [vocal 65]). Gounod's listeners would have recognized the carol and recalled the Latin refrain, "Gloria in excelsis Deo," contradicting Méphistophélès's blasphemy.

The baritone part of Valentin, Marguerite's brother, acquired Act II's "Avant de quitter ces lieux" for the English premiere (No. 6 from MOLTO MODERATO, p. 86 [vocal 56]). There is a danger of getting too saccharine in this cavatina, but it can be effective and has become one of the better-known numbers in the opera. Siebel, the young man who pines for Marguerite, is played by a mezzo-soprano. But at least some of his music is usually cut.

A quartet (No. 16, p. 199 [vocal 140 from MODERATO ASSAI]) follows two of the most well-known arias in French opera, those of Faust and Marguerite in Act III mentioned above. In the quartet, two couples sing alternating and then simultaneous duets. Faust and Marguerite sing romantically, and Méphistophélès and Marthe play out the comedy. Giacomo Puccini would write a similar blending of romantic and comic duets for Act III of *La bohème* almost forty years later. But Giuseppe Verdi had used this double-duet form to very different effect in *Rigoletto* and would do so again in *Otello*.

The chorus shines throughout. This includes most of Act II, beginning with the "Kermesse" through the critical meeting between Faust and Marguerite, as well as Act IV, with the church scene and the soldiers' chorus. The chorus also portrays the band of angels in the concluding apotheosis, of course.

Step into My Study . . .

Before the first day of rehearsal, the conductor and director and producer must come to a series of agreements with respect to cuts, an issue that looms large in this opera. Indeed, when renting orchestra parts, one must make special requests in some cases. In addition, restoring music means a longer opera and brings us over the three-hour cutoff that many companies try to observe for cost reasons. We will consider just two of the almost-universal cuts.

First, there is a "Spinning Wheel Scene" for Marguerite at the beginning of Act IV, long virtually forgotten until the Metropolitan Opera restored it in the 1960s, but still rarely performed (No. 19 [vocal p. 179]). The Spinning Wheel Scene would have been widely known to Gounod's educated listeners. It is part of Goethe's story, and Franz Schubert's lied "Gretchen am Spinnrade," setting Goethe's text, had been published in 1814. It also fills in the narrative a bit. That is, while we all get what lies behind her suffering in the church scene, the need for the audience to fill in the facts of the case is a consequence of the cuts. Siebel gets to express his selfless but unrequited love in this scene too.

Admittedly, the scene has been cut since very early in the work's history. Camille Saint-Saëns chalked up its disappearance during his own lifetime both to its being underappreciated and to sopranos' finding it fatiguing. It is true that an uncut *Faust* makes for a very long night. Originally, there was even a mad scene when the curtain went up at the prison and an additional Marguerite-Faust duet.[3]

Still, we can only hope that the Spinning Wheel Scene will be restored more often. There is about as good a case for this as for Gounod's poison aria for Juliette, which has slowly returned to *Roméo et Juliette* since the 1970s. It, too, portrays an important moment in the score.

There remains a foreshadowing of the Spinning Wheel Scene in Act I that also gets the ax all too often. It comes early in the opera when Méphistophélès conjures a vision of Marguerite in his own seduction of Faust (No. 4, from ANDANTE, p. 38 [vocal 23]). This cut is unfortunate because the scene contains a double preview. While the muted violins play the figure that imitates the rhythm of the spinning wheel, the horn sweetly (DOLCE) plays the love theme that we will hear in the Marguerite-Faust duet in the Act III quartet.

Digging beneath the surface of this music reveals Gounod's skillful dramaturgy: The Act I preview is in the key of E major, consistent with Faust's joy. The harp, supported by the violins' relatively regular and gentle rhythm, suggests Méphistophélès's magical powers. The later spinning song, on the other hand, is in the more somber key of E minor, consistent with Marguerite's despair and isolation, and the horn and clarinet reinforce the mood with plaintive moans. In addition, in Act IV we hear a more realistic spinning wheel sound. This is a result of the two violin sections alternating and overlapping and concluding each phrase with a note lower than the average for the phrase, creating accents that receive extra emphasis from the lower strings playing pizzicato.

The second major cut is of the trio of scenes usually referred to collectively as the "Walpurgisnacht Scene" that opens Act V (everything that comes before the prison scene, Nos. 27–29 [vocal No. 18]). It poses a different dilemma. Cutting its first-rate ballet music, written for l'Opéra de Paris a decade after the premiere, is a shame. But if a company cannot spend what is needed on a fine choreographer and dancers, the entire scene might be cut.

A well-danced grand ballet is a real treat for today's opera audiences who get to see one in only a handful of operas. (*Aida*, *La Gioconda*, and *Samson et Dalila* are almost guaranteed to come to the stage with their ballets intact, but there are not many others.) The complete suite is seven dances that take about twenty minutes; but a partial performance of four or five of them is a reasonable choice. The rationale for cutting the entire scene once it is decided that the ballet is to be cut is that, though it belongs to Méphistophélès, he does not have his most impressive or character-revealing music to sing. His character is revealed earlier in the opera.

In individual productions of *Faust*, however, acts and scenes may be further rearranged. These changes may be made to eliminate intermissions, to meet the production's dramatic requirements, or to make further cuts and then restore logic. The church scene and the death of Valentin have been switched in some productions for a hundred years. Given the libretto that remains after the usual cuts, this makes considerable sense. Moving from the church scene directly to the prison makes for better theater than we get by keeping the remaining scenes in their original order.

Happily, in whatever form this opera takes, there are still many pages of great music. With agreement all-around regarding what the production will include and in which order, I can return my attention to the music.

Both singers and conductor will see some commonalities between *Faust* and the operas of the bel canto school. In Gounod's work, more than in that of Bizet or Saint-Saëns, a delicate balance must be struck between elegance and refinement on the one hand, and an adequate amount of drama on the other. Finding appropriate dynamics and tempos means showcasing the beauty while not losing the forward motion.

There is a triple-forte indication at the end of the church scene of Act IV and, for me, this is both the emotional and dynamic high point of the opera (No. 21, on p. 285 [vocal 205]). The end of the trio in Act V also has a triple-forte indication (No. 31, on p. 454 [vocal 296]) so *Faust* admits of two dynamic high points. The end of the trio does not have the emotional content of the church scene however. The ending apotheosis is emotional in another sense and should leave the audience feeling uplifted, but its intensity is expressed more gently.

As to forward motion, *Faust* can become a tedious sequence of moments without continuity if we do not remain vigilant. The problem is rooted in its original structure with spoken dialogue between musical numbers. Thus, the vigilance is the same as is required in conducting bel canto operas where recitative breaks up the flow between musical numbers.

I look for places where firm, smooth, inevitable-seeming connections feel natural and exciting and work with the drama onstage. These will only enhance the audience's engagement. But as with bel canto operas, this should not be taken to mean that we must strive for mathematical relationships between all sections. Imposing such relationships where none exist is no better than ignoring them when they are present.

Above all, however, this music requires flexibility.

While there are metronome indications in the scores, there is a special caveat with respect to tempo in Gounod's music: While some conductors change composers' metronomic indications more readily than others, Gounod's tempos are among the most commonly changed. And speeding things up is often a far better idea than slowing things down. We can only leave it to historians and other scholars to explain why, so frequently, the metronome indications seem so extremely wrong to our modern ears.

Méphistophélès's "Le veau d'or" is a number that benefits from a little extra energy, for example. When taken at the speed indicated or a bit faster, it has a scherzo feel that can recall Berlioz and Rossini and look forward to Verdi's Iago. Marguerite's Jewel Song is almost universally taken at a faster tempo than the metronome indication, and to good effect. With this aria, the danger lies in overdoing it. If we go too fast, we lose the impression of innocence and naiveté. This is not a contest to see which conductor's Marguerite can get to the finish line first.

While going faster is often a good idea however, this is by no means a suggestion that we should perform *Faust* faster across the board. An example of where such a change is ill advised comes in the "Kermesse," which opens Act II (No. 5 [vocal p. 31]). Conductors have been speeding this up for more than a century, resulting in "an inharmonious and displeasing hullabaloo" according to Camille Saint-Säens.[4]

But a kermesse starts as a religious event, a mass, followed by festivities that spill out into the village square or another outdoor public place. Gounod's own leisurely indication for this Kermesse lends a kind of rustic charm and Germanic spirit to this scene. It is marked ALLEGRETTO (84 quarter notes per minute) but often taken much faster; e.g., up to 116 quarter notes per minute.

As to relationships between tempos, sometimes they are obvious—straightforward and logical both musically and dramatically. In the Act II "Waltz and Chorus" where Faust and Marguerite meet, the ANDANTINO between the fast waltz sections should have a solid, proportional relationship to what comes before and afterward, as suggested at that indication, with the new quarter note very close in speed to the earlier dotted half note (No. 9, on p. 134 [vocal 91]). We return to the opening 72 dotted half notes per minute at TEMPO DI VALSE, 29 measures later.

In Act III, there is a series of tempo changes that requires just a little more homework. This is in Scenes 2–3 featuring Méphistophélès and Faust (No. 11, from p. 161 [vocal 109]).

Scene 1 of the act (No. 10), belongs to Siebel, hoping that the bouquet he is leaving for Marguerite will convey his love for her. No. 11 begins with a bump up in speed, an ALLEGRO, as Méphistophélès and Faust re-enter. But at m. 15, we begin a slow-down in four steps, without specific metronome indications.

Siebel re-enters and grows ever more rhapsodic up to his final line about one kiss telling Marguerite what is in his heart. Note that Gounod even indicates COL CANTO on Siebel's final word (m. 40 of No. 11, vocal p. 111), leaving no doubt as to the passion the singer should express and the freedom the conductor should make room for. A modest pullback should last just that one measure.

At the top of Scene 3 in No. 11, we will get to an ALLEGRO and then an ALLEGRETTO four measures later marked 88 quarter notes per minute (both on p. 164 [vocal 111]). So the question is how fast we should be going after Siebel's ardent declaration; i.e., both before and after the ALLEGRO at the top of Scene 3?

I can make Scene 1 through Scene 3 (Nos. 10 and 11) smooth and connected, and honor Gounod's metronome indications, by recognizing that

Scene 1 (No. 10, Siebel's scene), begins and ends at 88 beats per minute, the very pulse that we return to at ALLEGRETTO early in Scene 3. The 100 dotted quarter notes for Méphistophélès at the top of Scene 2 is a digression. More specifically, in No. 11 (Scenes 2 and 3):

Top of Scene 2: $\frac{6}{8}$ ALLEGRO, ♩. = 100.
m. 15: POCO PIÙ LENTO.
m. 17: A TEMPO, ALLEGRETTO (suggested ♩. = 88).
m. 36: RITARDANDO (suggested ♩. = 80).
m. 38: PIÙ LENTO (suggested ♩. = 72).
m. 40: RALLENTANDO, COL CANTO.
mm. 41–46: TEMPO I (suggested A TEMPO, ♩. = 88).
Top of Scene 3: $\frac{4}{4}$ ALLEGRO (suggested 𝅗𝅥 = 88, but treat Méphistophélès's unaccompanied line [mm. 3–4] as recitative, slowing a bit as needed).
m. 5: ALLEGRETTO, ♩ = 88.

Note that "TEMPO I" at m. 41 means A TEMPO, a return to the ALLEGRETTO of m. 17 and the previous scene, not a return to the ♩. = 100 indicated briefly at the top of Scene 3. As important, it is a caution to not let the COL CANTO drag down the remaining six measures of the scene.

Thus, 88 beats per minute links together Nos. 10 and 11 preparatory to Faust's "Salut! demeure chaste et pure," LARGHETTO (No. 12, p. 166 [vocal 114]).

In this romantic music, the tempos may vary slightly and the relationships may be flexible, as long as the structure is respected.

My favorite things

Méphistophélès's "Ô nuit, étends sur eux ton ombre!" in Act III, with its foretaste of later French music like that of Gustave Charpentier and Gabriel Fauré. In particular, the harp and tremolo violins give atmospheric accompaniment to the horn. In addition, the orchestra is carrying the melody rather than the singer, a more modern approach than we see in most of this opera. (This ADAGIO section in No. 17 begins on p. 217 [vocal 157].)

Bizet: *Carmen*

> Imitation is for fools. It is better to write badly like oneself than like others. Besides, the more beautiful the model, the more ridiculous the imitation. There have been imitations of Michelangelo, Shakespeare, and Beethoven. Heaven knows what horror this rage for imitating has afflicted us with.
>
> —Georges Bizet[5]

Unlike so much of the French repertory, Georges Bizet's *Carmen* (1875) has remained wildly popular for nearly a century and a half. The work is loosely based on a novella by Prosper Mérimée, although Bizet and his librettists modified characters somewhat. For the stage director and designer, this is about as timeless as an opera can be. It has been moved to modern times successfully, most notably to the period of the Spanish Civil War. As often as one conducts it or attends performances, both singers and stage directors can bring original little touches that surprise and delight and stick in the memory.

Carmen's popularity and familiarity present a distinct set of difficulties for everyone involved with a production, however. No opera in the repertory comes with more baggage than this tale of the title character's seducing, abandoning, and being murdered by Don José, while the girl from back home, Micaëla, looks on helplessly. Where specific expectations are not met, disappointment can be great. But the work is so rich that it can sustain several different and valid approaches.

Stylistically, *Carmen* is more a verismo work than a work of the Romantic school. It may, in fact, be the first verismo opera. The story and the rebellious and wanton character of Carmen still have great dramatic power. And the realism that probably contributed to its shaky launch is at least part of the reason for its enduring popularity. Undoubtedly, it was the violent final duet, in particular, that shocked the Opéra-Comique audience. The scene's content would have shocked, but the extent to which the scene contrasted with the first scene of the act would have as well. (Characterizing the opening production as a fiasco would be overstating the case, however.)

Partly because of the composer's early death, disputes existed well into the twentieth century about exactly what the definitive score should contain. Today, the only major question is whether to perform the original dialogue or the recitatives Ernest Guiraud composed later. And the issue of cuts is less about authenticity or fidelity and more about the sheer length of the piece when performed uncut. A critical edition was published in 1964. Although it is not widely used, it is nice to have in one's library. The principal complaint about the critical edition is that some of what editor Fritz Oeser restored was actually cut or revised by the composer himself. Oeser's restorations would still be interesting if the opera were short, but it is not.

This brings us to one of the few problems with *Carmen*: Uncut, with three intermissions, it lasts four hours. Thus, for financial reasons, it is cut—excessively so in recent times. While some cuts may be reasonable, trying to force this opera into three hours is misguided. In addition to telling a story, the work is as full of atmosphere as *Aida* or *Turandot*. Cultivating this atmosphere and setting the scenes take some time.

The prelude and three entr'actes are as important to the total experience as is the story of José and his infatuation with Carmen. The three entr'actes are at the end of Acts I, II, and III in the score although they are generally performed as preludes to Acts II, III, and IV, respectively.

The choruses also help establish atmosphere. Among them, we must count the chorus in Act III, about the customs guard. It is a brilliant musical piece, and like the "Din-Don" chorus in Ruggero Leoncavallo's *Pagliacci*, it is something of a musical divertissement rather than a way of advancing the story.

A more rousing scene-setter is the Act IV opening. It was originally much longer than many of today's productions allow, with a parade and a chorus of vendors at the bull ring that is wonderfully evocative. Later, Bizet's own *l'Arlesienne* suite was added as a ballet after the Act IV opening chorus. When this ballet is included, it is inserted before No. 26 and some part of the often-cut No. 25 is performed to serve as a bridge between the entr'acte played as an Act IV prelude and the ballet. The words "A deux quartos" are changed to "Dansez, dansez" as needed in No. 25. (See the footnote and optional text on pp. 338–339 in the vocal score.)

Everything involving soloists in this rather large cast moves the story forward, however. This includes Carmen's four friends as well as José's superior officer, Zuniga. All of the singers require solid musicianship and a lively stage presence.

While Carmen was written for a mezzo-soprano, sopranos have sung this role. With either voice type, it requires a singer with an even vocal extension. That is, a mezzo must have a mezzo's notes plus a secure upper range, or a soprano must have better-than-average projection in the low range. Current fashion comes down decisively in favor of mezzo-sopranos. In addition, the title role requires a singer of striking personality, someone who can dominate the stage. Carmen must also be a good dancer. Although she does not need to be movie-star beautiful, she must convey a sexual magnetism without becoming a hip-swinging parody.

José requires range. His music is mostly lyric, but when it is dramatic it is very much so. Thus, tenors as diverse as Jon Vickers and Nicolai Gedda have sung the role. The main requirement in casting José is that the two lead voices be matched. While contrast is often a good thing, in this case, it can make balancing their scenes together more difficult. Both will sound best if a dark, spinto mezzo-soprano is paired with a dramatic tenor, and a lyric mezzo-soprano's partner has rather a sweeter timbre.

While Carmen understandably dominates any production, the gentle Micaëla, whom we meet in Act I, shows considerable growth in her character and in the music she sings in her second scene. (Her Act III aria, omitting the Ernst Guiraud recitatives, begins in No. 22 at [32] ANDANTE MOLTO [vocal p. 300]).

But as notable as is the music for both of the women in José's life, the contrast between them is musical dramaturgy at its finest. Micaëla sings simple and direct music. Carmen's is more ornamented, and she sings it while in almost constant motion. The contrast is particularly stark in their duets with José. His Act I duet with Micaëla is conventionally pretty (No. 7). The voices intertwine sweetly and come together in delicate harmony. Notably, as in much of Wagner's work, Carmen and José engage in a naturalistic back-and-forth conversation rather than in conventional duets. Their lines overlap very briefly on occasion as may happen in conversation—or arguments—but they do not sing together in harmony. Arguably the most original and revolutionary passage in the entire opera is the couple's final violent confrontation—no harmonizing there (No. 27).

The toreador Escamillo is a true bass-baritone. A bass needs high notes if he wants to sing this part, and a baritone without strength in the lower notes will simply not be heard. If he does not have enough volume, the dashing, swaggering superstar does not come through. Without enough range and volume, the life is sucked out of a part of the story and out of one of the most famous melodies ever written, the "Toreador Song" (No. 14). Note that this will be true not only if he is inaudible but also if a conductor tries too hard to tamp down the volume in the pit in an effort to compensate. There are limits to what a conductor can do when a singer is miscast.

There are many opportunities for individuals in the pit to shine. They include the first violin in Act I during the interrogation that follows Carmen's arrest (No. 9, [53], from m. 25 [vocal p. 92, m. 1]). The focus then shifts to the cello section, but I like to ask the first cellist to play that alone as well. Other parts that stand out from the orchestra in this opera are the English horn before José's Act II "La fleur que tu m'avais jettée" (No. 17, from ANDANTE at m. 19 of [41] [vocal p. 199]) and the oboe in the Act III–IV entr'acte (from m. 18, ESPRESSIVO).

The flute figures prominently when Carmen sings and also has several lovely solos. This includes the opening of the Act II–III entr'acte, which begins with a solo harp. In a purely orchestral passage like this, I usually will not conduct a soloist. I also prefer not to have to conduct much when the flute joins in, assuming the two instruments can be seated near each other. This is enjoyable for the featured artists and for everyone else in the pit. Once additional instruments enter, of course, I have to resume leading.

In the last twenty-five years or so, many companies have been returning to the original version with spoken dialogue. The *Faust* dialogue, by contrast, is almost never heard. In *Carmen*, both versions have their merits. Particular problems with the spoken dialogue are that French is difficult for non-natives to master and dialogue can be hard to hear, let alone understand, in large opera houses. The sung alternative is somewhat easier for an international cast (i.e., with few if any native French speakers) to pull off successfully.

Some will complain, however, that Guiraud's adding music that the composer did not have in mind in any given moment changes the piece, even if the music is a reprise of something Bizet wrote elsewhere. This is certainly not a concern to be dismissed lightly. Others have noted that spoken dialogue results in more natural and realistic theater. Thus, the dialogue-versus-recitative debate in *Carmen* has no simple resolution.

For me, a practical issue in the fully sung version is the pacing and speed of the recitatives. They are just that: recitatives. If taken too slowly, they can drag the action down. While they cannot move as fast as speech, they must move with a flexibility and pace somewhat like speech.

Step into My Study . . .

The structure of the opera is clear and beautifully supports the story. A single "fate motive" unites the work (first heard in the overture at ANDANTE MODERATO, m. 3 of [6] [vocal p. 4]). We run across its most astonishing reprise in the Act II English horn solo mentioned above. In this reprise, the melody is instantly recognizable, but Bizet's choice of the English horn turns it into an ardent, yearning love song. This choice of a single instrument dramatically alters the mood and goes to prove that there are no small choices in composition.

When Escamillo's Toreador Song is reprised at his Act II and Act III exits, it may be considered just a dramatic echo, like the reprises in *Faust*. But in the finale of Act IV, it is part of a more sophisticated musical structure, intertwined as it is with the fate motive (No. 27, from **[40]**, ALLEGRO MODERATO [vocal p. 389, bottom]).

Dances underpin *Carmen* too: the "Habanera" (No. 5) and the "Seguidilla" (No. 10) of Act I and the more complicated "Gypsy Song" at the beginning of Act II (No. 12). Later in Act II, Carmen briefly sings and dances the "Castanet dance" (No. 17). It is notable for its sparse scoring—just her castanets and pizzicato strings—and some extreme dissonance when the bugle calls to José from offstage. Let it be said, too, that in any catalogue of the dances in *Carmen*, we would also have to consider the flamenco-like Act III–IV entr'acte.

At the same time that *Carmen* is a joy to conduct, its score provokes a few questions large and small. A relatively small practical question arises with respect to the number of players needed in some opera houses. Several passages were almost certainly written with the expectation that musicians would travel between the pit and some offstage location. This happens in places for one trumpet in Act I and two trumpets in Act II, and for the trumpets and trombones in the final duet of Act IV. In the majority of opera houses, this is no problem. However, in the small ones (or more precisely, theaters with very small pits), there can be inadequate room to maneuver in and out of the pit expeditiously. And in very large houses, the distance can be too great to be sure that the musicians can make it in time with enough breath to play. In these situations, of course, more musicians must be paid, or a recording may be made, or the offstage music must migrate to the pit.

In addition, the first page of *Carmen* is notable for containing one of the more questionable metronome indications that the conductor faces in this score. The 116 quarter notes per minute printed in most editions is simply too slow. It sounds heavy, particularly when we get to the preview of the Toreador Song. It is true that colleagues whom I respect use this tempo, often conceiving the piece as a march. They have tradition—which should not be dismissed lightly—on their side.

This returns us to Fritz Oeser's critical edition. Oeser worked from sources believed to reflect Bizet's intentions as well as from records of the first production, which the composer supervised. In his preliminaries however, he tells us that there are no metronome indications extant in Bizet's hand. (He also points out that, sometimes, those in published scores are inconsistent with the verbal tempo indications.) This comes as a bit of a shock. By 1875, the year of *Carmen's* premiere and Bizet's death just a few months later, most composers had happily adopted the metronome. True, there were great composers who eschewed its use entirely, but if there are metronome indications in an 1875 or later score, we have had reason to believe that they came from the composer. Editors have exercised discretion in adding them, and placed them in parentheses or brackets to alert us to the additions.

In the 1875 vocal score, we see the metronome indications that have been handed down since then with no clue about their origins. Still, Oeser urges caution regarding even these. He cannot rule out that they are Bizet's, and he cannot rule out that they are not Bizet's.

In light of this history, and given that Oeser himself includes many—if not most—of the traditional indications (in brackets), it is reasonable to point out that Oeser omits any metronome indication at all next to ALLEGRO GIOCOSO (a playful allegro) at the top of the overture. He does this without any discussion or explanation for what is, at the end of the day, uncharacteristic of him. So there is ample room to question whether that ♩ = 116 is Bizet's intention here. For me, a tempo closer to 132 quarter notes per minute feels more apt. Admittedly, I play energetically.

That said, it is also reasonable to consider the traditional metronome indications carefully. I find most of them in this score work quite well. So I would not want to encourage discarding them wholesale. In fact, this is just a reminder that we should approach all scores with caution. Even those of us with a desire to give our all to observing the composer's intentions cannot always be sure about them. And the problem extends past the scores from earlier in the nineteenth century.

Because this opera began life with spoken dialogue and fewer sections to connect, the question of tempo relationships here, as in *Faust*, is less relevant than it is in *Samson et Dalila*. Indeed, trying to establish arithmetic relationships sometimes adds little and can even seem a bit contrived. Mostly, attentiveness to the printed indications will serve us very well in *Carmen*. Still, four sections that require some forethought and planning are discussed below.

Act I: Planning Ahead

The evocative, descriptive passage for the chorus of cigarette factory workers in Act I (No. 4, from [23], ANDANTINO [vocal p. 35]) is often played faster than the metronome indication of 60 dotted quarter notes a minute. There is no dramatic or musical reason for this change. Dramatically, the tempo Bizet indicates seems to depict a group of women returning from a break in factory work on a hot afternoon in Seville perfectly—languid and seductive. At least some of the women may be assumed to have been sleeping during this break. These women are well aware that a group of men is observing them closely. So they should be strolling, far more interested in teasing the men (easy marks, admittedly) than in returning to work.

Example 6.1A Cigarette workers' chorus in *Carmen* (Act I, No. 4, from m. 5 before 24 [vocal top of p. 36]). Dotted bar lines divide all measures from m. 4 before 24 and continue through the end of this chorus; i.e., until the basses enter at 27, ALLEGRETTO.

Example 6.1B (Continued)

Staging frequently contributes to confusion about this scene. The women are almost invariably seen emerging from the factory. But the original dialogue makes clear that the men (a lot of them) are awaiting the return of the women to work. When Zuniga asks whether women work in the factory,

José tells him, “Oui, mon lieutenant. Elles n’y sont pas maintenant; tout à l’heure, après leur dîner, elles vont revenir. Et je vous réponds qu’alors il y aura du monde pour les voir passer.” (See Oeser, p. 62 [vocal p. 30].) Alas, even when *Carmen’s* dialogues are performed, these words are virtually always cut.

Notably, the door to the factory is often elevated so that the chorus descends some stairs. Yes, the original stage directions use the verb *descendre* at ANDANTINO (in Oeser and Choudens [first edition]), but this is mistranslated in the Kalmus reprint and Schirmer vocal score available for download. Here, *descendre* does not necessarily have to involve literally moving downward or coming from above. This use of *descendre* is equivalent to English’s “walk down [the street],” definitely with a connotation of rambling along the stage in a relatively unhurried manner. So *descendre* does not mean descending and certainly does not mean that the women are leaving the factory. (It is a small matter perhaps but note that Carmen herself comes onto the scene last. This, too, is more consistent with ending a work break. We would hardly expect Carmen to be the last to leave her work station.)

The indicated tempo is also consistent with the angelic sound of an all-female chorus and the women’s poetic words about lovers’ sweet talk, raptures, and vows that are smoke mounting toward the sky. Thus, there is nothing happening onstage that compels a faster tempo, and the choice of many to zip through this chorus is less interesting dramatically than the speed Bizet indicates.

Even if I do not concern myself with the stage and the story, however, there is a technical rationale for respecting the score’s indication. If we look ahead, the indicated tempo is not just *not* too slow; it is actually the fastest possible if we want the chorus to hang together in the intended manner from beginning to end. (My own performance, in fact, will generally come in a little slower, about 56 dotted quarter notes per minute.)

The beginning of the scene (No. 4) is marked ALLEGRO, with 104 dotted quarter notes per minute, reasonably peppy. (The Kalmus reprint of Peters erroneously indicates ♩ = 104; the Schirmer vocal score has the correct ♩. = 104.)

At [22] (vocal p. 33), the men downshift to ALLEGRETTO MODERATO (104 quarter notes) with "La cloche a sonné" as they position themselves for the expected return of the ladies. A gradual slowing down continues with PIÙ LENTO for two measures followed by MOLTO PIÙ LENTO for two measures followed by a fermata over a rest, marked LUNGA. Finally, as the women enter, there are both a meter change from $\frac{2}{4}$ to $\frac{6}{8}$ and a tempo change to ANDANTINO, 60 dotted quarter notes per minute ([23], vocal p. 35).

If the indicated deceleration is not observed, it is in part because beating slowly can be difficult and speeding up unconsciously is easy. A solution is to begin beating the eighth note from a few measures before the women begin singing, whereas beating the dotted quarter note (twice per measure) is sufficient through the preceding music. Beating less frequently is often preferred. It lets the music breathe, if you will. Beating six times per measure, however, can be expected to help keep this tempo rock solid but unrushed. It also allows for subtle variations in phrasing. There is the opportunity to create a larger number of gentle stresses that work nicely with the words the chorus is singing in this relatively slow tempo.

Beating the eighth note presents a physical limitation, however: Even starting the piece at the indicated tempo, if I keep the pulse constant and beat each of the eighth notes in these measures, I will be moving at the rate of 180 eighth notes per minute, or three wrist movements per second; and that is moving rather quickly. If I start any faster, I am apt to hit a conducting wall and need to slow down—probably suddenly. This would mean a non-logical and therefore somewhat bumpy tempo shift where we should be gently and effortlessly sliding into the women's singing. Note the figures of ascending sixteenth notes in Example 6.1. These are the measures right before [24] where the women begin singing. There should be no discontinuity there, not even the slightest. There should be a leisurely propulsion.

Therefore, starting this section any faster than indicated is undesirable dramatically and risky in technical terms. Early editors of this score offered some food for further thought and planning in a section that has been recognized as a potential problem for a long time. As far back as the 1877 Choudens score, the editors introduced broken bar lines, cutting the measures in half. They even included the verbal suggestion to beat these half-measures in three, steering us toward beating the eighth note rather than making no change at all after the previous measures.

Why not just suggest beating the existing measures in six without adding broken bar lines? "In six" means tracing a relatively large, six-point pattern in the air. In fact, it is not practical to try to beat such a pattern in space at this tempo. "In three" means a simple triangle that can be traced in a small space; i.e., quickly. This works well with these notes in this tempo, although it requires some practice the first time one tries it and will not be practical at any appreciably faster speed.

Those dotted bar lines send a powerful message to conductors. For the record however, Fritz Oeser scrubs the critical edition clean of both editorial additions.

Act II: A Scherzo

There is a quintet in Act II at Lillas Pastia's tavern that merits discussion (No. 15). It is a rhythmically tricky section at the indicated tempo with a lot of words, and it requires good musicianship on the part of singers. In addition, it contains some manageable difficulties for the orchestra. So this scherzo will easily be one of the points in rehearsal where we stop and take more time.

What is not generally noted is that this pretty, upbeat quintet is in classic scherzo form. The music supports a comic dialogue among Carmen and her four friends regarding their next big criminal undertaking, and it follows the A-B-A scherzo form.

The metronome indication calls for a fast tempo: 152 dotted eighth notes per minute; then the trio section is marked 132 eighth notes per minute. The scherzo sections bear a time signature of $\substack{6\\16}$ rather than the $\substack{3\\8}$ we might expect from our German models. The phrasing is in groups of three sixteenth notes, but the conductor can generally be most helpful by beating once per measure. The trio section is in $\substack{2\\8}$ meter, and the beat pattern can be twice per measure at the slightly slower tempo.

To take this scherzo too slow is wrong. On the other hand, some want to take it as fast as possible, and sometimes faster, and then slow down for a dramatic contrast at the trio (at [32] [vocal p. 173]). But the trio bears the indication A TEMPO, MA UN POCO RITENUTO, which follows a MOLTO RALLENTANDO. A slightly slower trio is consistent with most symphonic scherzos going back to Beethoven. With a dramatically different tempo in the trio, we will miss a musical reference that Bizet surely intended. So I relax the tension but slow down relatively little. The tempos in the metronome indications serve quite well.

Bizet also injects a bit of a pun, since the middle section of this quintet is actually shared by three singers. Dancaïro and Remendado introduce the melody and then hand it off to Carmen. But Frasquita and Mercédès do not sing during this interlude. All five singers then join for a repeat of the scherzo music. So this trio is actually sung by a trio of singers.

Act III: Discontinuity

Bizet indicates disconnects within the Act III trio among Carmen, Frasquita, and Mercédès (No. 20). The trio begins and ends with Mercedes and Frasquita seeking to divine their fortunes in playing cards. The women are entertainingly light-hearted. In between, however, Carmen's ANDANTINO ([20] [vocal p. 271]), "Carreau! Pique! La mort," and ANDANTE MOLTO MODERATO ([21] [vocal p. 272]), "En vain pour éviter les réponses amères," should be more dramatic and unrelated to the tempos that come before and after. Carmen is in a different place psychologically. So while a constant pulse serves us well in many sections of this opera, discontinuity in tempo reinforces the drama of this scene, giving us a foretaste of even greater melodrama in the final duet.

Act IV: Melodrama and Recitative

The most challenging sequence in this opera is in the final duet where Carmen defies the enraged José (No. 27). This scene can be quite harrowing and following the tempo indications will increase the audience's visceral experience of instability. The music—in fact, the fluctuating tempo—is at the heart of the audience's experience.

Over the years, a certain sloppiness has accumulated around *Carmen's* final duet. While it is not a mathematically related series of sections, as in the great Mozart finales, Bizet is very specific about what is recitative—freer and rather speech-like—and what requires more strictly observed rhythms.

Although the stage action is far more melodramatic and veristic, this sequence may be considered the grandchild of the extended dialogue between Tamino and the Priest in Mozart's *Die Zauberflöte*. The structure of that duet, too, involves combining orchestral recitative with sections in specified tempos.

Thus, this duet requires something quite different from a series of proportional relationships and smooth transitions. While sometimes tricky, many of our mathematical relationships are just a matter of, well, math. And, for a conductor, explosions of sound are easy. To arrive at a series of tightly interlocking sections that propels the story forward relentlessly, while portraying nothing so much as instability, is rather more difficult and requires more skill and discipline. It becomes all the more important to find the single climactic moment and build toward that with controlled dynamics and a combination of sudden changes and smooth transitions.

The opening measures are marked RECITATIVO and COLLA VOCE. *Colla voce* is too often interpreted as "slow down" because that is often appropriate. It really is an indication to the conductor to give the singer some freedom, although it is not quite as wide open as an AD LIB indication. In this scene, in particular, it may mean any combination of lingering or lurching forward as the drama requires.

While encouraging the conductor to give the singers room to act, though, the score has a countervailing indication: SENZA LENTEZZA at m. 2. Literally, this is "without slowness" and may be interpreted as "don't drag." Nonetheless, most Carmens are inclined toward a funereal pace for recognizing José with "C'est toi!" in the first measure. In fact, the word given the greatest duration is "craindre" a few measures later; the rest of the words are written to move faster. Then a MODERATO tempo is established at m. 7 (96 quarter notes per minute), and soon we will see UN POCO ANIMATO (112 quarter notes at 31 [vocal p. 373]). This is an abrupt break in tempo as Carmen has finished telling José that their relationship is over and her words grow considerably more melodramatic.

If we take the first measure of this UN POCO ANIMATO at the indicated tempo, we show Carmen's stubbornness in the face of danger. Note that the indication COLLA VOCE—but not RECITATIVO—is repeated at m. 1 before [32] (vocal p. 377, m. 1), as Carmen vows ". . . non je ne te céderai pas!" So stretching her high A-flat makes some dramatic and musical sense. But immediately, we are returned to the first and unrelated tempo, 96 quarter notes per minute, as José replies "Carmen! Il est temps encore." Thereafter, we will only see COLLA VOCE and RECITATIVO indications in the final pages of the score. The singers should be singing in tempo through most of this finale. It will pay off.

For me, the single climactic moment that a conductor should have in mind from at least the beginning of this duet comes with the first restatement of the fate motive as José stops Carmen from leaving him for the last time with "Ainsi le salut de mon âme . . ." This is José's turning point (at [38], MODERATO, p. 567 [vocal 387]).

His instability is reflected in the music in two ways: First, the fate motive explodes out of the orchestra repeatedly (*ff*). Note that it appears four times in the mere 12 measures beginning at MODERATO. Although the orchestra does not get louder with each repetition, the tension should continue to mount through rigorously controlled tempo and carefully calibrated attacks. Second, we begin alternating between recitative and strict rhythm. Bizet gives the singers a rhythmic freedom that appears nowhere else in the opera.

The fury and chaos accompanied by strings, woodwinds, and French horn are thrown into sharper relief with the festive chorus and brass breaking in at irregular intervals with their play-by-play commentary from the bullring offstage. Notably, the offstage music has its own tempo, unrelated and also faster than almost everything else in this finale. When conditions permit, I even like to ask the conductor backstage to maintain that ALLEGRO GIOCOSO for the one measure in which the pit bursts in with its first restatement of the fate motive, MODERATO.

But just as a climax is impossible to discern when everything is loud in a performance, the chaos in the final 51 measures of this opera will be hard to appreciate if we have not exercised some control in the 75 percent of the scene leading up to it. This is not easy. The whole scene is melodramatic and, at the end, there are repeated instructions to give the singers freedom to emote. So it requires some thought and planning and careful consideration each time we ratchet up the energy. My goal is to ensure that José's turning point is recognizable as such and the tension builds until Carmen throws her ring at him, where the winds escalate to *fff* and José finally snaps completely (in the 2 measures before ALLEGRO MODERATO at [40] [vocal p. 389]).

My favorite things

The ever more insistent repetition of the fate motive in the final duet, discussed above. This sums up the whole opera emotionally and musically.

Saint-Säens: *Samson et Dalila*

> What gives Sebastian Bach and Mozart a place apart is that these two great expressive composers never sacrificed form to expression. As high as their expression may soar, their musical form remains supreme and all-sufficient.
>
> —Camille Saint-Säens[6]

Unlike *Faust* and *Carmen*, which were first heard as works with spoken dialogue, Camille Saint-Säens's *Samson et Dalila* was conceived as an oratorio and evolved into the opera we know today. The composer had to persevere in the face of almost universal rejection.[7] Today however, it remains one of his most popular works, along with the *Carnival of the Animals* and Symphony No. 3 (the *Organ* Symphony).

Samson lies somewhere between the classic oratorio and Hector Berlioz's music dramas for the concert stage (e.g., *La damnation de Faust* or *Roméo et Juliette*). At the same time, it supplies more vivid theater than an oratorio of either kind even if it feels, at times, like a series of tableaux. Act I is the most static, with a lot of choral writing. Act III also has little stage action except for the "Bacchanale" and the final pages. So while *Samson* can be a very effective opera with the right singers, we need to bring life to those tableaux. Still, *Samson* is not unique in this regard. We have, for example, Act II of *Tristan und Isolde* where, in spite of the greatness of the music, there is extremely little physical action for a director to work with.

Samson benefited from the composer's long-term exposure to authentic Arabic music. He was extremely successful at suggesting music of the Middle East—or the Middle East as imagined by nineteenth-century Europe—in the Bacchanale in Act III, Scene 2, particularly in the oboe solo of its opening (from p. 376 [vocal 204]). But dabs of exoticism appear elsewhere. For example, Abimélech's aria in Act I, Scene 2, is doubled by two ophicleides (from PIÙ ALLEGRO at [A], [vocal p. 50]). These short-lived brass instruments that replaced the serpent of Renaissance music may themselves be replaced by two bassoons or a French horn in the upper octave and a tuba in the lower range.

The influence of Richard Wagner is evident most notably in that this opera is virtually entirely through-composed. Except for applause after Act III's Bacchanale, we cannot stop after any aria or duet in *Samson*, even the biggest. The listener must feel connections to a greater extent and for longer stretches than is the case in *Faust* or *Carmen*. Saint-Saëns gives us clues about knitting the pieces of *Samson* together however—either explicit metronome indications or note-value relationships. On the other hand, it is characterized by simpler harmonies and fewer shifts in key than Wagner would have given us. So it is more like the tone poems of Franz Liszt in that regard.

Saint-Saëns wrote that the storm that gathers in strength throughout Scene 3 of Act II was inspired by the storm in Gioachino Rossini's *Otello*.[8] That may be so, but this entire section is quite reminiscent of the opening storm of *Die Walküre*. For one thing, it has a recurring figure of the same kind. For thunder, Saint-Saëns achieves something like the sound of the two rolling timpani in *Die Walküre's* storm with a bass drum and timpani in a two-instrument conversation. The bass drummer is directed to play with timpani mallets (at [S], p. 306 [vocal 167]). This gives a sound that is not quite like either a typical timpani or a typical bass drum. In addition, there is an homage that is more hidden in this storm, a figure that sounds very much like the moaning chorus that interjects itself throughout the storm in the last act of Verdi's *Rigoletto*. In *Samson*, this figure is given to the horn and lower strings (from [V], m. 2, p. 315 [vocal 169]).

The vocal requirements for *Samson et Dalila* are closer to those of Wagnerian operas than to classic French opera of the time. Dalila requires

Example 6.2 Dalila's principal aria in *Samson et Dalila* includes two melodies used motivically (Act II, Scene 3): (a) Introduction of the first motive (at N, p. 286 [vocal 157]). (b) A reprise of the second motive (at m. 4 before Q, p. 297 [vocal 163]).

a dramatic mezzo with a very strong low range, like Fricka of Wagner's *Das Rheingold* and *Die Walküre* or Azucena of Verdi's *Il trovatore*. The part requires a creamy, rich middle and bottom range and very good breath control. Like Wagner's and Richard Strauss's women, her vocal lines are conceived as long, legato phrases. In fact, some words in her most important aria are very difficult to sing as written. We usually hear them rephrased with a repetition of "réponds" to get in a breath. The alternative phrase is printed below the original in Example 6.2(a).

On the other hand, high notes are not a very big issue for this character. She has two written B-flats, but they do not require the same tonal beauty as Samson's high notes. The first is in her duet with Samson near the end of Act II when she calls him a liar (m. 12 before Z, p. 332 [vocal 177]). It is sung in anger, even if feigned. The other is almost a scream, together with the chorus and High Priest, as the temple comes crashing down (m. 9 before the end of the opera). In the Act II aria, "Amour, viens aider ma faiblesse," a B-flat is often substituted for the written G-flat at "je le brave" (Scene 1 at D, m. 7, p. 186 [vocal 108]). If this B-flat is to be sung, it must be done beautifully and with the entire phrase legato. However it is certainly not necessary to risk it if the mezzo is not one-hundred-percent secure.

Although Dalila was Saint-Saëns's original focus, and although she has the two most-excerpted arias, it is Samson that remains the greater role for an actor and, overall, the more important role. Samson is a dramatic tenor like Wagner's Tristan, or at least spinto like Canio in Leoncavallo's *Pagliacci* or Lohengrin in Wagner's opera of that name. Although the part requires a tenor of power with a strong lower range, he must have a secure, ringing top register. Three times he is asked to sing high B-flats. In one instance, in particular, the approach is difficult and the note must have a certain lyrical warmth. This occurs in Act II on his "Je t'aime!" at the end of "Mon coeur s'ouvre à ta voix" (Example 6.2[b]).

The High Priest of the Philistines is a dramatic baritone like Iago or Macbeth. Abimélech, another leader of the Philistines, is a lyric bass like Gounod's Méphistophélès. As described above, this means a bass with a higher range and greater flexibility. There is also a classic, deep bass in this opera, the Old Hebrew, who has the thankless task of trying to warn Samson about Dalila. He needs beauty of tone and a good legato line.

Finally, let us not forget the chorus. Since this work was conceived as an oratorio, it is no surprise that the chorus plays a major role (in Acts I and III).

Beyond its through-composition, some of its orchestration, and its vocal requirements, *Samson* resembles a Wagner opera more than the other two operas discussed in this chapter in one other regard. That is in its use of motives, which is more sophisticated than we see in *Carmen* with its single unifying motive, or *Faust* with its simple reprises.

Samson, the High Priest, Abimélech, and the chorus all have themes that reappear. Dalila's Act II "Mon coeur s'ouvre à ta voix" contains two melodies that are used motivically. At the beginning of the aria, Dalila is turning up the heat on Samson with "Ah, réponds à ma tendresse, verse-moi l'ivresse" (Example 6.2[a]). Lest we miss the nature of Dalila's character, notice the tritone, the "devil's interval," in the fourth and last measures of the example.

The second melody in the same aria that is used motivically is introduced at [N], m. 13. It contains expressive leaps that resemble those Wagner wrote for Wotan near the end of *Die Walküre*. Dalila's leaps are a little less extreme, however; she sings sevenths. Example 6.2(b) illustrates this theme at the end of the aria and Samson's topping Dalila with an octave leap. Notwithstanding Samson's declaration of love on "Je t'aime" however, it is also notable that there are a couple of moderately jarring dissonances after Samson joins her.

Step into My Study . . .

Musically, I view *Samson et Dalila* as a study in contrasts. The Israelites and the Old Hebrew often sound Bachian or Handelian and some of the Israelites' more woebegone passages are even chanted. The opera opens with 31 measures of repetitive, sighing music in the orchestra before the Israelites begin singing behind a closed curtain. They softly implore God to hear the prayers of his children. In these opening measures and in the grist mill scene of Act III, Saint-Saëns aims with some success for the kind of weight and heartbreak that we hear in the opening of the *Saint Matthew Passion* of Johann Sebastian Bach. In contrast to the somewhat Baroque sound of the Israelites, the Philistines' paganism and decadence and, of course, Dalila's seductiveness, are expressed music far more characteristic of the Romantic period. This begins from the moment Dalila enters with a chorus of Philistine women in Act I to the rousing Bacchanale of Act III.

The Philistines' fugue-like chorus at the end of Act III (Scene 3, after the Bacchanale) differs from their music up to that point in the opera. But it is not the dirge-like music of the downtrodden Israelites either. If the music of the Israelites can sound Handelian or even Bachian, the orchestra here at times glitters like Mozart's at his most romantic and playful. For example, the chorus and principals glorify their god in Act III accompanied by such colorful instruments as the glockenspiel, bells, triangle, and harp (e.g., from ALLEGRO MODERATO at [N], m. 9, p. 476 [vocal 257]).

A conductor studying Samson for the first time will soon run into a few technical issues. The first is that Saint-Saëns has the cellos begin the opera with a note that is below that of its lowest string. This doubles the B that the basses are playing, adding weight to this low sound, but requires that the cellos must tune their low C string to B. The indication to tune back up comes after only seven measures of rest, allowing only about twenty-five seconds (at [A], m. 21 [vocal p. 14]). This looks worse than it is. The reason is that, given the way that the parts are written, the cellos can play all of the necessary notes on other strings for some time. It will, in fact, be many pages before the cellos absolutely must be retuned (at [B], m. 13 [vocal p. 19]), just before the curtain rises. And, before that, they will have another 17 measures of rest to finish that job. In any professional orchestra, that is adequate time to retune.

The second issue presents a bit more of a challenge for the conductor. In the Act II music for Dalila's "Mon coeur s'ouvre à ta voix," the strings have four-note figures that last for just one beat (Scene 3, from ANDANTINO, m. 2 before [M], p. 283 [vocal 155]). The required lightness is achieved, in part, because the strings play in unusually small groups. The usual five string sections are exploded into as many as twenty-one distinct string parts on thirteen staves, and the subsections toss the ball among themselves, creating momentary pullbacks as the ensemble climbs the scale.

This instrumentation can be problematic in smaller companies because only in the biggest companies will we find enough string players to make this sound good and a pit big enough to hold them. It may be added that the rest of the opera does not require as many string players. Simply omitting parts is anathema, but asking string players to play two notes at a time will not give the lightness and delicacy that aptly portrays Dalila's skill at seduction. Happily, there are satisfactory ways to redistribute the assigned notes. For example, sometimes while the first violins are divided, the second violins are playing nothing. At other times, idle violas can double second violins or cellos. When the pit orchestra is not of symphonic size, rewriting the parts to employ all of the musicians more fully will yield the best results.

Last, the opening tempo and how to beat it both require some careful consideration. Consistent with the added weight in the lower strings discussed above, the tempo that opens the opera is MODERATO MESTO at 66 quarter notes per minute. This is quite slow for MODERATO, but *mesto* means sad in Italian. The next tempo indication is a couple of dozen pages later where the chorus moves into the opera's first recognizable melody, ALLEGRO NON TROPPO at 126 quarter notes per minute (at [D]). I beat this in two, 𝅗𝅥 = 63.

When opening with about two dozen pages of slow vamping, however—that is, without melody—it can sometimes be difficult to gauge the right tempo. This may, in part, explain the inclination of some conductors to take the opening too slowly and then make too sharp a contrast at the tempo change. But the opening should be quite close to half the speed of the upcoming melody—almost imperceptibly faster than half that speed—and we should use the weight in the lower strings as much as possible to achieve the right *mesto* mood.

At the beginning of my career, an old-timer shared a very useful, practical tip: Mentally, I hum the tempo of the upcoming melody and beat that tempo from the top. Here, the difference between 63 and 66 half notes per minute is nearly imperceptible. So having firmly established that melody's beat in my head, all that remains is for me to nudge the tempo up very slightly for the opening and/or adjust to slightly slower than double tempo when I get to the melody.

High Points and Relationships

I feel that the emotional high point of this opera is Scene 1 of Act III, at the grist mill, and conveying the emotional climax is largely a matter of pacing and articulation and phrasing. (The dynamic high point, or the loudest indication, is ***fff*** and occurs only once. This is in the last 13 measures of Act II, the blinding of Samson, and for the orchestra, all of the dynamic peaks should fall a bit short of that level.)

At the grist mill, Samson is alone and blind, at the lowest point in his life, repentant and devoted to God. He hears the offstage chorus that represents the voice of Israel. The scene begins at a painfully slow tempo (ANDANTE SOSTENUTO, with 76 eighth notes per minute). At first, ANDANTE seems anomalous; the metronome indication is closer to what would normally be labeled LARGO or ADAGIO. But Samson is pushing at the wheel of the mill and moves it bit by painful bit. So I think of this ANDANTE as effortful rather than simply a moderately slow pace equivalent to relatively effortless walking. And the written accents reinforce that impression. The tempo picks up a bit at various places, with the chorus chiding Samson, but it eventually returns to the very slow initial speed. Finally, an orchestral interlude at four times the speed of the Israelites' music brings us to the final scene in the temple of the Philistines (from ALLEGRO at [L], p. 360 [vocal 194]).

Perhaps because adjusting tempos in French music is done so routinely, interpreters can neglect Saint-Saëns's indications. We should at least check them in Saint-Saëns's work, because most are very effective. In Act I, Scene 1, for example, there is a tendency to drag after Samson exhorts the Israelites to put their faith in God and to fight, where the ALLEGRO is reasonably marked 138 quarter notes per minute (at [I], p. 47 [vocal 39]).

Another case is the ALLEGRO AGITATO of Dalila's Act II aria "Amour! viens aider ma faiblesse!" (top of Scene 1, p. 177 [vocal 104]), with a metronome indication of 160 quarter notes per minute. The editors of the vocal score have added ANIMATO over her first line, "Samson, recherchant ma presence," and it is a welcome reminder that the tempo should not slow. We should not over-interpret AGITATO, of course, which can refer to intensity of emotion rather than simply speed. Nonetheless, nothing about the drama or the music gives us reason to slow at this point.

On the other hand, a tempo that might well be reconsidered in this opera is one of the last. The conclusion of *Samson et Dalila*, in fact, has one of the most effective passages imaginable, the Bacchanale, and one of the most problematic tempos a conductor can face. It helps to step back and consider the entire final fifteen minutes or so of the opera: After the Bacchanale,

Samson is led in and the Philistines taunt and ridicule him. They also begin a sacrificial rite with "Gloire à Dagon vainqueur!" (from [H], ALLEGRO MODERATO, in Scene 3, p. 455 [vocal 240]). The "Fugato," as it has come to be called, continues with one small interruption until Samson, with his strength restored, pulls the temple down on everyone.

The problem arises at this Fugato. The well-known Bacchanale ends so wildly that introducing the Philistine sacrifice to their god Dagon, with this fugue-like choral passage at the indicated 112 quarter notes a minute (at [H]), is anticlimactic. Both because of the effectiveness of the dance and the relatively upbeat intervening music—as fast as 96 half notes per minute briefly (at [E], m. 37, p. 437 [vocal 226])—this ALLEGRO MODERATO, at 112 quarter notes per minute, feels deadly to many of us.

Some might argue that anything we do with the music that follows the Bacchanale is bound to be hopelessly anti-climactic. Still, there being no room for hopelessness on the podium, moving the Fugato to a noticeably faster tempo yields a much more satisfying result. As it turns out, 120 quarter notes per minute is consistent with the ALLEGRO MODERATO indications of most of the Bacchanale. In addition, this pace remains satisfying through the transition to $\frac{6}{8}$ (at [N], m. 24, p. 479 [vocal 259], with the indication to keep the sixteenth note constant) and the final tempo change of the opera to ALLEGRO MODERATO (144 quarter notes per minute with a return to $\frac{4}{4}$, at [P], m. 23, p. 489 [vocal 271]).

My favorite things

The first measures of the opera: The bassoons play a single note; then the horns play the interval of a third; and the flutes play a minor triad followed by a minor triad in second inversion in the clarinets and bassoons. This sets the stage for the B-minor mood of the next section. The build-up in intensity reminds me of the opening of *Das Rheingold* where the great river begins in the horns and expands through harmonic and motivic repetition. In this instance, it is the story of the Hebrews that is described.

Chapter 7

Puccini

> Music? Useless if I have no libretto. . . . If only I could be a purely symphonic writer! . . . Almighty God touched me with His little finger and said: "Write for the theater—mind, only for the theater."
>
> —Giacomo Puccini[1]

"Verismo" generally refers to an Italian school of opera that began with *Cavalleria rusticana* by Pietro Mascagni and includes works by (at least) Francesco Cilea, Umberto Giordano, Ruggero Leoncavallo, Italo Montemezzi, Giacomo Puccini, and Riccardo Zandonai. At this writing however, only *Cavalleria rusticana* and Leoncavallo's *Pagliacci* now enjoy anything close to the popularity of Giacomo Puccini's operas. There are those of us who hope that a few more verismo operas will re-emerge as some less frequently encountered bel canto operas have in recent years. But this chapter focuses exclusively on Puccini with respect to the verismo school.

After *Edgar* and *Le Villi*, Puccini finally found what would be his own style in *Manon Lescaut*. The opera is more symphonic than most Italian opera up to that time. It has one of his two great orchestral interludes (the other being in *Madama Butterfly*) plus many longer-than-usual passages for the orchestra and beautiful solo passages for individual instruments. While Leoncavallo,

Mascagni, and Giordano used orchestral interludes to good effect, no composer of standard repertory opera except Richard Strauss wrote small tone poems like Puccini's.

Puccini never stopped evolving. His sense of form would continue to improve with his next opera, *La bohème*. He would explore different orchestral techniques, and change his orchestral palette, to tell his stories and reflect their settings. His use of exotic orchestral sound and his deft technique reach a high point with his final opera, *Turandot*. It is also noteworthy that *Turandot* is the last work of the form called "Italian grand opera." It is firmly rooted in that tradition, and there is simply nothing that resembles it after this date. In it, Puccini retreated a little from continuous, seamless melody and left more breaks for applause. Yet, it has passages that are quite forward looking, most notably the Ping-Pang-Pong scene of Act II and the music immediately following Liù's death (before the final duet by Franco Alfano).

Like many artists, Puccini was repeatedly drawn to the same themes. Virtually throughout his entire opus, he gives us loves lost for one reason or another. Notice that I eschew the cliché that Puccini's operas are all about women who suffer and die for love. This generalization may be accurate enough with respect to Liù and Butterfly, but after that, it breaks down. Meanwhile, Verdi's Violetta and both of his Leonoras also suffer and sacrifice for love. Indeed, the whole idea that Puccini was obsessed with women is also somewhat overdone. Richard Strauss gave more great roles to women than Puccini did. And if we may draw conclusions from how women dominate his operas, Strauss was even more taken with the female voice than Puccini was.

Puccini's melodic inspiration seems to have been inexhaustible, and he uses melody in myriad and inventive ways. He gives us quotes, previews, reprises, puns, and variations that are at times subtle and, at other times, attention grabbing.

The Madrigal in *Manon Lescaut* is the Agnus Dei from his own *Messa di Gloria*, for example (Act II, from [11]). In addition, two themes in Act IV come from his string quartet *Chrysanthemums* (from [1] in the first violins and from m. 3 before [20] in Manon's line). Very late in his career, Puccini quotes his own *La bohème*, almost any part of which would have been instantly recognizable to his audience. The sheet music vendor and solo violin quote Mimì's signature aria in *Il tabarro* (beginning at [25], m. 10). In *Turandot*, we hear an echo of Rodolfo's trying to revive Mimì after she has fainted during their first meeting. Pang sings the same major third on the same word ("così") when he and Ping tell us about singing at Turandot's wedding (Act II, Scene 1, from m. 3 before [21]).

His external references and puns are no less entertaining. We shall see his references both obvious and subtle to "The Star-Spangled Banner" in *Madama Butterfly*. A sly reference to "The First Noël" appears in *La bohème*, as illustrated in Example 7.2. In *La rondine's* first act, Puccini quotes a figure that appears persistently in Richard Strauss's *Salome* (e.g., from [35], m. 11, in the English horn).

For decades, Italians have heard a pun underscoring Tosca's assent to Scarpia's Act II demand as she stands mute, exhausted, and defeated. The orchestra sings A–C, known throughout much of Europe as *la–do*. But *la do* in Italian also means "I give it" or "I'll give it" (from [56], mm. 2–3). And the same translation may be given to the notes played after Tosca tells Cavaradossi of the sham execution she expects. This is usually staged to suggest that Cavaradossi is skeptical about Scarpia's beneficence. Cavaradossi may be thinking "I'll give it" regarding *la vita*, his life (Act III, from [22], m. 9, in the lower strings, after the word "fucilato").

Note the three delicate notes from the harp in the two measures before Musetta begins her Act II aria in *La bohème* (m. 2 before [21]). I am grateful to French actor-director Bernard Uzan for pointing out that Puccini is here illustrating a tradition from classical French theater: *les trois coups*. Given that the lights were candles, theatre management needed a way to alert the audience to settle down because the performance was about to begin. Thus, someone knocked loudly on the floor three times with a large *baton*, first backstage and then again before the start of the performance. Can anyone seriously doubt that Musetta is putting on a show in this scene?

Uzan also raises a question that comes up often in art: Was Puccini consciously thinking about classical French theater or did he come up with these three notes without even thinking? I have often pondered a similar unknowable about the composer's intent and conscious choices: In the three operas to which we will give the greatest attention, there is a small but fascinating commonality in that Mimì, Tosca, and Butterfly all first appear vocally from offstage. We hear them before we see them. What does this mean? Are they hidden? cloistered? veiled? Was there some practical reason? Is it just one of many efforts at verisimilitude? Did the composer intend it to mean anything at all? The three entrances are all different in mood, after all. There are many offstage voices in opera for all kinds of story-related reasons, and Puccini uses the technique elsewhere, too. Introducing these three different heroines in this manner stands out as quite different, however.

Puccini uses motives to represent characters and unite works. While Puccini's gift for melody and keen sense of drama are well accepted, his subtle use of motives is not nearly as universally recognized. This may be, in part, because his attention to motivic development was variable, waxing and waning throughout his career. Nonetheless, Puccini's use of motives, while not as extensive or complex as that of Wagner, advances Italian opera beyond where Verdi had taken it. Indeed, Giacomo Puccini and Richard Strauss stand together after Richard Wagner in sophisticated use of motives in their operas. Puccini's results are less complex, but this relative simplicity reflects Puccini's taste more than any lack of skill. Few if any composers equaled the orchestral complexity of Strauss.

An almost universal signature of Puccini, however, was to end his operas with a quote from an earlier part of that opera. These references seem to sum up the main idea of the work for Puccini. With Manon Lescaut's final words (from [25] of Act IV), for instance, we recall the life that the title character has lost, one of wealth and luxury, in a slow, sad variation of the dance master's music. Puccini gives us such quotes in the three operas discussed below, and Alfano maintained this formula in his ending to *Turandot* with the melody from the tenor's aria "Nessun dorma."

For a conductor, Puccini's quotes and puns, as well as reprises of motivic and non-motivic material, make for one of the more enjoyable study experiences. They also mean that even fairly straightforward passages that I have conducted before—sometimes many times before—will suddenly yield some refreshing new insight. Sharing these insights with the audience, by balancing the stage and pit and balancing within the pit, is an obligation I can embrace with unalloyed pleasure.

This introduction would be incomplete without a mention of the extra-musical reasons for Puccini's dominance over his era, however. With respect to plot, his most successful works remain strikingly fresh and relevant, and most of the time, he tended to de-emphasize the violent or grittier aspects of the stories he chose. In addition, if the truth be told, some of Puccini's operas are remarkably economical to mount. All kinds of reasons may be given for the absence of *Il trovatore* from the season brochures and the paucity of productions of so winning an opera as *Aida*, but both are substantially more expensive to produce than *Madama Butterfly*. Thus, music, storytelling, and economics conspire to make Puccini's works bread and butter for every opera company in the world.

Conducting Puccini

The bigger challenges in conducting Puccini are those commonly encountered in music of the late Romantic era: Increasingly greater skills were required of individual instrumentalists, and ensemble became more complicated. The practical difference is that smaller companies that will not chance a big Richard Strauss work, or will do so only rarely, need to perform Puccini far more regularly. Thus, a perfectly fine symphony orchestra that performs Beethoven without a hitch may be in for a shock with Puccini. Leaving aside any question of artistry or interpretation, a conductor can improve the odds of good results by being consistent. This does not mean metronomic consistency. If nothing else, we have to make small adjustments depending on the singers. But it does mean that some homework will pay off on the podium. I also recommend anticipating when cues will make a difference, beating time in the same manner from rehearsals to performances, and maintaining roughly the same proportions among sections.

There is little excuse for getting Puccini's tempos or tempo relationships wrong, however. With or without a metronome indication, I have a pretty reliable rule of thumb: Puccini's tempos tend to correspond to the speed of speech—slow speech, fast speech, or average speech, but not a great deal faster or slower than one might reasonably speak, and certainly not fluctuating wildly within a sentence or two. This is true of Richard Strauss as well. By contrast, both Wagner and Bellini require singing that is often slower than anyone would reasonably speak. If we are competent with the language and try speaking Puccini's lines at about the speed that seems right given the drama however, we will get solid guidance on the speed. This obviously will not be a specific tempo, but it will be a range that makes sense. When we hear tempos dragged down beyond where anyone would speak and then rushing forward in a manner that could not possibly follow in any reasonable conversation (even in theater), the tempos are being distorted. They might make sense with some composers' music but not that of Puccini (or Richard Strauss). In addition, the lingering over unaccented syllables that one sometimes hears distorts the sentence, which is detrimental to our understanding of both the drama and the music. These are just two reasons that being acquainted with a language is helpful in conducting complete operas.

With respect to tempo relationships, proportionality remains the best approach. Whether through lack of internal discipline or the operation of bad influences (also known as tradition), interpreters on the stage and in the pit may not only ignore Puccini's tempo indications, but may also invent tempo relationships of their own. Performers want to add decelerations and accelerations at every transition to create relationships where there is no justification in the score. But there is much to be gained from some respectful attention to what the score actually says. With composers of the late Romantic era, we can know with some certainty what they intended. Along with Debussy, Ravel, Mahler, and Richard Strauss, Puccini is generous with indications.

If I had to give advice to a conductor embarking on Puccini's works for the first time, I would begin with the need to cultivate the flexibility needed to be a good accompanist. This means hearing the breathing as much as the singing and developing the physical flexibility needed to make continuous fine adjustments. When singers and conductor share a working knowledge of the language and basic assumptions about style, it becomes somewhat easier to agree upon and execute the subtle rubato that makes all the difference in this music. But the conductor needs mastery of his or her physical equipment as much as the singer does. Admittedly this is a skill that is needed in all music, but nowhere more than in Puccini's works.

I would also caution a conductor new to Puccini's music to resist the temptation to sub-divide too much; it is necessary less often than it is done.

Beating more than necessary will tend to result in a somewhat more accented sound without any conscious effort. The singers and orchestra also need to breathe, but beating too frequently acts as a kind of corset. Yes, the wearer can breathe but the corset is no help and can get in the way in the biggest and most intense moments. Beating fewer times per measure—all other things being equal—will leave room for the almost imperceptible fluctuations within a phrase or measure that will result in a more idiomatic performance. So strive to sub-divide as little as possible.

And, *coraggio*!

La Bohème

The architecture of Puccini's *La bohème* (1896) is as close to perfect as we have in opera. It ranks with Mozart's *Le* nozze *di Figaro* and Richard Strauss's *Elektra* in its dramatic flow and unity of story and music. In one way, it is even superior. For different reasons, both *Figaro* and *Elektra* are usually performed with cuts, whereas *La bohème* is so concise and the roles are so well balanced that any cuts would be unimaginable.

When compared with Puccini's other operas, *La bohème* is more disciplined, elegant, and accomplished. There is not a moment of what can be described as filler as there is, arguably, in Act III of *Tosca*. Nor does it seem as episodic as *Manon Lescaut*, or as stylistically inconsistent as *La rondine*. In *La bohème* we encounter none of these anomalies. The work is equal parts comedy and tragedy, completely credible dramatically, and perfectly integrated musically like a Mozart-Da Ponte opera.

With its diverse cast of lovable characters, and generous amounts of both comedy and pathos, there is no end of opportunity for an inventive stage director. I have seen and conducted this opera many times and I can still chuckle at what directors and tenors can do with Rodolfo's feigned search for Mimì's key in Act I, for example. The list of golden moments for singing actors in this opera is long.

It helps if all four of our bohemians, and the ladies in the lives of two of them, can look young and energetic. Vocally, Mimì and Rodolfo have the highest notes and the highest tessitura, or average pitch—so much so that Rodolfo's Act I aria is often transposed down a half step. This is a little like the transposition problem for Manrico in *Il trovatore*. We must alter an harmonic progression to reach this lower key (beginning with the violins at [29], m.19). Still, if a Rodolfo has the stamina and the charm and the ability to sing most of the notes, it behooves us to give the audience the best that we can, and that may mean transposing rather than compromising the performance.

Musetta's big Act II aria lets a short role steal the show for a while (beginning at [21]). This is some of the canniest writing for the voice imaginable. In fact, her highest note in Act II, where she soars over soloists, chorus, and an orchestra at relatively full throttle, is a B-natural. She does not appear in Act I. She has only a small part in a comic argument in Act III (from [31], m. 9 [vocal p. 219, last measure]). She also sings a short song in Act IV (a prayer, from [29], m. 3). So, understandably, sopranos want to milk Act II's "Quando m'en vo." They thus are inclined to drag the tempo well below Puccini's metronome indication, hoping to magnify Musetta's seductiveness. This can be carried too far. It slows down a lively and comic scene and rather saps some of Musetta's equally important youthfulness and impetuosity. A good singing actress will, instead, focus on vocal nuance and body language to show us why Marcello has such a hard time ignoring her—and why his buddies are so entertained by the whole encounter.

Colline's "Vecchia zimarra" in Act IV (from [19]) is another effective aria that benefits from our sticking close to the tempo indicated and not dragging it down too much. It is marked ALLEGRETTO MODERATO E TRISTE, at 63 quarter notes a minute. This is by no means the slowest tempo in the scene. At the speed indicated, the aria remains a young man's aria and does not pretend to be something like King Philip's "Ella giammai m'amò" (*Don Carlo*).

Most of *La bohème* is delicate and, with its relatively large cast of characters, the composer uses the woodwinds to supply many different timbres. One of the most delicate and colorful passages occurs at the opening of Act III, the cold, dark scene that follows the boisterous fun of Act II. There are many pages of scene setting before Mimì's entrance (at around 6), and the orchestra generally sounds quite light. The colors arise from an ever-changing arsenal of instruments, including the harp, woodwinds, triangle and timpani, clinking glassware, bells of two kinds, as well as tremolos in the lower strings and, from offstage, both Musetta and a chorus of women. This music is less tuneful than we are used to hearing in a prelude, almost completely about mood setting.

Motives

Structurally, *La bohème* is Puccini's most motive-rich opera. The list of beautiful melodies, both motivic and non-motivic, is long, but some of the more inventive and sophisticated reprises of motives are illustrated in Example 7.1:

(a) Schaunard's motive, introduced in Act I (m. 3 of 10), is utterly transformed when it reappears poignantly in Act IV.
(b) Marcello has about as minimal a motive as may be imagined, just the single interval of the perfect fourth, that we first hear just before he sings his first words (Act I, beginning at m. 12). It reappears frequently, especially in Act III where he is the linchpin dramatically and musically.
(c) Mimì's motive first appears in her Act I aria (at 35). It is set in a new tempo to tremendous dramatic effect in Act III, signaling that a romantic comedy is about to get very serious.
(d) Musetta's primary motive starts life as just a pair of fragments in the flute (Act II at 16 and from m. 2 before 18). They are repeated over twenty-nine measures, but then become a recognizable melody. This motive announces her entrances and evokes her character more often than the melody of her big aria in Act II. The second fragment reappears in Act IV, and a change of a half step in the last note creates a certain sadness consistent with the text.

The vibrant and robust opening of Act II is built on four motivic seeds that we first hear in Act I (from 16 until m. 14 before 17). The four themes that Puccini will expand and elaborate upon are introduced quietly and at a relatively slow tempo, just before the landlord knocks as three of the four

Example 7.1 Inventive reprises, *La bohème*: (a) Schaunard's motive in Act IV. (b) Marcello's motive at the top of Act III (in piano reduction). (c) Mimì's motive in Act III. (d) Musetta's motive in Act IV.

roommates in the garret impishly foreshadow a night out on the town. The Act II opening also includes one of my favorite Puccini coups: a rhythmic variation of "The First Noël" (Example 7.2). Did Puccini associate this English Christmas carol, long spelled *à la* française, with Paris? We know that he studied and collected music from all over the globe, and if he had not heard the carol before May of 1894, we know that he visited London before he finished *La bohème* (for that city's premiere of *Manon Lescaut*). Most important, for me, is that the notes are there on the page and they are hard to ignore.

Example 7.2 Christmas and *La bohème*: (a) A Christmas carol. (b) The pitches of the carol in the rhythms of *La bohème's* Act II opening. (c) The opening of Act II of *La bohème* (Trumpet in F rendered in concert pitch). The first three notes of the melody are in an inner voice and the remainder are at the top of each chord.

Step into my study . . .

The indication RUVIDAMENTE at the top of the score is sometimes over-interpreted. The word means rough. The playing should be energetic and the attacks aggressive, which creates a certain amount of bow noise in the strings and aspiration in winds. This is apt for our bohemians, dead broke but full of gusto. We should not be aiming for the most violent sounds of *Pagliacci*, *Cavalleria Rusticana*, or even Puccini's own *Tosca* and *Il tabarro*, however. Think youthful exuberance, not brutality.

There are a couple of matters of stagecraft that are worth mentioning, and they both come up in Act II. This act may run for little more than a quarter of an hour. Thus, where the stage machinery permits, diving directly into Act II from Act I makes perfect sense. Rodolfo and Mimì depart the garret to head directly for the Café, after all.

Assuming that we have an intermission, or at least a break where the curtain comes down for a few minutes to allow a set change, Puccini is quite specific about when the curtain is supposed to rise in Act II. It does not rise until the twenty-eighth measure of the Act, after the trumpets have played the opening bars and the chorus has sung for ten measures. This instruction is sometimes observed and sometimes not. It being the domain of the stage director, I will not weigh in with edicts. However, if audibility of the chorus is the issue (and some of those curtains are quite soundproof), one successful strategy is using a scrim. This presents the audience with a black screen but permits those onstage to see the conductor and be heard as if there were no curtain at all. At the appropriate moment, the lights can come up and/or the scrim can rise on the bright, festive scene.

It is notable that the score does, indeed, specify an outdoor café on Christmas Eve, and many of us have wondered about the weather. Would it not be too cold for an outdoor café and parade? One effective solution directors have come up with is to depict a jammed Café Momus so that outdoor tables and chairs are accommodating an overflow crowd. Others have tried to set the scene in a galleria of some kind. This makes the parade a little hard to pull off convincingly, however. (Film would be another matter, of course.)

How could a composer who seems to have considered every staging detail leave us with this dilemma? Well, Paris would not be as cold as New York or London or any number of other cities. But in her Puccini biography, Mary Jane Phillips-Matz, drawing on tenor-conductor Herbert Handt, supplies further information of interest. She tells us that the Paris of *La bohème* has a great deal of Puccini's native Lucca about it. In particular, at Christmastime the central square in Lucca resembles the Latin Quarter setting of the opera. It is full of vendors' stalls and carts and crowds of people buying snacks, toys, and so on. More to our point here, with Lucca's Mediterranean climate, it can be so mild in December, that people can sit outside the cafés as the characters of *La bohème* do in Act II.[2]

Puccini strove for authenticity in his music with remarkable success. We know that his research into new locales was far from casual. He systematically studied Japanese music and consulted Japanese colleagues for *Madama Butterfly* and ended up writing melodies that are impossible for most of us to distinguish from authentic Japanese melodies. He is known to have studied both American and Native American music for *La fanciulla del West*. Legend has it that as he labored over *Turandot*, he wrote to Giulio Gatti-Casazza, the Metropolitan Opera's general director, asking him to sally forth to New York's Chinatown on a hunt for Chinese music to augment what he had already found.[3]

It would appear that if we like Act II of *La bohème* however, we will have to allow this young *Lucchese*—and his two librettists—some license.

Tempos and Tempo Relationships

Puccini is more careful to specify smooth connections in *La bohème* than he is in the other operas we are considering here. There are seven specifically indicated:

Act I, [20]: ♩ = ♩. LO STESSO MOVIMENTO

Act II, [27] (vocal p. 155, m. 5, ANCORA PIÙ LENTO): one measure of $\frac{2}{4}$ = ♩ of the previous tempo (indicated by the bar lines)

Act III, [6], m. 4: 𝅗𝅥 = ♪

Act III, [24]: ♪ = ♩, LO STESSO MOVIMENTO, double speed

Act IV, [11], m. 12: one measure of $\frac{4}{8}$ equals two of the preceding $\frac{2}{4}$ measures

Act IV, [11], m. 20: COME PRIMA, two measures of $\frac{2}{4}$ = one measure of $\frac{4}{8}$.

Thus, while the spirit of *La bohème* is unmistakably Italian, its organization is more like that of the works of Mozart, Brahms, or Richard Strauss, just as its use of motivic unity reflects the influence of Wagner to some extent. Ironically and inexplicably, these relationships are almost always observed in Acts I and II but are rarely executed as written in Acts III and IV.

At Mimì's Act III entrance for example, Puccini clearly indicates his intentions as to tempo, as illustrated in Example 7.1(c). The music should slow down very dramatically at this point, mirroring the plot's turn away from fun-loving bohemian Paris and toward death. In fact, at LENTO MOLTO, it should slow to one-quarter the speed. I can achieve the intended smooth transition and dramatic effect only if I do not begin too slowly or permit myself to slow too much before Mimì's entrance.

The composer starts this act ANDANTINO MOSSO (specifying 112 quarter notes a minute) followed by one indication to move a little faster and a few fleeting pullbacks. If I maintain a speed a bit faster than the starting speed at [5], m. 2 (A TEMPO), then downshifting to one-quarter speed at the LENTO

MOLTO indication is both satisfying and not unreasonably slow. I can realize the intended change in mood, anticipating the tragedy to come in a seamless manner.

It is fair to ask about the RALLENTANDO at [6]. I consider it close to impossible to execute a noticeable rallentando and then observe the tempo relationship given. Rather, I make a small ritard.

Since *La bohème* is written in four acts with no scenes or set musical numbers, pinpointing the finale is a little subjective. Act IV begins in the middle of a conversation between Rodolfo and Marcello followed by their beautiful duet. With the entrance of Colline and Schaunard, levity returns but all too briefly. We may identify the denouement as beginning with Musetta's abrupt entrance—with Mimì trailing behind—decisively altering the mood.

After Colline's "Vecchia zimarra," all of the friends will leave the lovers to their last conversation. As Schaunard departs last, closing the door, a short orchestral interlude commences. It combines themes introduced in Act I: a poignant reprise of Schaunard's motive (Example 7.1[a]), followed by reprises that recall the meeting and romance of Mimì and Rodolfo. The composer's discipline is on full display here. The interlude may be likened to a sketch by a great painter. In a few moments, he encapsulates the tenderness and sadness of the situation and, indeed, of the entire opera.

A few measures later, we hear a melody not heard earlier in *La bohème*, Mimì's "Sono andati" (from [21], m. 4). Even though it appears only twice in the opera, it serves the important purpose of ending the opera. Notice Mimì's grace note on the first syllable of "dire" (m. 10). This is written as an acciaccatura. As a rule, a grace note like this would be approximately a thirty-second note or even shorter, before the beat. However, in this slow, sad music—with these very poignant words—there is another reasonable approach: a short note sung on the beat. There would be nothing incorrect about singing before the beat, but this touch—on the beat—suits the drama. It injects a little sadness as she tells Rodolfo that she deceived the others to get rid of them because she has so much to tell him. Meanwhile we all know she is dying.

The ending of *La bohème* is, in some ways, Puccini's most successful at wrenching the listener's heart. (Subjective, admittedly). It also depends mightily on a tenor with voice and passion. On Marcello's "Coraggio" Puccini employs a full complement of brass and even cymbals to accompany a quote of "Sono andati" and Rodolfo's howl of grief. This is the dynamic high point of this opera and nothing else should be louder than this.

My favorite things

In the last act, the RALLENTANDO two measures before [21] and transition into the next section. They epitomize the lovers' yearning and, for me, serve as the emotional high point of this opera. I confess to emphasizing this RALLENTANDO—and the ***pp*** and DOLCISSIMO at [21]—with all my heart.

Tosca

If *Tosca* (1900) suffers from any flaw it is the same one that we find in Puccini's *La rondine* and Montemezzi's *L'amore dei tre re*: The last act is really not equal to the previous two acts. Yes, Act III of *Tosca* opens with a beautifully evocative orchestral depiction of Rome at first light and follows that with one of Puccini's finest tenor arias, "E lucevan le stelle." (The words actually precede the justly famous melody in a short recitative, but the melody is universally referred to as "E lucevan le stelle.") The problem lies in a duet after this aria that seems to go on too long and then a rather clichéd execution and suicide. I freely admit, of course, that this judgment is far from universal.

To me, the challenge in this act is to keep the interest of the audience throughout this duet and not fall into stock gestures and musical bombast at certain points. Such an opportunity for noise springs up in the lovers' singing "Triomfal di nuova speme" (at [29]).

The execution of Cavaradossi that follows should be riveting. This seems to be accompanied by the loudest music in the opera although that is an impression made by the guns. The loudest indications in the score are for the end of Act I's "Te Deum" and for Act III's final bars. Nonetheless, the execution is certainly one of the loudest moments and dramatically important.

Yet, the action often fails to rise to the occasion. The goal for both the visual and musical team should be to make the final fifteen minutes equal to everything that went before and, even, a culmination.

Both of the lovers should be spinto singers—with voices of ample volume and some bite. Tosca requires a heavier voice than Liù of *Turandot*, Mimì of *La bohème*, or Butterfly of *Madama Butterfly*, in part because of some heavy brass writing and her intense scene with Scarpia in Act II. I will have more to say about Tosca's principal aria, "Vissi d'arte," in connection with motives. Here, I will just address the complaint that the aria is disconnected and unrelated to the rest of the scene. The score indicates that the aria should be sung at 40 quarter notes per minute (ANDANTE LENTO APPASSIONATO), but many want to perform a reasonably slow aria much more slowly. This is neither a lullaby nor a dirge. Tosca will rally, so tension should not leave the scene completely, and it does not have to if the aria is performed close to the indicated speed.

Cavaradossi also requires a slightly more dramatic voice than other familiar Puccini tenors; i.e., Rodolfo of *La bohème* or Pinkerton of *Madama Butterfly*. His tessitura is a bit lower. In addition to his duets with Tosca and his major Act III aria, he has a lovely short aria in Act I, "Recondita armonia" (from **18**).

He also has a very dramatic moment in his short appearance in Act II (beginning at **42**, m. 9). Tenors often like to race to the final vowel in the repeated word "Vittoria." It is, in fact, somewhat easier to hold the last syllable than to articulate more than one syllable on the same high note. It is the *o* that is assigned the longest duration, however, reflecting the way the word is pronounced in Italian. When we hear that *o* given its proper weight, it means that the tenor has better vocal technique, better control, and an appreciation for the language. Furthermore, it is at least as thrilling since it sounds like he is holding the highest notes even longer. The score by the way, indicates COL CANTO to the conductor when he sings "Vittoria" twice. There is, in fact, little orchestra after a run up to his first "Vittoria" until the beat before the tempo indication, so I can give the tenor whatever support or space he needs to shine. In the pit, we get to savor a great vocal moment while remaining poised for a sudden re-entry. Even relatively jaded instrumentalists who think they have heard it all will perk up noticeably when a great tenor nails this perfectly.

Scarpia is a classic bass-baritone, like Escamillo of *Carmen*, Jochanaan of *Salome*, or the Holländer of Der *fliegende Holländer*. Such a bass-baritone ranges higher than a bass and lower than the classic Italian baritone. These characters also need big personalities. If they do not have enough vocal and dramatic power, the drama is vitiated. No conductor can be of much help.

Act I ends with the exciting and justly admired "Te Deum" in which Scarpia soliloquizes on his twin goals of hanging Cavaradossi and possessing Tosca. This is another of Puccini's particularly skillful passages. One thing that can add a little spice, if Scarpia is up to the task, is for him to sustain the F on his last syllable (the last syllable of "Iddio" at [88]). If he does, he creates a dissonance that is perfectly in keeping with both the drama and all of the music that has led up to this point. He can then join the chorus on "Patrem" slightly later than the score indicates, in keeping with his being lost in his own thoughts and shocked out of his reverie by the chorus and its religious content. I would rather see interpreters tweak this passage not at all, however, than try too hard to intensify the effects with which Puccini left us. Overkill is to be avoided at all costs.

In addition to the chorus in the church, *Tosca* has a children's chorus earlier in Act I. Many operas have children's choruses, but the short Act I "Cantoria" of the altar boys with the Sacristan is a particularly tricky section rhythmically as it changes meters several times (from [51] until Scarpia's first words). Complicating matters is the fact that it must be staged as chaotic, as the boys (they would be eight to fourteen years old) tease the Sacristan and generally make mischief. Puccini helps us out, though, by writing the chorus for some children plus a few adult sopranos and tenors.

On the other hand, the Shepherd Boy whose song opens Act III (at [3]) is a short part and not very demanding. In a large city, a boy soprano generally can be found. In a smaller city, we may have to ask a young woman with a light voice to sing this song with minimal vibrato. Since the song is sung from offstage, appearance is no problem and getting the right sound is the only concern. It is to be noted that his song supplies one of those moments that reward repeat visits to a work of art. The song is in Roman dialect. Obviously, the listener can enjoy these lovely moments without knowing this. Even Italians would not notice the *absence* of the dialect. Standard Italian would serve just fine. For those acquainted with the language, however, this choice represents one of those little extra touches that accumulate to make a work just that much more rewarding.

Step into my study . . .

For good reason we remember the brass in *Tosca*. It is particularly present during scenes with Scarpia, and the conductor's goal has to be to keep it exciting but hold back enough to make the climaxes distinct. The music also has to have propulsion without excessive weight. Furthermore, this power must be contrasted with the flirtatious sweetness of the Act I love duet and the poetic calm of the opening pages of Act III. It is tempting to lapse into sentimentality with these breaks in the tension and that, too, is a mistake.

There are two dynamic high points in this opera: ***ffff*** at the end of Act I and ***fff*** at the end of Act III. It is in the torture of Cavaradossi that I find the emotional high point (coming to a head with Tosca's high C at [36], m. 3). Admittedly, finding the emotional high point of an opera is more subjective than finding the dynamic high point. In addition, Act II of *Tosca* offers many candidates, beginning as it does with foreboding and progressing to torture, attempted rape, and homicide. So there is certainly room for interpreters to differ on this point.

The final bars of the opera carry with them two traditions, one good and one not-so-good. Apart from the distortion of tempo discussed below, the better tradition is known as *dopo la parola*. It gives the singer room to finish a particularly dramatic note when a big orchestra is about to come crashing in. In this tradition, the singer's last syllable is extended as if it bore a fermata, and the orchestra's entrance is delayed. While this tradition of giving a singer room to finish is often associated with verismo opera and big orchestras, it goes back farther and was employed in Mozart's *opere serie* and in Baroque music.[4]

It makes a lot of sense. There are only two caveats: First, we never want to lose momentum, so we cannot wait until the singer has stopped completely. You know you are becoming a good accompanist when you can hear the singer *begin* cutting off. Second, as in evaluating whether to follow any tradition, the decision must be grounded in the immediate circumstances. If a singer, in this case the soprano, is having vocal difficulty, the orchestra should come in as written, letting her get on and off the note quickly. This too requires educated listening. It is also where experience and quick reflexes can help.

There is also an instrumentation issue to be considered in planning a *Tosca* performance. In the opening of Act III, the orchestra depicts Rome at dawn. After a few measures of introduction, we have the Shepherd Boy's song and then bells representing at least ten different churches at varying distances (from [4]). For anyone who has lived in or visited Rome—and certainly anyone who has tried to sleep in once the bells have gone off—they describe Rome almost by themselves. Some companies own or can obtain the enormous bells required, and these have been used to great effect. But this is hardly an option for most smaller companies, and few will be able to play all of the pitches on the bells they have available.

At the LARGO indication for example, the E written for the bell is extremely low ([7], m. 4). It is, in fact, the lowest E on the piano keyboard, almost three octaves below middle C. An electronic instrument may be substituted. This is less than ideal, however. As a rule, it will not blend well with whatever acoustic bells are available, so one is stuck with an all-electronic sound and great difficulty imitating the distances associated with the bells. The alternative to substituting is to transpose any out-of-range notes up or down one or more octaves as needed to get into range. For that very low E, a tam-tam played softly may also substitute.

When I have enough bells, players, and rehearsal time, I distribute the bells backstage, under the stage, in the theater, and in the pit. If this is possible, changing the pitch of the bells is vastly preferable to using an electronic instrument to get the pitches in the right octaves. When appropriate, there is simply nothing to compare with having sound come from unexpected places. It is, in fact, one of the things that live theater can uniquely supply.

As to *Tosca's* structure, the opera is characterized by through-composition to a greater extent than *La bohème* is. But stopping for applause at the two biggest arias is almost inevitable. These are Tosca's Act II "Vissi d'arte" and Cavaradossi's Act III "E lucevan le stelle." In order to stop after "E lucevan le stelle," a small cut is made (from 3 measures before [14]) to eliminate a short bridge to the next section, MODERATO CON MOTO. While not absolutely necessary, a similar small cut is often made after Act II's "Vissi d' arte." (Cut from the second half of the first measure of [53] and resume at the following ALLEGRO AGITATO.)

Tempos and Tempo Relationships

Tempos and tempo relationships are fairly clear and straightforward in *Tosca*, even if they are not always indicated by the composer. The principle of striving for proportionality and seamlessness, absent some good reason to do otherwise, remains a reliable guide. In addition to being esthetically preferable, keeping the tempos in proportional relationships countervails any tendency to lapse into either the sentimentality or the bombast that are the dangers in this opera. Both sentimentality and bombast almost invariably mean bending the tempo excessively and disrupting the audience's sense of forward propulsion in addition to any exaggerated changes in volume.

There is one small time-beating dilemma in this opera, however. It occurs at the opening—in the fourth measure, in fact. The problem is that after three opening chords at 69 half notes per minute, there is a long rest followed by a change in time signature from $\frac{3}{2}$ to $\frac{2}{4}$ with the indication VIVACISSIMO CON VIOLENZA at 168 quarter notes per minute. The silence lasts through a quarter rest plus two half rests and a fermata, but some musicians are tacet even a bit longer. So when I start the VIVACISSIMO with only an upbeat, any orchestra will react more slowly than my beat, resulting in a tempo far less exciting than the one given. In fact, rarely is the indicated speed even approached. The trick here is to use that long rest to beat an entire measure in the upcoming $\frac{2}{4}$ meter. This will help all of those resting musicians re-enter in unison and with precision at a tempo near or at 168 quarter notes per minute.

But one of the most unfortunate traditions to attach itself to *Tosca* concerns tempo. It is the tradition in which the principal theme of "E lucevan le stelle" is played at the same tempo in each of its four renditions, sometimes even distorting the rhythms. There may be no other opera where interpreters have rewritten reprises like this or, indeed, rewritten just one set of reprises while leaving others as written. In fact, Puccini gave it various combinations of tempo markings and note values in Act III. Admittedly, there is some judgment needed here because while there are many tempo markings, only one contains a metronome indication. Still, there is enough information given:

In the strings at 7, coming from 𝅗𝅥 = 40 at 4 with a relationship at 7, m. 4 (𝅗𝅥 = ♩).
In the clarinet solo at 11, DOLCISSIMO, VAGAMENTE, ♩ = 40 from 7, m. 4.
In the tenor's line at 12, m. 2, CON GRANDE SENTIMENTO, VAGAMENTE.
In the entire orchestra after Tosca's final word, "Dio," ANDANTE MOSSO (at 41 [vocal score, last page, m. 1]).

The slow tempo and the holding of certain key notes makes for a beautiful clarinet solo when well played. When the tenor gets to this melody, it is usually yet slower, and justifiably so. Unsurprisingly, the composer indicates great freedom for the soloists, both tenor and clarinet. The mischief comes in at the other two points in the score with this melody, its first statement in the strings and its last at the conclusion of the opera (the not-so-good tradition I referred to earlier).

The theme's first appearance in the strings accompanies Cavaradossi's Act III entrance onto the stage, just before the cello quartet and well before the clarinet solo. But this first instance of the melody has a steady rhythm, with unmistakable accents added by a low bell, as well as a specific relationship set up a few measures later at LARGO, where the new quarter note will be equal to the preceding half note. The score indicates a steady—and far less romantic—rendition to accompany the condemned prisoner than the clarinet will play later. (I would also note that church bells do not do rubato.)

In addition, in the last measures of the opera the melody is sometimes erroneously dragged down to the clarinet's tempo and, again, we hear the clarinet's phrasing instead of the more steady rhythm called for in the score. This reprise has no metronome indication, but we do have the indication ANDANTE MOSSO, TUTTA FORZA CON GRANDE SLANCIO at 41.

(*Slancio* may be interpreted as flinging, hurling, leaping, or soaring.) Some older vocal scores indicate ANDANTE SOSTENUTO, reinforcing a tradition that is at odds with the orchestra score. By 1956, the Ricordi reprint (same plate number as the 1905 score available for download) corrected the indication to ANDANTE MOSSO.

Moreover, the music is written in sixteenth notes rather than the earlier eighth notes. So the melody should move noticeably faster at the end of the opera than in any previous instance. Its energy and urgency are reinforced by its hammering rhythm: repeated sixteenth notes as Tosca jumps from Castel Sant'Angelo vowing to see Scarpia before God. To slow down these last few measures—and alter the rhythm so that it resembles the earlier love song—is to become ponderous in an opera that needs no extra ponderousness. It also misses a kind of hysteria—or maybe victory—in Tosca's suicide.

This set of tempos was so firmly entrenched by the 1970s that, when I indicated my intention to execute each instance of this theme as written, the great chorus master of La Scala, Roberto Benaglio, told me that it would be a "bold" choice. But he said it with a smile. Like a lot of other misguided traditions, the imposition of a single speed and rhythm at each instance of this theme has grown less popular in recent years. As is also common with misguided tradition, I still meet those who cling to it. For reasons I cannot quite understand they put greater stock in hoary hearsay about what the composer intended than in the evidence before their eyes (i.e., what is in the score).

Motives

Structurally though, the single most salient characteristic of this work is Puccini's use of intervals as motives. These are summarized in Example 7.3. The kinship among *Tosca's* motives also sets this opera apart from *La bohème*, which has diverse motives for diverse characters. The lives of Angelotti, Cavaradossi, Scarpia, and Tosca are fatally intertwined; and their motives are correspondingly subtly related in that they are based on related intervals. We will see something similar in the intervallic motives of Octavian and Ochs in Richard Strauss's *Der Rosenkavalier*.

Example 7.3 Intervals that operate motivically in *Tosca*: (a) Scarpia: the augmented fourth (piano reduction from m. 1 of the opera). (b) Love: the perfect fourth (multiple parts from 37, m. 3, in Act I). (c) Desperation or panic: seconds (piano reduction from m. 4 of the opera).

A)

B)

C)

Scarpia's music is anchored firmly in "the devil's interval," aptly enough; it opens the opera as illustrated in Example 7.3(a). Puccini uses the perfect fourth to render a stark contrast between Scarpia and the lovers; their motive, taken from their Act I duet, is illustrated in Example 7.3(b). He uses seconds to portray panic or desperation during Angelotti's Act I entrance (Example 7.3[c]), in Tosca's "Vissi d'arte" (from 51 of Act II), and during the torture of Cavaradossi (also in Act II, in the flute from 15, for example). Seconds also dominate the "E lucevan le stelle" theme we first hear as Cavaradossi awaits execution (Act III from 11), although this melody ends with a perfect fourth. We hear seconds as Cavaradossi recalls his trysts with Tosca (from 12, m. 2) and later when he proclaims "E non ho amato mai tanto la vita!" (from 13), here again ending with the perfect fourth.

The most sophisticated combination of intervals occurs in the final measures of Act II, however. Scarpia's motive almost ends the act, but not quite. Puccini engineers some ambiguity, creating conflicting emotions in the listener, by giving us two quite noticeable harmonic changes in just the last 11 measures of the act. As this scene draws to a close, minor keys reflect Tosca's state of mind. At 65, Puccini repeats the tritone three times as Tosca finishes placing candles around Scarpia's corpse and the crucifix on his chest. As the drum rolls begin offstage, An E minor chord is repeated three times. Any conventional mind would have ended with the last E minor chord. Rather abruptly though, Puccini moves back to the F-sharp minor that prevailed earlier. What dominates in the orchestra is a move from C-sharp up to F-sharp, a distance of five semitones and, therefore, the perfect fourth.

Does this instance of the perfect fourth represent love triumphant? If this were in a major key, it would feel like daybreak: Good has vanquished Evil. It does not feel that positive however. It is more ambiguous because, at the same time, Puccini lays some stress on the fact that we are resolving in a minor key. In more technical terms: He achieves this stress on the resolution in the minor key by including the same two notes that made the perfect fourth (C-sharp up to F-sharp) in the opposite direction, C-sharp down to F-sharp. This is the dominant-tonic cadence, which resolves to F-sharp minor. This resolution plays out in the lower strings with a little help from the horns and trumpet. (Everyone is playing quite softly to very softly at this point.)

Thus, there are two strands of thought embedded in this one final chord: relief (the lover's interval of the perfect fourth) seasoned with some dismay and fear (a minor key).

My favorite things

The "Te Deum" that closes Act I—with a great Scarpia. This is the finest scene Puccini ever wrote for a baritone.

Madama Butterfly

Madama Butterfly has a more tortured history than the composer's other great successes. The orchestral scope of the work, with its symphonic intermezzo in Act II, caused great criticism at the premiere (1904). It went through four rewrites, some major and some minor. Having conducted the second of the three versions (the Brescia version, 1904) in 1984, in its first performance in the United States in over fifty years, I feel that the final version (1907) is still the preferable one to use. The earlier versions have more japonaiserie, but the last is more universal. The earlier versions also have more music and more characters that do not move the story forward.

As originally conceived and rejected by Puccini's audience, *Madama Butterfly* was written in two acts. In his revisions, Puccini split Act II after the "Humming Chorus." Act III would begin the following morning with the intermezzo serving as an Act III prelude. Increasingly however, if the soprano has the stamina and the set permits, *Madama Butterfly* has reverted to two acts, which is preferable for a number of reasons. The two-act structure separates Act I from events occurring three years later. Then, the two later scenes—events of twenty-four hours or less—flow in a more realistic drama. The poetry and eloquence of the intermezzo—painting Butterfly's fervent yearning but telescoping the many hours of her watching and waiting—is heard in its proper dramatic context.

Puccini may simply have been ahead of his audience. Ironically, on opening night, the intermezzo seemed to bog the story down and stop the action. For modern audiences, it does quite the opposite. Today's opera lovers can certainly enjoy this second act of less than eighty minutes intact; nowadays, just about everyone in the audience will be acclimated to films of two hours or so. The real challenge in this relatively long act is for the cast.

Indeed, audiences seem to perceive this opera as being closer to one long symphonic poem than the composer's other works. Yes, it is characterized by through-composition for large swaths of the score. Even where there are breaks that allow applause, however, audiences are not inclined to break in. "Un bel dì vedremo" provokes applause (Act II, Part 1, from 12) but it also is entirely reasonable to applaud after the later "Che tua madre" (55 in Part 1). Yet people rarely do. There being a break, I am always alert to the possibility of applause and ready to accommodate it, but some combination of through-composition and the sheer intensity of the scene seems to militate against it.

Act I concludes with Puccini's most rapturous love duet (from 111). It is long—Puccini's longest by far. In addition, it is almost entirely a dialogue; the lovers unite only at the climax of the duet. Syncopated figures in the orchestra are used in much the same way that Wagner uses syncopation in the *Tristan und Isolde* love duet, to portray Pinkerton's anticipation and the mild impatience of a young bridegroom.

We cannot conclude this introduction without mention of the Humming Chorus that brings Part 1 of Act II to a close (from 90). It is an effect that is quite rare in opera. *Rigoletto's* storm comes to mind, but there are not many more.

Tune-Smithing

The abundant melodies in *Madama Butterfly* include authentic Japanese tunes and some that, most impressively, just seem to be authentic. Any composer can borrow a tune, of course. But Puccini regularly invested considerable energy in researching music from other locales for his operas and making it his own. That is the take-away for our purposes. I must leave it to scholars to write about this at length, in part because they are still making discoveries after all these years.[5]

Puccini's inventiveness is not limited to Japanese atmosphere. It is usually easy to identify "The Star-Spangled Banner" when it appears, for example. The third reference is fleeting, however, something extra for the devoted listener to discover upon revisiting the opera. After Sharpless has pressed Butterfly to reconsider Yamadori's marriage proposal and she has run offstage to get her son, the few measures that the orchestra plays include a rhythmic variation of "The Star-Spangled Banner." It is just a whiff of the melody in an arpeggio, but the reference is unmistakable (Act II, Part 1, at 50).

The waltz that accompanies the Sharpless-Yamadori dialogue in Act II, Part 1 (from 36, m. 5) is even subtler and more dramatically important. Embedded within this waltz is a hint of a form that would come to be called the "hesitation waltz." The TENUTO indications create something that sounds a little like rubato, and it requires a similar kind of flexibility from the conductor. Realizing this effect is more difficult however, in that the singers do not sing exactly the same rhythm; they should go on singing in a more speech-like rhythm with an almost imperceptible stretching of the single sixteenth rest in m. 4 of 37.

With this waltz and its hesitations, the orchestra contrasts considerably with the more intense and tense conversation that takes place between the two men. The mood is gentle and dreamy, and the waltz evokes a heroine quite detached from the reality that is bearing down on her and so concerns Sharpless and Yamadori. That is, it may be said to have more dramatic meaning than "The Star-Spangled Banner," delighted as we may be to hear the composer embed the American anthem in this Italian music with a Japanese accent. Yet this hesitation waltz, along with a subtler hesitation figure during Act I's Goro-Pinkerton dialogue (from [5] of Act I), often goes unobserved, resulting in a far less poetic and meaningful accompaniment.

Singers and Singing

As is widely recognized, the role of Butterfly is Puccini's hardest in many ways. She gets the first part of Act I to prepare, but then she has one of the most difficult of entrances in the long bridal pageant (from [39]). Once onstage, she almost never leaves. The biggest break she gets is for the Pinkerton-Sharpless-Suzuki trio of Act II, Part 2 (from [22]), but there is little other respite. Moreover, she must have great range, with the lyrical beauty of voice to portray a fifteen-year-old and then the great power needed for most of Act II.

Pinkerton is a somewhat short role. Nonetheless, he must sing beautifully and ardently. If he is also very winning and dashing, it helps to explain Butterfly's immediate, total, and unquestioning infatuation. (It is telling that she converts to Christianity before she even meets Pinkerton. She has staked everything on him.) Butterfly's love of Pinkerton is an obsession almost on the same scale as Des Grieux's love for Manon Lescaut. The pure, sublime love we see in Butterfly is really her love and ultimate sacrifice for her child. The somewhat more complex love she feels for Suzuki also adds richness to this most fascinating of Puccini heroines.

Near the end of the Act I entrance of Butterfly, the score contains an high note on the soprano's last syllable (from m. 1 before [41], LARGO). If the soprano wishes to sing the optional line, however, it is ill advised to try to slow too much. So instead of forcing the soprano to slow down, I omit the fermata and the RALLENTANDO in that measure and maintain a steady tempo. If Butterfly is in good form, she has plenty of room to hold that final syllable after the LARGO indication when she knows it is secure. Then the cut-off is up to her.

When the melody that ends Butterfly's entrance repeats at the end of the act, Butterfly has a high C and Pinkerton has an optional high C (from m. 1 before [136], LARGO). It is reasonable for both of the singers to hold their high C's through the entire final measure. Overall, the whole passage is a bit faster in this reprise, and holding the notes is consistent with the build-up in intensity at this point. On the other hand, I would still not force the singers to slow down at the fermata. Here, too, it is best if they hold the note as long as they can after the LARGO indication and judge the cut-off for themselves. (I would note that if Pinkerton does not sing the optional high note in the measure before [136], he should cut off as written even if Butterfly holds the high C—just because of the way in which the Italian syllables scan.)

Both Suzuki and Sharpless are richly human with anxieties and a certain helplessness. Suzuki is a part for a true mezzo-soprano, a voice on the dark side that blooms in the lower notes. She has very low notes that must cut through the orchestra in the Act II, Part 2, trio (from [22]). Later in the act, when she sings "Piangerà tanto, tanto," asking Sharpless and Kate to leave, she must ascend to a high G with full dramatic force ([30], m. 5). A dark sound also works best in the exquisite "Flower Duet" that she sings with Butterfly as Act II, Part 1, is coming to an end (from [71]). When the two voices have distinctly different timbres, it only enhances our ability to hear them alternately blending and weaving around each other. Very lyric mezzo-sopranos have neither the heft nor the right color to sing Suzuki.

Step into My Study . . .

Among the standard orchestral instruments, Puccini gives the greatest weight to the strings in this opera. He breaks with the Germanic model common from Mozart through Brahms, however, where the strings form the orchestral backbone because they have most of the sound while the woodwinds and brass are used mainly to provide color. In *Butterfly*, Puccini uses the strings to provide color and create effects more than in his other operas up to that time. In addition to bringing us the melodies, they are a source of constantly shifting light and mood much like Japanese screens. The music at Butterfly's entrance achieves such an effect, in part, with sustained chords and tremolos. This scene also reflects the trend toward more chromaticism; the music moves up in pitch and the ensemble passes through multiple keys, painting a picture of first Sharpless and then Butterfly climbing that hill.

Expression in the Orchestra

Sometimes the conductor can add a bit of color by certain choices of technique. For example, in Act II, Part 2, right after Butterfly's words "Piccolo Iddio, amore mio, fior di giglio e di rosa," the strings play loud pizzicato chords (54, m. 7)—in fact, COLLA MASSIMA FORZA, QUASI CON ESAGERAZIONE. At this place, snapping the strings makes a sound like the Japanese shamisen, as Butterfly gives up on the Western world she tried to join and moves inexorably toward suicide. Snapping the strings, of course, is usually to be avoided. This is one of the very few instances in which I would ask for such an articulation. The way in which Puccini phrased this indication, however, strongly suggests he was looking for a jarring sound.

In contrast to the delicacy of so much of this opera, the timpani has an unusually prominent part near the end, after Butterfly learns the truth and directs Suzuki to leave and keep her son company (from 3 measures before 50). However, the timpani part here poses a bit of a dilemma, depending on how much rubato the conductor chooses to employ. I feel this passage should be intensely emotional and flexible with its multiple indications like MENO MOSSO, ALLARGANDO, STENTATO, and RALLENTANDO. Indeed, for me, this is the emotional high point of the opera, as Butterfly decides on suicide and goes about preparing.

The timpani line is not suited to a great deal of rubato, however, and in such a performance, it can sound too prominent, too intrusive, and even downright strange. There is a longstanding tradition that solves the problem while, ironically, pushing the timpani further into the foreground. After a couple of measures of setting the speed, the conductor leaves the timpanist to maintain a steady drumbeat; i.e., the timpanist does not follow the conductor exactly. Thus, as the conductor leads everyone else in the orchestra, slowing down or speeding up as the case may be, there are more or fewer timpani hits per measure. The timpani portrays something like a terrible and relentless force of nature that is outside the orchestra in a sense.

Notwithstanding these couple of suggested tweaks, attempting to intensify Puccini's effects will backfire more often than not because one can easily careen into exaggeration and even bump into parody. One example is the decision to use cymbals where they are not written in the score.

Young conductors like to add cymbals to big moments, and I can plead guilty to such youthful indiscretions. Puccini does use cymbals in *Madama Butterfly* and the other two operas we are considering in this chapter. But he does not use them at the end of "Un bel dì vedremo" (at [16] in Act II, Part 1) or at Butterfly's spotting the vessel *Abraham Lincoln* in the harbor in the same scene (at [70]). Adding cymbals when not written in *Madama Butterfly* is usually a mistake. It now strikes me as undisciplined and indulgent because too many dynamic high points blunt the impact of all. It is also unduly affirmative. After all, Pinkerton does not return to Butterfly.

For me, the two dynamic high points of this opera are the spotting of Pinkerton's ship in the harbor (***fff*** TUTTA FORZA without cymbals) and the end of the opera (TUTTA FORZA at [58], which I interpret as ***ff***, followed by cymbals and ***fff*** for the entire orchestra in the last two measures of the opera). Puccini uses a wide range of percussion in this opera, including the timpani discussed above, a cannon, and Japanese pitched tam-tams in addition to a standard unpitched tam-tam. But he is careful with the spice that cymbals add, and his interpreters should be, too. Our watchword should be that of Sharpless to Pinkerton: "Giudizio."

Unity: Melody

Beyond its through-composition, what most unifies *Butterfly* is the reprising of melodies. These are not motives, not even for the title character. Or it might be said that they are all about the title character herself, but none stands out as motivic, distinct from the others. Melodies may reappear within the same section or scene or much later. A conductor has to resist any temptation to play the reprises at the same tempos as heard in their first appearances. The transformations in these reprises—including tempo changes—are packed with meaning. So this discussion parallels the discussion of the "E lucevan le stelle" reprises in the section on *Tosca* above. A few examples are outlined in Table 7.1.

In the music cited in Row 1, the difference is mostly in tempo. Beating the original statement in six, rather than in two, works best for me. The reprise should sound more urgent (and a bit louder). Beating in two here can help give the music more forward drive.

Table 7.1 Unifying melodies in *Madama Butterfly*. Where the score lacks a specific metronome indication, a suggested tempo is enclosed in square brackets.

(1) within Act I, Scene 1	From [123]: in the love duet on "Stolta paura, l'amor non uccide," ANDANTE ♪ = 112.	From [133]: later in the duet on "Via dall'anima in pena" ANDANTE MOSSO APPASSIONATO ♪ = 120.
(2) across scenes in Act I	From [40]: the principal love theme on "d'amor! d'amor venni alle soglie" [♩ = 90].	From [134], m. 9: at the climax of the love duet, on "Oh! quanti occhi fissi," LARGAMENTE, CON CALORE ♩ = 92.
(3) across scenes in Act I	At [41]: in the orchestra at the end of the bridal procession, before everyone bows to Pinkerton, LARGO [♪ = 60].	At [136]: in the orchestra after Pinkerton's "Ah! vien! sei mia!" in the love duet, LARGO ♩ = 69.
(4) from Act I to Act II	At [41] [♪ = 60].	Part 2 intermezzo, from 4 measures before [7]: almost three times as fast, ♩ = 112.
(5) from Act I to Act II	See Example 7.4.	

(*Continued*)

Table 7.1 (Continued)

(6) from Act I to Act II	From $\boxed{40}$: first statement of the principal love theme [♩ = 90].	Part 2, at $\boxed{51}$: cellos play the love theme against the timpani, MENO [♩ = 60].
(7) from Act I to Act II	From $\boxed{108}$: as the Bonze and chorus exit after he denounces Butterfly, ALLEGRO ♩ = 126.	Part 2, at $\boxed{52}$: orchestra reprises his melody, RUVIDO [♩ = 52].
(8) in Act II, from Part 1 to Part 2	Part 1, from $\boxed{56}$: on "E Butterfly, orribile destino," UN POCO AGITATO [anchored in ANDANTE MOLTO MOSSO ♩ = 112 at $\boxed{55}$].	Closing of the opera at $\boxed{58}$: ANDANTE ENERGICO ♩ = 88.

In Row 2, we have a tempo change and an even greater difference in intensity in the reprise. In the first statement of this, the principal love theme, we are coming from LARGO at 60 quarter notes per minute at $\boxed{39}$, but we are also moving from $\frac{4}{4}$ to $\frac{6}{4}$ meter at $\boxed{40}$. If I hold the speed of the measure constant from $\frac{4}{4}$ meter to $\frac{6}{4}$ meter, what results is 50 percent more quarter notes in the same time. That is, the music is faster, in the neighborhood of 90 quarter notes per minute, moderated only slightly by the SOSTENENDO at $\boxed{40}$. Butterfly's triplets in the measure before $\boxed{40}$ facilitate the transition, so focusing on keeping her eighth notes in $\frac{6}{4}$ the same as her triplet eighths in the preceding $\frac{4}{4}$ helps me realize the intended propulsion over a seamless transition. Notice that 92 quarter notes per minute is indicated for the reprise, which is also $\frac{6}{4}$ preceded by 60 quarter notes per minute in $\frac{4}{4}$ time. The difference between 90 and 92 quarter notes per minute is, of course, not even measurable. I think Puccini just wants us not to lose that *calore*. To me, it says "don't slacken."

The two passages in Row 3 contain the high notes discussed above and, as suggested in that discussion, the first concern is supporting the singers. The reprise is somewhat more sophisticated on two fronts. First, the earlier orchestration paints a picture of extreme delicacy, with no brass and with such instruments as glockenspiel and harp (the latter preceding each note with a grace note). The reprise is more robust. It has ample brass and much more pitched and unpitched percussion to express the passion that has been building throughout the duet. Second, the tempo is different. Although there is nothing specific in the score, the first statement (at 41) is universally performed at a dramatically slower speed than the section's opening 60 quarter notes per minute (at 39). I find that dropping to half speed, beating in eight, works beautifully. At the reprise, longer note values, combined with a slightly faster tempo, means that the melody should feel similar but just a little more animated, as befits the end of the love duet. This difference is of the same kind as we hear in Tristan und Isolde's "Liebestod" of Act III and the virtually identical music that appears at the end of that opera's Act II love duet (Chapter 5).

By comparison, the same theme from the end of the bridal procession appears again in the Act II intermezzo (Act II, Part 2), where it is almost three times as fast (Row 4 of Table 7.1).

The music referenced in Row 5 is illustrated in Example 7.4. This is the most sophisticated of the cases in this table because Example 7.4(c) combines Example 7.4(a) with a rhythmic variation of (b), the principal love theme.

In the reprise of Row 6, it is important not to lose sight of the MENO and *appassionato* in the cellos (which follow a LARGAMENTE). The cellos, with only the timpani in the background, must communicate heartbreak as they play the love theme slowly in a somewhat altered rhythm. This contrasts with the VIVO tempo at which Butterfly has just banished Suzuki to play with her son (47) and the ALLEGRO VIVACE that will accompany the boy's reappearance shortly (at 53).

The reprise of Row 7, at 52, follows the MENO at 51 and an ALLARGANDO that will continue until Butterfly's son re-enters ALLEGRO VIVACE (which begins at 53). So while *ruvido* indicates a little roughness, we are

Example 7.4 Echoes of Act I in Act II, *Madama Butterfly*: (a) Act I, from 39, m. 4. (b) Act I from 40. (c) Act II, Part 1, from 9, combines (a) and a rhythmic variation of (b).

still in a passage that is more about heartbreak than anger. I like the strings to employ more downbows than usual, yielding a more accented sound. Also note that if the timpani has been traveling to its own beat as described above, m. 9 of 51 is the time to resume following the conductor (the beginning of the ALLARGANDO).

Row 8 begins with a theme heard in the aria "Che tua madre." I like to ask my Butterfly to sing in a more accented manner than normal about the horrible destiny she fears. This means we will generally clock in a bit slower than the indication. It also means that I cannot begin too slowly at 55. If I do not keep the tempo up at that point, then Butterfly will not be able to act with her voice as much as she and I might like at 56. The reprise in Row 8—the end of the opera—is much slower (and louder) of course.

This ending of *Madama Butterfly* contains something of an anomaly: The resolution from B minor to G major is completely unexpected. The final chord is considerably more unrelated to what goes before it than even the final chord of *Tosca*'s Act II. Verdi experimented with leaving us hanging a little in order to segue into the next scene in *Aida*, and Wagner, of course, is noted for writing long stretches of music with postponed resolution. On the other hand, this is quite startling and uncharacteristic of Puccini's closing curtains. I have never heard a satisfactory explanation for this final G major chord. At best, the explanations are wildly speculative. My personal best guess is that the chord mirrors the great divide between the two cultures that clash in this opera.

Tempo

Moving smoothly from tempo to tempo is also fundamental to conveying unity. Just one tempo relationship is expressly indicated in *Madama Butterfly*. In Act II, Scene 2, when Butterfly is preparing to commit suicide but is interrupted by her son's running to her, the tempo is halved after her startled "piccolo Iddio! Amore, amore mio" (at 54).

The score has many metronome indications, however, and honoring them will result in the necessary proportionality among sections when called for. One indication that is rarely—if ever—performed, however, is in the Act II intermezzo, easily the most impressive orchestral passage in the opera. When the intermezzo can directly follow the gentle stillness of the Humming Chorus, its opening three notes come as something of a shock as we embark on an exploration of Butterfly's anguish followed by a tone painting of the sun rising over Nagasaki.

After the 19 measures of introduction that begin with those three notes, the metronome indication is 132 eighth notes per minute (at 2), vastly slower than we usually hear. Many performances clock in at about 153 eighth notes per minute. Evidently, this passage has always been a bit up for grabs, consistent with its central place in the failure of the original production and with all of the rewrites. Piano-vocal scores have metronome indications as slow as 100 eighth notes per minute. The right tempo, in my experience, lies somewhere in between but close to the 132 found in the final published orchestra score. It is to be noted, however, that the tempo may be modified somewhat relative to the size of the string section at hand. A lusher sound can sustain a slower speed.

To take it too fast, however, is to miss the dramatic point; this prelude should break your heart. In addition, Puccini wanted contrast. The music will be faster with the birds chirping at daybreak, only to slow down again as the dialogue between Suzuki and Butterfly begins. Even the ALLEGRO MODERATO (at [6]) is on the slow side, at 112 quarter notes per minute, so that the dawn can break over time. (The score is quite specific about the birds chirping, then first light, then the sky reddening and, finally, at exactly which measure the sun breaks through.)

There are about 60 measures between the indications of 132 eighth notes per minute and 112 quarter notes per minute. In the last dozen of these measures, indications are both MENO ANCORA and RALLENTANDO MOLTO. These rubato indications give us time to get down to about 112 eighth notes per minute. This means we can sweep into ALLEGRO MODERATO at exactly twice the speed. This will feel like a small surge but will result in an ALLEGRO that is still not very fast.

My favorite things

The love duet of Act I, in particular the part the oboe plays when it doubles Butterfly on "bambino" (from the last note in m. 8 of [128]). The effect is spine tingling.

Chapter 8

R. Strauss

Direct *Salome* and *Elektra* as if they had been written by Mendelssohn: Elfin music.

—Richard Strauss[1]

Along with only Wolfgang Amadeus Mozart and Pyotr Ilyich Tchaikovsky, Richard Strauss was successful at composing for both the concert hall and the opera house in equal measure. His symphonic tone poems and instrumental works mainly belong to his youth. But in his final years, he wrote three masterpieces for the concert hall: *Metamorphosen* for twenty-three solo strings, the Oboe Concerto, and the *Four Last Songs*. From shortly after the turn of the twentieth century, however, he blossomed as an opera composer.

While Strauss's tone poems show the influence of Wagner, in *Elektra* and *Salome* he took that Wagnerian spirit to a more extreme and dissonant level than he had before. They are works of powerful drama and rhythmic incisiveness. They also combine raw, almost savage, emotion and power with sections of impressionistic color. Then with *Der Rosenkavalier*, he turned to Mozart for inspiration. Although Der *Rosenkavalier* is even more intricate, in a good performance, the audience should barely notice the intricacies amidst the infectious melodies and comedic stage action bubbling along. It should sound tuneful, sparkling, and ebullient. Then he mixed things up with *Ariadne auf Naxos*, using a chamber orchestra to accompany two completely different sets of characters who figuratively and literally march to the sound of different drums.

Still, Strauss achieves his effects in both comedies and melodramas with the same tools. One of the most salient is his changing, alternating, and conflicting rhythms. With these, he masterfully portrays Herodes's losing his mind (*Salome*), delineates Octavian's adolescent libido (Der *Rosenkavalier*), and renders a variety of disputes and conflict. Strauss's rhythms and tempos may sometimes be difficult to execute but, happily, this composer is liberal with indications that clearly mark the road we are to travel. So there are relatively few difficult-to-figure tempo relationships or transitions between sections.

Back on the stage, and for the sake of both the drama and the demands on the vocalists, we should remember that Strauss, like the composers of the verismo school, usually wrote to simulate the speed of speech. If you sing the lines to yourself, you are likely to hit upon a reasonable tempo. He also gave us metronome indications often enough to validate this approach. There are excited passages that call for fast singing and sometimes characters may linger as appropriate dramatically, but rarely is a passage in a Strauss opera much slower or faster than anyone would reasonably speak the lines. It follows then that, as in the music of Puccini or Debussy, indications such as "calmer" or "tightening" or "moving ahead" often have as much to do with mood as speed. Above all, and in spite of both intensity and the need to manage many moving parts, there should be a certain flexibility in this music as there is in verismo works, without lapsing into any exaggeration in tempo or dynamics.

Audiences do not walk away humming meters and tempos, of course. They remember gorgeous melody and color, exquisitely matched to the drama and setting of the work, juxtapositions both witty and beautiful, and a great deal of sound. The last of these means that Strauss's operas are easily made loud throughout. Still, he rarely writes *fff*, certainly not for the full orchestra. So the basic discipline of identifying the one or two biggest moments and keeping the rest just a bit below that level becomes downright critical in performances of Strauss's music.

As far as balance is concerned, at least as much as balancing the pit and stage, balance within the orchestra can be a problem for the conductor of Strauss. While Wagner presents the orchestral musicians with technical difficulties, once mastered, the music almost always sounds as it looks on the page. In Strauss, the texture is thicker yet must emerge as transparent, even crystalline. So when musicians see held chords with a loud dynamic indication (especially in the brass) for example, this often means that they must attack the note aggressively but immediately bring the volume down to something that allows us to hear other moving lines—especially, of course, the melody.

I will point to a number of demanding passages for singers and conductors in the pages that follow. But let it be clear: everyone is challenged by Richard Strauss. Rehearsal pianists can be blindsided by notes that are unexpected given the key signature, for example. Sometimes the composer does not change the key signature because we are just passing through one key on the way to another. This is part of the reason that much of Strauss's music is replete with accidentals. But at other times, the composer's reasoning is less clear. (The solution here is to treat the rehearsal pianist even more kindly than usual in rehearsing Strauss's music.)

Even before Arnold Schoenberg's *Pierrot Lunaire* (1912), Strauss experimented with atonality in both *Salome* and *Elektra*. And while Sergei Prokofiev and Igor Stravinsky are sometimes credited with launching the neoclassical style between 1917 and 1920, that only works if we ignore *Der Rosenkavalier* and both versions of *Ariadne auf Naxos*. It is easy to see why Schoenberg demurred when he was labeled a revolutionary, claiming that only Richard Strauss was a revolutionary in their time.[2]

First Operatic Successes: *Salome* and *Elektra*

Richard Strauss's two well-known one-act operas have much in common. Both *Salome* (1905) and *Elektra* (1909) tell dark tales of grudges and vengeance. They both make enormous demands on their star sopranos and demand the highest levels of musicianship of everyone else in the cast. Like virtually all of Strauss's works, they present the conductor with tricky rhythms to get the cast and orchestra through. And once we have absorbed the music, we must figure out how to manage the almost nonstop intensity—mostly, but not entirely, a question of volume.

Salome

Salome—the girl who demands and receives the head of John the Baptist ("Jochanaan" in this libretto) in return for dancing for her stepfather—has had a stupendous run in art and literature. Oscar Wilde's play, on which this opera is based, premiered in Paris in French in 1896, more successfully in German in Berlin in 1902, and as Strauss's opera in Dresden in 1905. The opera shocked audiences everywhere and was a great success for Strauss, whose first operas had been a disappointment relative to his concert music.

That Strauss was, like most musicians, awed by *Tristan und Isolde* is evident in *Salome* in particular. The *Tristan* theme appears in the first violins and cellos on the opening page of the opera as Narraboth concludes his opening line about Salome's beauty (mm. 5–7). A look at the orchestra score will confirm that MOLTO ESPRESSIVO appears only over the lines with this melody. Nineteenth-century German composers like Strauss and Brahms often used *espressivo* to indicate the lines that should be "brought out," or made more prominent with a bit more volume. The indication implies more volume than it might for the Italians or French. So there can be little doubt that Strauss intended his audience to recognize the melody. The theme reappears while that same character pleads with Salome not to stay near the cistern-prison that holds Jochanaan (in the lower strings from ACCELERANDO, m. 4 of [76]). It is to be noted that Narraboth commits suicide over his impossible love, making him arguably the character most like the dying-for-love romantics featured in *Tristan.*

The title character's part would be known for the Dance of the Seven Veils if for nothing else, of course (beginning after m. 8 of [247]). For some years, sopranos have been vying to dance it better and better and perform a genuine striptease. This is a considerable accomplishment; the usual practice when the work was new was to have a dancer ready to slip in and out of the scene. If the Salome looks good, that is just the beginning. Recall that she will nag Herodes for her reward at great length after the dance, growing ever more demanding, even petulant. Then she must launch into the long final aria. Generally, the soprano preparing to both sing and dance the part will enter into a period of training as strict as any athlete who performs without musical accompaniment. The Salome who looks, dances, and sings credibly and beautifully deserves the biggest shout-out the audience can muster and all of the support her colleagues can supply.

A note about her character: Keep in mind that Strauss is said to have expressed a preference for having an innocent sounding Salome. I urge my Salome to think along those lines. A younger, more child-like Salome is actually even more frightening. A good actress will find multiple ways to strike the right pose. Musically, Salome should eschew the portamento at the end of the opera on "Liebe" in "Doch es schmeckte vielleicht nach Liebe" (at 357, m. 3, in the vocal score but absent from the orchestra score). Just a bit later, I ask her to take the optional higher note at 360.

The grand final aria for a leading character makes *Salome* different from *Elektra* and many other operas (from the pickup to 314). The aria may seem unsurprising at first blush. By the time that Strauss was composing his operas, though, it was rare to end operas this way. Moreover, Salome's final aria may be the grandest, longest such scene in the standard repertory. Had it been much shorter, *Salome* would be like *Elektra* in being composed of two equal parts. One virtue of the great sweep and length of the aria is that it serves to balance the long scene in which Herodes tries so hard to convince Salome to ask for anything in the world other than Jochanaan's head.

Salome is not the only singer in this opera who faces challenges, and some are as much musical as vocal. One is pitch. Sometimes it can be difficult—and a bit scary—for a singer to find a pitch amidst all the dissonance while standing at some distance from the pit. There can be a temptation to shout lines in order to facilitate such difficult moments in the music, and the angry text often supports this choice.

There are two such problematic moments in what may be described as the Nazarenes' scene, about half way through the opera. The scene follows a contentious theological debate among the Five Jews. The Nazarene begins his message of salvation (from [209]), and then the orchestra reprises a barcarole-like theme introduced earlier as Jochanaan described the Savior and urged Salome to seek him on a boat on the Sea of Galilee (from [132], m. 2). The First Jew vociferously denies that the Messiah has come while the orchestra and First Nazarene continue in a decidedly unrelated sequence of keys. Note that the indication SCHREIEND for the First Jew translates as "screaming" or "screamingly." But since there are notes written, he should sing clamorously but on pitch (at [209], m. 4).

The Nazarene continues by describing the Savior's miracles. Herodes expresses horror that the dead are being raised and orders that this practice stop, singing in A minor against the company still in A-flat major (the measure before [212]). This is about as dissonant a combination of notes as a composer can assemble.

For either Herodes or the First Jew to merely yell these two phrases deprives us of the more painful dissonances achieved by singing the pitches Strauss wrote. They express the polarization in the scene. So these two tenors, too, deserve appreciation and support when they make that extra effort to sing their lines as written.

It may be added that there is a musical irony in this scene, because these pungent notes are embedded in some of the most beautiful music in the opera. This is the music of the First Nazarene himself. In particular, when he gets to relating the water-into-wine miracle and the lepers healed at Capernaum, the harps, which have been relatively silent for many pages, add a touch of the celestial as he unveils his story (from [210]). Management needs to cast a bass with strong low notes, good volume, and some beauty of tone in what appears on paper to be a relatively minor part. Otherwise, the harps supply only pleasant background filigree. Only when the First Nazarene's melody is prominent can the full *wunder* of the counterpoint and orchestration come through.

So we might say that the Lord himself has a motive in this opera, appearing first in the orchestra that accompanies Jochanaan [132] and later sung by the Nazarene [209]. Indeed, for a short, one-act opera, *Salome* has a highly developed and elaborate motivic structure. At the opening, the clarinet and then Narraboth have a melody about Salome's beauty that comes back fast, loud, and jerky when Narraboth kills himself and, later, at the end of the orchestral interlude in a dark and sinister rendition in the contrabassoon. Another melody is foreshadowed at the end of the interlude and is reprised at each demand for the head of Jochanaan. A pair of themes expressing Salome's desire for Jochanaan also runs through the opera. One appears just before and during their duet and another dominates her dance. In the "Dance of the Seven Veils" in particular, Strauss weaves together all four of Salome's motives. While motives revolve predominantly around Salome by any accounting, Jochanaan's appearances are also signaled by a consistent theme.

Step into My Study . . .

Rhythms are often tricky for all concerned in *Salome*. When Herodes is losing his mind, for example, he has different meters in each measure: first, when he suddenly panics about the climate and his cloak and his crown and so on (from 235), and again when Salome has him exactly where she wants him and keeps demanding Jochanaan's head (from 281).

Strauss also employs conflicting rhythms. For example, when the Second Soldier begs Salome not to try to speak with Jochannan, three different meters are being played simultaneously (from 42). The speed of the Second Soldier's quarter note in $\frac{2}{2}$ equals that of the eighth note in the $\frac{2}{4}$ measures, while the oboe and English horn play $\frac{3}{4}$. With an arrangement like this, the conductor beats once per measure and each musician maintains that pulse in his or her own meter.

Conflicting rhythms represent more than a time-beating problem. On the podium, we must also determine which parts are of greater importance and balance them accordingly. I consider the nature of the instruments involved or the natural sound of the player in the orchestra at hand. Both of these considerations tell me which line or occasionally which note or notes must be brought out or played more softly. If needed, I may lighten the volume a little on long, sustained notes.

There is a moment at the end of the dance that is rather tricky to pull off cleanly. As the dance ends, there are fifteen measures in which the orchestra lightens considerably, some playing trills. The indication is ETWAS LANGSAMER (at the second K, m. 4). By the last measure, the orchestra is playing half notes, and at SEHR SCHNELL, we have several measures of sixteenth notes with more instruments joining in. One of the most useful pieces of advice I can share with a fellow conductor is to begin beating the new tempo (with small gestures) in the measure that precedes SEHR SCHNELL. This not only cues all of those musicians counting rests, but it also alerts them to the exact tempo.

Happily, one of the two loudest moments in *Salome* occurs in the interlude when nobody is singing (6 measures before 149). The other comes at the end of the duet between Jochanaan and Salome. In his final line, he curses her with "Du bist verflucht" and descends into the cistern. On Jochanaan's final syllable, everyone in the orchestra is playing loud, louder, or pretty close to as loud as possible (m. 6 before 141). In addition, the bassoons, bass trombone, tuba, cellos, and basses have the melody. They must clearly cut through the rest of the orchestra if the audience is to hear that melody and other quick-moving lines.

After balancing within the orchestra though, I still have the problem that the last syllable of Jochanaan's curse upon Salome is inevitably going to be drowned out by the orchestra. In the contest between orchestra and singer, we may sometimes employ the technique discussed in Chapter 7: *dopo la parola.* We can let Jochanaan finish his climactic phrase before the orchestra crashes in. With the right Jochanaan, this can suggest the wrath of God himself and add to the dramatic punch of the moment.

The argument to the contrary is that Strauss was talented at "painting" with music in his operas much as he did in the tone poems of his youth. He also often painted humorously and *Salome* has its humorous moments. Thus, it is possible that Strauss was mischievously foreshadowing Jochanaan's fate by cutting him off that way. That is, one is certainly justified in following the score as written at this point. But if I have a good Jochanaan, I will always prefer to "play it straight."

Finally, there is an anomaly in the second violin part worth mentioning: It appears a little before we hear Jochanaan sing for the first time and again just before his entrance. Strauss writes an unplayable low E (at 25 and at m. 5 of 63). There is no single explanation for why composers do this, and Strauss does it often. Strauss surely heard the E in his head, and he may have preferred writing a complete phrase for the conductor, the violinists, and himself. In any case, there is also no single solution when we come across such a note in a score either. In this instance, since the same music is doubled in the violas, clarinets, bassoon, and horn, I ask the second violins to skip that phrase and reenter in the next.

My favorite things

Salome's final aria. One highly dissonant chord on the third beat of the bar before 361 sums up the entire work and serves as the emotional high point for me.

Elektra

Strauss may well have modeled *Elektra* on *Salome*. After two less-than-successful tries, after all, *Salome* had been his first success in opera, and he next turned his attention to *Elektra*. To begin with, similarities may be found in the motives of *Salome* and *Elektra*.

Example 8.1 Agamemnon and related motives: (a) The second theme of desire in *Salome*, the A-clarinet part in concert pitch. (b) The Agamemnon motive in *Elektra*, from 36, m. 7. (c) Aegisth's motive in *Elektra*, from 198a, m. 5.

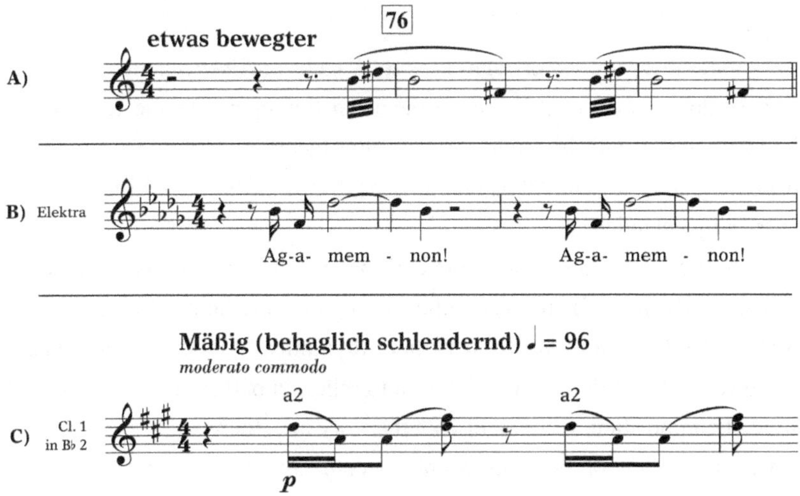

The Agamemnon theme that opens *Elektra* and is later sung by the title character is something of a musical anagram of one of the themes that dominates *Salome's* Dance of the Seven Veils (Example 8.1 [a] and [b]). The two themes are closest in rhythm, and at the heart of each motive are three pitches that are related. They form something of an inversion in minor. Although this is not a strict dodecaphonic inversion, it sounds like one. Of course, minor scales, keys, intervals, and chords are usually perceived as more somber or foreboding than their cousins among the majors. And this suits a theme for the heroine of *Elektra*. Strauss then plays with the Agamemnon motive further and transforms it into Aegisth's theme, casting it in a major key and giving it a sauntering accompaniment with a rather mincing rhythm (Example 8.1[c]).

Strauss opens the opera with shifting meters, changing accents, and syncopation, depicting dark moods and toxic relationships. In this, it is different from *Salome*, which opens rather gently with Narraboth's admiration of the title character's beauty. On the other hand, as in *Salome*, a big interlude marks the middle of the work (beginning at **259**), and an important new motive is introduced as the action resumes. After the *Elektra* interlude, we first hear a motive about Orest. The motive is in a minor key when introduced (at **1a**) and as Chrysothemis arrives to announce that Orest is dead (from **3a**). It returns, still in minor, when Chrysothemis describes strangers outside (from **13a**). But when she returns to correct the story of Orest after Aegisth is killed, she sings the complete motive in major (at **220a**, m. 5).

While there are fewer references to Wagner in *Elektra* than in *Salome*, Strauss does return to the *Tristan* theme in this opera. In the first scene, he combines it with his short Agamemnon theme in multiple instruments beginning at **6**. We hear it as the maidens discuss Elektra's foul moods and unfriendly behavior.

The work has long, flowing melody and even features Strauss's signature waltzes, especially for the last child in this unhappy home, Chrysothemis, who yearns for a normal life. It is more rhythmically incisive than *Salome* is, however. What throws the rhythm into relief, in part, is a straightforward style of composition. Consistent with the story line, there are fewer passages where subsidiary or decorative lines accompany the main musical idea.

It follows that the principal idea stands out and commands our attention to a greater extent.

Several standard cuts have been around since the earliest performances and are included in most recordings. They are virtually all in the first 60 percent of the opera and include musically interesting material, to be sure, but they make sense. This is especially true in the long and kaleidoscopic Elektra-Klytämnestra duet. Thus, *Elektra* presents a special case when it comes to cuts. While there is no good reason to make cuts in *Salome*, the *Elektra* cuts believed to be sanctioned by Strauss himself give some help to the soprano in this most punishing of roles.

Perhaps the most difficult passage for the soprano signing on to perform Elektra is the quiet, lyric singing required in the duet with Orest, which is bookended by almost an hour of violent, relatively loud singing beforehand, and then a return to the truly dramatic, loud, and very loud singing in the last part of the opera.

Chrysothemis is also a demanding role. In fact, while there are lighter and heavier Salomes and the conductor can accommodate them, a lighter-voiced Chrysothemis cannot be heard at her most intense moments. There is little the conductor can do to help out in these moments without vitiating the drama. In fact, if I find that I have two beautiful female voices that can pull off the parts of these two sisters and there is some contrast between them, I consider myself to have hit something of a jackpot.

Although Klytämnestra's part is shorter than that of either sister, it has great impact. The opera is really about the conflict between Elektra and her mother.

As for the men, they are needed but, paradoxically, almost irrelevant. Aegisth appears but briefly (although he does provide an opportunity for Elektra to dance and gloat). Orest arrives intending to murder his mother and her lover. He does not tell us this in a grand aria worthy of his intentions, however. Instead, after some dialogue that leads to their recognizing each other—the opera's emotional high point—Orest listens to Elektra's aria about what she has become after years in what, for her, is virtually a prison. There is nothing like Rigoletto's "Vendetta" here. Chrysothemis, too, is mostly a foil, but she sings more than does her brother, who is central to the story.

Step into My Study . . .

With this opera, Strauss created something at least as wonderful as *Salome* but even more formally perfect. It seems clear that he aspired to Greek tragedy in the loftiest sense. The work is a little longer, but perfectly symmetrical in its two halves. It has no subsidiary characters with their own stories and digressions. Even the maidservants, functioning as a Greek chorus, comment only relatively briefly on events and the circumstances and character of Elektra. A single, stark story unfolds relentlessly, as does the music.

As in *Salome* and in his writing generally, Strauss's music approximates the pace of speech. There may be urgency in the dialogue but it remains realistic and naturalistic. The scene in which Elektra tries to convince Chrysothemis to help kill their mother and her husband, for example, depicts a range of emotions and moods across many pages of music (from **34a**). It begins with a rapid exchange that segues into a quick waltz taken from Chrysothemis's earlier aria. This waltz accelerates as Chrysothemis pleads with Elektra to free them by making peace with their elders. Elektra's music slows down here as she shifts from strong-arming to sweet-talking. The music then speeds up until the end of the scene as Elektra's frustration escalates. Thereafter, it is the orchestra alone that continues at breakneck speed, reflecting Elektra's near hysteria.

Balance problems are real in *Salome* but they are even greater in *Elektra,* so care must always be taken not to overpower the stage. Happily, nobody is trying to sing at the two loudest moments in the opera: after the confrontation between Elektra and her mother that ends the first half (at **259**) and in the very last measures of the opera. Nonetheless, and even with the most considerate of conductors, this work demands voices of heroic size.

This is, however, glorious orchestration coming from a creative original. The string writing in *Elektra* is especially striking. The standard string orchestration for the era would have been first violins, second violins, violas, cellos, and basses. Strauss gives us no fewer than four new sections: third violins, second and third violas, and second cellos. This gives the strings a slightly darker color than normal. Shortly after Chrysothemis enters, after the death of Aegisth, the first violas become fourth violins, which restores the usual balance in favor of the violins (at 235a). This means that these four violists must bring violins and switch instruments at this point. Similarly, at Aegisth's death, Strauss adds three more trumpets, resulting in a total of six separate parts where there had been three (at 214a). This brightens the sound but also increases the volume.

It is important to restrain the orchestra in *Elektra*, but there are occasions when the orchestra can contribute something extra to the audience's experience by emphasizing a line or adding effects. The trick, especially in Strauss's music, is to find such emphases and effects that are dramatically apt but do not depend on volume alone. So for example, I like to ask the string players with loud PIZZICATO indications to snap their strings to imitate the overseer's whip (in the three measures before 25). As mentioned in our discussion of *Madama Butterfly*, snapping is not a string articulation to be used often or lightly. I can count the number of instances where I would use it on one hand. As a rule, one must caution the strings to avoid snapping the strings when they see both *ff* and PIZZICATO. But when it reflects something happening onstage, it will not distract the audience and is thus worth considering.

Before we leave the *Elektra* orchestra, another anomaly should be noted. Strauss writes yet another extremely low note for the violins, a low F. This not-quite-unplayable note first occurs after Elektra sings her Agamemnon motive (at 1 measure before 37). But the only way to play that note is to retune the instrument, an instruction that Strauss includes in the score. There is not adequate time to tune and retune, however. Nor is it practical for all twenty-four players to have a second violin nearby, all perfectly in tune, virtually anywhere other than a recording environment. The only possible solution is to omit the note in the violins since the violas and English horn play the same note in this passage.

My favorite things

The final bars of the Elektra-Klytämnestra duet (from 257 to 259). The high C for Elektra on the word "Jauchzt" and the resolution on a high B-flat bring us as close to true catharsis as we have in opera.

Der Rosenkavalier

Der Rosenkavalier is one of a handful of most technically difficult works in any conductor's career because it combines technical complexity with great length. It rewards all of the effort amply, but is a major undertaking. On the up-side, for a while, everything else will seem easy after a successful production of *Der Rosenkavalier*.

Scholars find its roots in the works of several French authors, including Molière and Beaumarchais. For most of us, the connection to Beaumarchais's *Le Mariage de Figaro* and Mozart's opera based thereon is most salient, and by his own account, Strauss used Mozart as his model.[3] Nonetheless, Hugo von Hofmannsthal created what amounts to an original tale, setting it in mid-eighteenth-century Vienna. The opera's 1911 premiere was an unqualified success.

Performers must be mindful throughout this opera of the tension between the twentieth-century musical language and the intended ambience. At the same time that we strive for Viennese *Schwung und Schlagobers* we must keep the balance, elegance, and delicacy of eighteenth-century Europe in our mind's eye. Think, for example, of Fragonard and Boucher paintings as well as Mozart's music.

The central building block of the opera is ascending or descending seconds. This includes the two most important motives, which belong to Octavian and Ochs, the rivals for Sophie's love. Indeed, the opera opens with Octavian's ascending seconds.

Given the history of this opera, and what we know its composer and librettist intended, it is hard to resist comparing Octavian's motive with the music of Mozart's Cherubino. In "Non so più" (*Le* nozze *di Figaro*, No. 6), Mozart gives Cherubino a figure of three descending seconds. Strauss gives Octavian a figure of three ascending seconds in the theme that opens the opera and is repeated throughout. When it becomes a waltz in Act I, it is expressed more gently than it is at the opening of the opera; but it is unmistakable (at the pickup to [95]).

The *Salome-Tristan* homage discussed earlier is fairly obvious. The Octavian-Cherubino reference, on the other hand, is subtler. Remember, however, the similarities between the two characters: Both characters are young men played by women. In addition, both are in love with older, married, and well-born mistresses who are compelled to renounce their dalliances. Octavian's fate is far happier than Cherubino's is in the Beaumarchais trilogy, however. Hence, Octavian's rising seconds contrast with Cherubino's descending seconds.

We can also contrast Octavian's motive with that of Baron Ochs, his putative rival for Sophie's love. Octavian's theme ends with three ascending seconds. Ochs's motive ends with three descending seconds (e.g., horn in E-flat from 64 of Act II). Strauss juxtaposes these two motives the most in Act II. (For an example, see the pickup to 23 through m. 2 of 26.) For its final appearance, however, Ochs's motive is somewhat mischievously embedded in the launch of Act III's great waltz medley right after his angry final exit from the tavern with, "Leupold, wir geh'n" (246, m. 7).

The interval of the second appears at other memorable moments. The initial idea in the Italian Tenor's love song of Act I is dominated by ascending and descending seconds (from 233). The Marschallin sings descending seconds in the final trio on the words "[rich]tigen Weis'" as she contemplates letting Octavian go as she knows she should (at 285, mm. 7–8). At the beginning of the waltz that ends Act II, Strauss writes three-note figures of an eighth note, an eighth note, and a half note (from the pickup to 253). The concluding half note of each figure is lower in pitch by a second: The first figure ends with a G-sharp half note, the next with an F-sharp half note, and so on through E and D-sharp. The last three-note figure ends with a dotted quarter note on C.

These ascending and descending seconds serve as the glue that binds together this marvelous opera, as the seconds and fourths of *Tosca* serve to unify that opera. In building on such germs, Strauss's work also resembles that of his countrymen, Ludwig van Beethoven and Johannes Brahms.

Another distinctive feature of this opera is the challenge that Strauss set himself: write for three female voices and keep it interesting. To this end, he revived the pants role of previous eras in the character of Octavian. In the 1940s and early 1950s, Octavian was sometimes sung by a soprano, so recordings and even films are available. (Jarmila Novotna and Sena Jurinac were among the last sopranos famous for the role.) Today, Octavian is like Bizet's

Carmen, virtually the exclusive domain of the mezzo-soprano. However, it must be sung by a mezzo with a lyrical voice and comfort with a relatively high average pitch like that of Romeo in *I Capuleti e i Montecchi*. As in other operas, using a woman in this role operates to make a very sharp distinction between a young man and all of the other males involved in the plot. In this regard too, the obvious antecedent is Mozart's Cherubino in *Le nozze di Figaro*. From the mezzo's and conductor's point of view, the difference is that Octavian's voice needs to be the more robust of the two because of the larger orchestra involved.

In this world of women, apart from the Marschallin's cousin Baron Ochs, the men have secondary roles. It may be argued that Sophie's father Faninal is something more than what the Italians call a *comprimario*, but his part is considerably less important than that of Baron Ochs.

Baron Ochs comes across as loquacious, pompous, and somewhat crude. His name, after all, translates as "ox" and is used for "oaf." So he is sometimes played for sheer buffoonery. The part requires great command of the stage and personality, however. His part may not be the longest in opera, but he may have the most words. While Strauss again writes mostly at a rate consistent with real speech, he also uses speed for comic effect, cramming more words for Ochs into the same tempo in which others sing in a more conversational manner. Ochs's greatest such tour de force occurs in his Act I exchange with the Marschallin (from **104**). At the PRESTO (**148**, m. 5), Ochs and the orchestra take off in a purely virtuoso moment worthy of the "Largo al factotum" of Rossini's Figaro. His display reaches its peak with a sustained high F held for eight and a half measures (from m. 1 before **190**).

Strauss's audience would have found the Italian Tenor's aria to be typically, even stereotypically, nineteenth-century Italian (Act I from **233**). We accept this as we accept other anachronisms in the Marschallin's eighteenth-century drawing room because, after all, Strauss is showing off his ability to write a simply glorious melody as well as those clashing styles.

Earlier in *Der Rosenkavalier's* history, we sometimes heard a bad Italian Tenor—tasteless or vocally inadequate. Some think that this was intended or, at least, tolerated. Just as we can cut the misogyny and racism that is explicit in Emanuel Schikaneder's libretto to *Die Zauberflöte*, however, my position is that we can ignore any caricatures that have attached themselves to the Italian Tenor. In fact, the melody and its accompaniment are so beautiful that it is preferable to think of him as a very fine tenor indeed. He can provide not comic relief but beauty relief in the midst of quite a raucous scene and then, in the reprise, against the scrappy argument between Ochs and the Notary (in much the same way that Lauretta's "O mio babbino caro" levitates out of and transcends a near-riot in Puccini's *Gianni Schicchi* [from 40]). So the Italian Tenor is something like the First Nazarene in *Salome*, a minor part in the great scheme of things perhaps, but one that can lift a good production yet higher when management goes to the trouble and expense of casting it with the right singer.

Last, there is the chorus. Unlike *Salome*, which has no chorus or *Elektra*, which has a short part for a chorus of servants of the house of Klytämnestra, the chorus in *Der Rosenkavalier* acts in small groups: servants, various waiters and customers, a trio of children, and so on. This is not unlike the way Verdi used the chorus in *Falstaff* and Puccini did in *Manon Lescaut* and, especially, in *La bohème's* second act. (Bizet did it before these composers, but the relevant music in the opening of Act IV of *Carmen* is very often cut.) Of course, the importance of each chorister's accuracy is only magnified when he or she is part of a small group—or even singing short solos.

Step into My Study . . .

True to form, Strauss tests the musicianship of all cast members as least as much as their vocal and language skills. One of his more clever uses of changing rhythms comes at the beginning of Act I when Octavian is singing about striving and yearning and finding the Marschallin's hand. Here Strauss is representing not horror or insanity as he did with Herodes's music. Rather, he shows us, through our ears, adolescent ardor. Beginning at 20, he makes the business of changing meters trickier by alternating $\frac{4}{4}$ and $\frac{3}{4}$ every measure for a few measures but then repeatedly reversing the pattern in an irregular manner. This means that, just when we begin to feel a stable rhythm, we experience the disequilibrium of adolescent love and libido again.

I beat this irregular pattern three times per measure in $\frac{3}{4}$ time and twice per measure in $\frac{4}{4}$ time. That results in about the clearest beat for the orchestra, especially for those musicians who are counting their way through multi-measure rests. Everybody still needs to prepare and remain alert, of course.

An instance of conflicting meters occurs in Act III, after the prelude and opening have perfectly previewed the manic mood and farce to come. An offstage ensemble plays waltzes while the orchestra and singers continue in a conversational style in $\frac{4}{4}$ meter (from [56]). Still this is gentler and far less dissonant than the conflicting meters that accompany the Second Soldier's begging Salome not to try to speak with Jochannan. Each waltz figure coincides with one beat of the $\frac{4}{4}$ measures in a highly regular fashion. Beating this in four makes sense.

On the other hand, there is a section where two musical threads sound appropriately and starkly at odds but are actually cast in the same meter. It occurs in Act I, when the Italian Tenor reprises his aria against Ochs's argument with the Notary over the marriage contract, ending with Ochs's fist-slam on the table (from [246]). The argument is talky while the aria is fluid and the two styles account for the apparent conflict.

Whatever the challenges however, Strauss supplies sufficiently clear guidance. For example, in Act I, up to [205], m. 3, the music has become ever more delicate until we transition magically into a waltz. This transition feels magical only if we heed the indication to keep the eighth note at a constant speed, but the indication is there for all to see.

The *Rosenkavalier* orchestra is smaller than those of the two one-act operas discussed above or *Die Frau ohne Schatten*; but it is large nonetheless. The music is busy and complicated almost every minute of its running time, but what requires my unrelenting attention is maintaining the delicacy that so much of the music demands. It would be easy to lose that with so large an orchestra and elaborate an orchestration.

This is somewhat complicated by the fact that the conductor must sometimes follow the singers, something that is especially true of the scene between the Marschallin and Ochs in Act I. That scene requires a great deal of subtle rubato that is mostly text driven. Too much manipulation of the tempo will make the scene sound mannered, but without suppleness, it can become leaden.

In contrast, much of the music of Acts II and III is more conductor-driven. The first part of the bifurcated Act III—the farce at the inn—has the most difficult music in the opera. It is capped off with the opera's dynamic high point; this is the rousing medley of many of its waltzes that begins when Ochs leaves. Only then does the work calm down and only then can the conductor take an extra breath here and there. In the trio that follows, the Marschallin, Octavian (as himself), and Sophie sing their independent but intertwining lines and build to a transporting climax. This trio is also the emotional high point for me and it seems that Strauss might have agreed since it is the music he arranged to have played at his own funeral.[4] It is followed by the duet for Sophie and Octavian that serves as a kind of delicate coda to the act.

As is often the case, supporting the singers through this long work means keeping the music from bogging down. Conductors and Marschallins should not subtly decelerate during the final trio, for example. It is natural to want to linger over this music, especially if the soprano is having a great night. But even assuming that it does not get so slow that we lose the audience, pacing it is critical. It will only be possible to broaden in the climax if we have not gotten too slow between [291] and [292].

My favorite things

The waltzes at Ochs's exit in Act III (from m. 6 of [246]). They epitomize Vienna, and nothing so evokes the city even to this day. Although the opera is set before the Viennese waltz flowered, Richard Strauss shows himself to be the master of this form as much as Johann.

Ariadne auf Naxos

Ariadne auf Naxos's roots lie in a 1912 Stuttgart production of Molière's *Le Bourgeois gentilhomme*. It took until 1916, however, for its creators to distill it into the two-act opera commonly performed today in which the comic Prologue explains what happens in Part 2, the "Oper." Nonetheless, the work retains a spirit not far removed from that of Molière's comedy.

It is to be noted that there are no directions in the score about the fireworks that the libretto refers to for the finale, and when I first performed this opera, indoor fireworks were rare. The first time I saw them, however, I was sold. Fireworks, as well as lighting and video effects, are getting easier and easier to pull off and therefore more common. They are well worth a little extra in budgeting and rehearsing this opera. This duet is rapturous. It is a dynamic high point but also an emotional high point since it is unexpectedly touching after the hijinks just moments earlier. Fireworks put the conclusion well over the top theatrically.

The acrobatic troupe is modeled on traditional *commedia dell'arte* characters and led by Zerbinetta. The Composer, a mezzo-soprano in a pants role, leads the serious performers. With this character, Strauss and his librettist poke gentle fun at the tendency for youth to take itself too seriously as well as at what were, by then, already stereotypes about the Romantic era. Thus, they create a rather more intellectual kind of humor alongside the clownish humor of the *commedia dell'arte* troupe. The whole has a third level of humor in the conflicts among the performers created by the rich host-producer. That is, *Ariadne auf Naxos* is also a comedy about show business, a backstage farce.

All of this humor—in both the libretto and the juxtaposition of contrasting musical styles—is accomplished with astonishingly limited forces in the pit. It may be added that, of the four operas discussed in this chapter, only *Ariadne* is updated almost effortlessly. It is timeless.

Strauss's playful side is also on display as he embeds the three ascending seconds of *Der Rosenkavalier's* Octavian in the orchestra. The motive appears at the end of the Prologue's duet between The Composer and Zerbinetta (Example 8.2). This is quite poetic. The Composer, after all, is an intense young man; his impulse to kiss Zerbinetta is about to be thwarted; and he is portrayed by a mezzo-soprano.

The Composer is a short role, but difficult. The duet he sings with Zerbinetta followed by his aria is a taxing sequence. As the ringleader of the comedy troupe and an "Older Woman," Zerbinetta moves with greater confidence than does the youthful Composer. She dominates whenever she

Example 8.2 In the Zerbinetta-Composer duet of *Ariadne's* Prologue, the accompaniment (reduced to piano here) includes a quote of Octavian's theme from *Der Rosenkavalier* at 103, mm. 3–4.

is onstage. Hers is a soubrette part with somewhat more than the expected allotment of high notes and requiring even more agility than the average coloratura. As one Strauss biographer entertainingly described the role, it has ". . . breakneck embellishments that out-Rossini Donizetti."[5] Her roughly quarter-of-an-hour aria must sound effortless, of course.

There is nothing *faux* about the singing for the faux-Wagnerian Oper embedded in the second part of this opera. This is a parody on the highest level, composed with immense love for its subject. Soprano Ariadne and tenor Bacchus require spinto voices with beauty, sheen, and volume for their rhapsodic duet at the end of the opera. Still, they do not need the heft of Brünnhilde or Tristan because the orchestration is lighter than in those Wagner operas, and a conductor should be able to control any balance problems.

Indeed, it is of great interest to compare the operas *Elektra* and *Ariadne auf Naxos*. Both scores are masterful and perfectly capture the moods of the stories. Yet the first has an orchestra of 115 players while the second has a chamber orchestra of 37. These 37 players sound quite robust and—just as important—create two very different sounds reflecting the opera's two worlds apart.

Ariadne is scored for eight woodwinds, two French horns, one trumpet, one trombone, six violins, four violas, four cellos, two basses, two harps, three keyboard players, one timpani, and three percussionists. When Zerbinetta sings, the piano is very prominent and the strings are reduced to a few soloists to give a music hall sound appropriate to the *commedia dell'arte*. In the Oper, the greater use of the harmonium, harps, and full string complement with multiple lines, gives this section a pseudo-Wagnerian weight remarkable for so small an ensemble. At moments, six violins are each playing separate parts, for example. In this manner, Strauss accomplishes something close to what he achieved in his late work *Metamorphosen* (1946), where twenty-three solo strings sound like a full orchestra.

The score gets specific about two instruments. It calls for American-made harps. This design has become standard, so the harps pose no issue. We can have a balance problem with the harmonium, however. Strauss specifies a particular brand made in Stuttgart, which was a bit more powerful in sound than the standard European instrument of his time or the average harmonium available in most orchestras today. Therefore, in many of today's productions, the harmonium may be barely audible in some important sections. In such cases, it is preferable to use an electronic instrument where volume can be controlled.

Step into My Study . . .

Equally impressive as Strauss's talent for orchestration and economy of means is the musical foundation that supports the collision derby of a story. *Ariadne auf Naxos* may be thought of as a study in compound meters, representing the cast of comic characters, alternating and competing with simple meters representing the operatic performers. The opera crowd and the comedy troupe travel to the sound of different drummers. Literally. If this juxtaposition of meters is not especially obvious to all listeners in the first part (Prologue), it becomes quite salient in the second part (Oper) when the two troupes actually perform simultaneously.

It may be added that *Ariadne* serves as a fitting close for this book because it demonstrates the common thread from Mozart's work to this point in music history. While *Ariadne's* music can get complex, it is also characterized by a linking of section after section of music with a constant pulse in a manner that parallels the Mozart-Da Ponte operas. Since the same practices were not universally expected at the time that *Ariadne* was written, however, Strauss (like other later composers) is careful to express these relationships at a great many tempo and meter shifts throughout the opera. Thus he leaves no question as to his direct link to his great Austro-German forebears. There are moments when the listener should feel exactly the same surge of energy and inevitability as in a wonderful performance of a great Mozart finale. And breaks in the steady pulse may be as brief as when Figaro pretends to have hurt his foot in the Act II finale of *Le nozze di Figaro* (as discussed in Chapter 2).

Shortly after the beginning of Ariadne's aria "Es gibt ein Reich" in the Oper for example, a tempo of 84 quarter notes per minute is established (at [62]). Although the comedians' bursting onto the scene seems disruptive ([75], m. 5), the same 84 quarter notes per minute is maintained with little variation until Zerbinetta's line beginning "Großmächtige Prinzessin" ($\boxed{100}$, m. 9).

Weaving some of these elements together is straightforward technically, and Strauss anticipates many questions for the conductor. For example, he often indicates the rubato that will facilitate a tempo change between two metronome indications. The music leading into Harlekin's aria in the Oper is a case in point (between $\boxed{46}$, m. 6, and $\boxed{54}$, m. 5). Strauss supplies NICHT SCHLEPPEND and ACCELERANDO indications to prepare for a shift from 92 to 52 quarter notes per minute (in $\frac{3}{4}$ and $\frac{2}{4}$ meter, respectively). This allows me to bring that 92 quarter notes per minute up closer to 104 in order to be able to connect the sections seamlessly by downshifting to half speed at the indication ALLEGRETTO, ♩ = 52.

At the conclusion of Harlekin's aria as well, Strauss supplies a dozen measures of rubato and near-recitative before we get to ANDANTE MOSSO at 96 quarter notes per minute (at $\boxed{60}$, m. 2). I have plenty of time to decelerate in order to reach a tempo that permits something close to doubling the speed at ANDANTE MOSSO. He even supplies a relationship along with the metronome indication: with the quarter note of the new $\frac{4}{4}$ section almost equal to the eighth note of the preceding $\frac{2}{4}$ section.

(NB: This score does not use the term TEMPO PRIMO as the Italians generally do, to refer to a tempo given for the same music considerably earlier. At $\boxed{59}$ of the Oper, it may be considered a synonym for A TEMPO, a return to strictly observing a given tempo after a brief deviation.)

Strauss also often helps ease the performers from a simple meter to a compound meter and through related tempo changes by using triplets in the last few measures of the simple meter. These may appear intermittently or in only certain musical lines, so the transition is gradual. For example, in the Prologue, there is some uproar over proposed cuts, and the music teacher tries to placate his singers. In his last several measures before his $\frac{4}{4}$ music gives way to the dance master's $\frac{6}{8}$ music, we find eighth-note triplets in some musical lines, and the triplets dominate in the moments before the time signature changes (at $\boxed{73}$). Triplets also alter the listener's perception of speed and reinforce the differences between the hyper-serious Composer and the ebullient Zerbinetta (e.g., in the Prologue, before and after $\boxed{87}$).

At least as much as in any opera, however, the intersections need to be approached with planning and analysis. Disjointed music will not get across the disconnects of this story. The insanity of the characters' being thrown together can only become real when the musical transitions are as smooth as the handoffs in a relay race. We have, at least, the comfort that this most demanding of composers was very explicit about what he wanted. Difficult as the music can sometimes be, he leaves us with few questions about his intent. Still, there are instances when decisions must be made. Five examples follow.

Finding an Initial Tempo

Following the short orchestral opening, there is a combination of recitative and spoken dialogue with the orchestra playing chords or bits of melodies that will appear later. The Haushofmeister (the majordomo of the household) explains the requirements of the evening. This must be performed flexibly, and the conversations must seem natural. Strauss gives us no metronome indications in the Prologue, although he often tells us in words to speed up or slow down and he occasionally reminds us to remain in the same tempo.

After a few measures of recitative, there is an ALLEGRO section where the music begins mirroring the back and forth between the competing interests in the story. The dance master reassures his comedians that all will go smoothly, and the music teacher does likewise with his troupe (beginning at 70). After this point, almost all of the sections of the Prologue alternate between the two foundational meters (i.e., $\frac{4}{4}$ and $\frac{6}{8}$). Yet Strauss indicates the same pulse for virtually all. This has three implications for the conductor:

First, while there may be slight rubato within any section, the listener should feel no change in pulse at any of the connections where the dramatic and musical ball is tossed between the competing performers singing their respective rhythms. Second, there is a range of tempos that could be correct in getting the opera started but once I have settled on a pulse it should not vary by much. But third, the range is not vast. Even though there is not a single metronome indication in the Prologue, if I am going to observe all of the other kinds of indications and honor the relationships that appear frequently, the range of possible tempos with which I can begin the opera is limited.

One approach would be to consider the foreshadowing of the Composer's aria that is embedded in the third measure of the Prologue. Most Composers want to sing the aria in the range of 120 quarter notes a minute or so. So beginning at about 120 or 126 would be a reasonable way to approach this question of the tempo at the top of the opera.

A Matter of Style

At the end of the Zerbinetta-Composer duet with the rude interruption by the Oper characters and the music teacher calling for the cast members to take their places, the meter and tempo both change (m. 2 before **104**, illustrated in Example 8.2). The indication in this part of the Prologue is SCHNELL with the new quarter note meant to be somewhat faster than the previous half note. So SCHNELL (fast) means changing to a speed that is a bit faster than half tempo.

Here, it is at least as important to recognize that if the music teacher's tempo is too fast, what will result will be something that sounds more like Rossini than Strauss. Note that Strauss gives the music teacher mostly sixteenth notes, which will sound faster than the earlier notes even at a strictly consistent speed. Indeed, one cannot sing this in German as fast as one might in Italian.

Missing Relationships

Coming from the music teacher's music, the Composer's aria concludes the Prologue. It contains two meter changes, first from $\frac{4}{4}$ to $\frac{6}{4}$ (at **111**) and then to $\frac{2}{2}$ (expressed as ¢ at **112**). The tempo changes to SEHR SCHWUNGVOLL. This "very energetically" should be interpreted as zest or verve in addition to simple speed.

Strauss does not supply a relationship here. But notice that a melody heard in the preceding duet with Zerbinetta is repeated in the orchestra. It is played by the violins and second cello from the pickup to **111**. If I maintain a constant pulse at the meter change, I will render that melody so that it is recognizable, and that makes a lot of sense to me. Therefore, the acceleration and impetus of the melody get me to a speed where a measure of the $\frac{6}{4}$ section takes about the same time as one of the $\frac{2}{2}$ measures beginning at [112].

Planning for the Long Haul

One long arc begins at the entrance of the comedians after Ariadne's aria through Zerbinetta's bravura aria, the trio of Najade, Dryade, and Echo and, finally, the Ariadne-Bacchus duet (i.e., from [75], m. 5, through the end of the opera). Strauss gives us a number of metronome indications, but not quite all. Specifically, the last he supplies before Najade, Dryade, and Echo enter at [188] is during the comedian's scene at [166], m. 3 (ETWAS LEBHAFTER, POCO PIÙ MOSSO, ♩. = 88).

So, how should I smoothly get from the comedians' 88 dotted quarter notes per minute to Najade-Dryade-Echo's 138 half notes, marked SEHR SCHNELL (and VIVACE for good measure)? Strauss supplies a few rubato indications, the most pivotal of which is a POCO PIÙ MOSSO at [181]. Here, I want to get to about 92 dotted quarter notes per minute, returning to 88 at [186]. That will allow a solid, logical connection when Najade, Dryade, and Echo enter (at [188]), where the new quarter note will equal the previous eighth note.

At the entrance of Bacchus, we arrive at the final duet (at [215]). All of the sections of the final duet are interrelated to build to a spectacular climax. However, there is a great deal of rubato within the sections, most of which Strauss indicates. For example, a few measures before Ariadne's entrance while Bacchus has an extended high A at 104 half notes per minute, the score indicates PIÙ MOSSO (at [219]). Ariadne enters 4 measures later and sings briefly before Nyade, Dryad, and Echo re-enter with a metronome mark of 48 half notes per minute (at [221]).

Reversing that PIÙ MOSSO after Ariadne has gotten her vocal footing, and even relaxing that pace to a bit below the 104 half notes indicated at [215] will allow a smooth transition into roughly half tempo.

Context, Context, Context

The last problem in the duet and in the opera comes after the NOCH SCHNELLER that moves Ariadne through a long, high passage. After singing from offstage (usually), Bacchus has entered and Ariadne greets him thinking him to be an emissary of death. The speed through this passage will be determined by Ariadne's breath control. Then, the task will be to transition to MÄSSIG LANGSAM in the next section. There is an inconsistency in the indications, however. They are:

$\boxed{275}$: $\frac{3}{4}$ SEHR SCHNELL (MOLTO ALLEGRO), 𝅗𝅥. = 80
$\boxed{276}$, m. 5: NOCH SCHNELLER (PIÙ ALLEGRO)
$\boxed{278}$: $\frac{4}{4}$ MÄSSIG LANGSAM (MODERATO), ♩ = 72 (♩ = 𝅗𝅥. des $\frac{3}{4}$)

But this is internally inconsistent. There can be 72 quarter notes per minute at $\boxed{278}$, of course. If the new quarter note is to equal the dotted half note in the previous section, however, then there must be about 80 per minute (as indicated at $\boxed{275}$).

So what, exactly, does this mean? As a rule, I take a new metronome mark very seriously, but try to give it the right context and preparation. It happens that after giving Ariadne all the support I can through this difficult passage, I have 5 measures after her last note before MÄSSIG LANGSAM. I can use these to decelerate unobtrusively until we slide directly into the new tempo without seeming to have hit a bump. A CALANDO is appropriate. This is a gentle deceleration, less obvious than a RALLENTANDO. Specifically, I can tap the brakes to about 72 dotted half notes up to the MÄSSIG LANGSAM. This positions me to make the transition to a tempo that is one-third as fast but unchanging in pulse.

This discussion illustrates how much metronome indications should mean to musicians. They give us the composer's expectation of a speed at any given moment, but more. When analyzed and compared with others in the same score, they show us how the pieces fit together. Thus, even if I have reason to change a speed, the relationships become all the more important in that they reveal the plan, the big picture, the architecture, and how the performance should hang together. They become all the more important as works get bigger or increasingly complex, or both, as we so often encounter in Richard Strauss's music.

Thus, metronome markings are a gift from a composer who uses them. It is imperative that we acquire the ability to come close to duplicating the pacing indicated. We are only human, of course, and machine-like exactitude for hours on-end is not possible or even desirable. We need to allow for expression, and in music with words, we must attend to the story being told.

So we might say that metronome indications are like rules: They may be disregarded at times, but only with good reason by those who have complete mastery of their craft and an understanding of the style of the work under consideration.

My favorite things

The conclusion of the opera (from 328). It raises this chamber opera to the grandest level. In a loving tribute to Richard Wagner, the orchestra seems like an ensemble of one hundred.

Postscript and Acknowledgments

> My excitement at these concerts was something new, for I came to understand that music, like every art, is a genuine requirement of man.
>
> —Dimitri Shostakovich[1]

I was born into a world of music and—apart from the incalculable satisfaction I get out of studying and listening to music—few things in life give me more pleasure than knowing that I have succeeded in sharing this rich and wonderful world with others. Friends and relatives can testify that, at an early age, I began accosting them with "Listen to *this*!" as they came through the door. And, still now, it makes my day when a colleague expresses appreciation for my giving him some new insight or a listener tells me that the enriching experience of listening to great music was further enhanced because my pre-performance talk guided her listening. This book is born of that same love and impulse to share music.

I owe both my love of and fluency in music, first, to my grandfather. Having grown hard of hearing, he had been forced to retire from playing trumpet with the Metropolitan Opera orchestra at about the time of my birth. He spoke to me and taught me to read music and sight sing in four clefs by about the age of three. His misfortune was my incredible good luck. That kind of immersion training at a such a tender age cannot be duplicated. His love of music and me has sustained me throughout my whole life, even decades after his death.

I had music on both sides of my family. My mother was a pianist; in fact, she was playing rehearsals for my uncle when she first met my father. She was a gentle, patient, and very generous human being, qualities I try to emulate with varying degrees of success. She was also a person of sincere spirituality. Like my grandfather, she believed in the redemptive power of art and love.

Soon enough, I met my uncle Nicola, my father's brother. He was many things to me: a role model, a surrogate father for the time I studied in Italy, a teacher, a colleague, and a friend. He was a person of style and taste both in his music and in his personal life. Above all, he was an example of a musician dedicated to the highest standards and a tireless warrior for those standards.

Before I began my career, adults outside of my family helped shape my music making. Ada Kopetz-Korf was my piano teacher from the age of thirteen and a second mother, and she remained my great good friend until her passing. She was herself a natural pianist and poetic soul, and she helped me in many different ways: with my piano playing but also with my bouts of nerves and the usual teenage anxieties. Most important, she taught me to recognize my own strengths and follow my own star.

Nicolas Flagello was my composition teacher in conservatory. He was a marvelous composer, a gifted pianist, a linguist, an excellent amateur painter, and a deep thinker. Like Samuel Barber, Leonard Bernstein, and virtually all of the composers of his era who had a commitment to tonality and the use of music for emotional connection, he was out of fashion, with the strictly serial composers in ascendance. His encouragement and collegiality helped build the confidence so essential to any performer—even though my fugues were nothing to write home about.

My relationship with composer-conductor Bruno Maderna, whom I met at Salzburg's Mozarteum academy, was similar. His musical language was decidedly avant-garde, but his personality was unabashedly romantic, and his musical tastes were catholic to say the least. He, too, buoyed me through late adolescence and—for better or worse—gave me insights into the music business.

Early in my professional career, at the Dallas Opera, I met chorus master Roberto Benaglio, who had previously spent twenty-five years at La Scala. He was an inspiring personality. With directions about inflection and dynamics, he could transform a chorus of many into a distinct character in the drama. We could talk about music generally, and his knowledge of opera was about as deep as it can get. While living in the apartment next door for a time, I observed that he began each day playing a half-hour of Bach on the piano. When I remarked upon it to him, he replied, "It keeps me healthy." The older I get, the more I agree.

My good friend and valued interlocutor, conductor Richard Woitach made an introduction for me in 1983. He prevailed upon Erich Leinsdorf to go over *Salome* with a complete stranger, preparatory to his first foray into that corner of the repertory. Leinsdorf promised me one hour. This turned into six sessions of about two hours each. He shared not only a wealth of practical information about *Salome*, but a treasure trove of musical insight, and he refused to take a dime from me. He was possibly the most concise and articulate teacher I have ever known.

In much the same way and for many of the same reasons, I will always treasure esteemed musicologists Linda B. Fairtile and Philip Gossett. Each unstintingly shared a deep knowledge of history, leavened with a musical sensibility and an understanding of performers.

There have been too many colleagues whom I have learned from and treasure to enumerate. So I will have to skip forward to the gestation of this book. There have been a number of people who encouraged me, served as sounding boards, and lent assistance. First among these is public relations expert Nancy Shear, one of the most positive people I have ever had the pleasure and great good luck of having in my life. Also of inestimable service were Dan Guss and Raphael Zinman in her office.

Editor Karen DeVinney at University of North Texas Press embraced this project wholeheartedly, and demonstrated admirable patience with utter novices. Music engraver Bill Holab gets credit for helping to polish the final product. And I can never sufficiently thank colleagues Christopher Cano, Arthur Fagen, and Francesco Milioto for doing me the honor of evaluating an early manuscript.

My manager, John Miller has been supportive in this effort as in all efforts over many years. For a regular dose of encouragement, I could also count on my neighbor Andrew Schulman, a guitarist and author himself. And friends Judy Andriola, Jim Corcoran, and Christoph Irmscher demonstrated remarkable stick-to-itiveness as lay readers, going well above the call of duty as friends.

And last, there is my wife Jeanne. After more than four decades with me, and with no formal music education, she digested a mountain of technical and historical information and regularly found a practical way to overcome obstacles. And I learned what a technical writer does.

Appendix: Scores Cited

See the preface for a discussion of our choice of scores. For each work below, the scores cited most often in this book are listed first. Entries are prefixed with **O** for orchestra score, **V** for piano-vocal reduction, or **M** for manuscript (facsimile). There are also notes about finding citations as well as some errata in the entries below. But this is not a systematic review of every page of each score. We report the problems and anomalies that arose in the course of documenting the citations in this book.

Many scores, including all principal references, are available free on-line, mostly through the Petrucci Music Library of the International Music Score Library Project (IMSLP). Therefore, each work's IMSLP file numbers are supplied below. Simply enter *https://imslp.org/wiki/Special:ReverseLookup/<IMSLP number>* into your browser's address bar. Any file number listed under a work will take you to a web page that links to all of the files for that work. And please consider joining IMSLP in support of its valuable work.

The Bärenreiter critical editions of Mozart's orchestra scores are available through the Mozarteum Foundation and the Packard Humanities Institute. Further instructions are supplied below.

Bach, Johann Sebastian

Ach Gott, vom Himmel sieh darein, BWV 2.

O *Bach-Gesellschaft Ausgabe, Band 1*, pp. 53–72. Ed. Moritz Hauptmann. First edition, Leipzig: Breitkopf und Härtel, 1851. Plate B.W.I. IMSLP No. 00721.

Beethoven, Ludwig van

Symphony No. 9, Op.125.

O *Ludwig van Beethovens Werke, Serie 1*: Symphonien, Nr. 9. Leipzig: Breitkopf und Härtel, 1863. Plate B.9. IMSLP Nos. 61850, 61851, 61852, 61853.

Bellini, Vincenzo

I Capuleti e i Montecchi. Libretto by Felice Romani.

O 3 vols. Boca Raton: Edwin F. Kalmus and Co., Inc., n.d. IMSLP Nos. 597369, 597370, 597371, 597372, 597373, 597374, 597375, 597376.

Notes: The Ricordi vocal and Belwin Mills reprint have a table of contents that does not supply musical numbers. But their ten sections correspond to the Kalmus musical numbers. The Kalmus has no table of contents, but after the overture: No. 1 ("Coro d'introduzione") is on Kalmus p. 51; No. 2, 79; No. 3, 126; No. 4, 179; No. 5, 194; No. 6, 270; No. 7, 295; No. 8, 409; No. 9, 449; No. 10, 522.

V Milan: G. Ricordi, n.d. Plate 42043. Reprinted Melville, NY: Belwin Mills n.d. (ca. 1970). Catalog 9399. IMSLP No. 130658.

Notes: The Ricordi vocal scores prior to the Toscani reduction contain the same rehearsal numbers as the Kalmus orchestra score, but the Belwin Mills reprint omits these.

M A facsimile edition of Bellini's original autograph manuscript, vol. 3 in *Early Romantic Opera*, eds. Philip Gossett and Charles Rosen. New York: Garland, 1981.

Notes: This is the manuscript identified as the principal source for the Ricordi critical edition of 2003.

O Ed. Claudio Toscani, vol. 6 in *Edizione critica delle opere di Vincenzo Bellini*. Milan: Casa Ricordi - BMG Ricordi S.p.A., 2003.

V Reduction Claudio Toscani, based on the critical edition of the orchestra score. Milan: Universal Music Publishing Ricordi S.r.l., 2003.

Norma. Libretto by Felice Romani.

O Milan: G. Ricordi, n.d. Plate P.R. 1385. IMSLP Nos. 130342, 130343.

Notes: *Norma* has twenty scenes after the overture:

Act I: Scene 1, p. 33; Scene 2, 65; Scene 3, 95; Scene 4, 115; Scene 5, 156; Scene 6, 163; Scene 7, 197; Scene 8, 208; Scene 9, 229.

Act II: Scene 1, 265; Scene 2, 274; Scene 3, 275 (not numbered); Scene 4, 308; Scene 5, 323 (numbered 5a); Scene 6, 335; Scene 7, 344; Scene 8, 362; Scene 9, 364; Scene 10, 371; Finale, 392.

V Milan: G. Ricordi, n.d. Plate 41684. Reprinted New York: G. Schirmer, Ed. 2253, n.d. Plate 44001. IMSLP No. 112077.

Notes: This score has the same twenty scenes after the overture:

Act I: Scene 1, p. 10; Scene 2, 27; Scene 3, 49; Scene 4, 56; Scene 5, 86; Scene 6, 91; Scene 7, 110; Scene 8, 116; Scene 9, 132.

Act II: Scene 1, 159; Scene 2, 166; Scene 3, 167; Scene 4, 188; Scene 5, 196; Scene 6, 205; Scene 7, 211; Scene 8, 221; Scene 9, 223; Scene 10, 229; Finale, 241.

M Manuscript from the Biblioteca Conservatorio L.Cherubini, Firenze. n.d. IMSLP Nos. 108290, 108291.

M A facsimile edition of the original autograph manuscript and the surviving sketches, vol. 4 in *Early Romantic Opera*, eds. Philip Gossett and Charles Rosen. New York: Garland, 1983.

Bizet, Georges

Carmen. Libretto by Henri Meilhac and Ludovic Halévy.

O Leipzig: C.F. Peters, n.d. (ca.1920). Plate 9028. Reprinted Boca Raton: Edwin F. Kalmus, n.d. (after 1987). IMSLP Nos. 30415, 30416, 30417, 30418.

Notes: The twenty-seven musical numbers are listed in the table of contents with the Prelude being No. 1 and the three Entractes being unnumbered.

V Ed. Ernest Guiraud, trans. Theodore Baker (1851–1934). New York: G. Schirmer, 1895. Plate 12117. IMSLP No. 06512.

O First edition, Paris: Choudens Père et Fils, n.d. [1877]. Plate A.C. 3795. Reprinted Budapest: Könemann, 1994. Plate K 1005. IMSLP Nos. 20318, 26096, 26097, 26098, 26099.

O & V Ed. Fritz Oeser. Publication facts are the same for the orchestra and piano-vocal scores. Kassel: Alkor-Edition, 1964.

Donizetti, Gaetano

Don Pasquale. Libretto by Giovanni Ruffini, after Angelo Anelli.

O Milan: G. Ricordi, n.d. (ca.1920). Plate P.R. 36. *Reissue* 1961. IMSLP Nos. 111627, 111628, 111629.

V Milan: G. Ricordi, n.d. [1870]. Plate 42051. Reprinted New York: Edwin F. Kalmus, n.d. (after 1969). Catalog 6161 (Belwin-Mills after 1976). IMSLP No. 111941.

Notes: The orchestra and piano-vocal scores share rehearsal numbers, which restart at [1] with each act. Musical numbers are the same beginning with "Introduzione" through No. 10, but then diverge. The eleventh title in the piano-vocal score is part of No. 10 in the orchestra score. Then the "Recitativo e duetto" is No. 11 in the orchestra score; the "Serenata" and "Notturno" are combined in No. 12; and the finale (the fifteenth title in the piano-vocal score) is No. 13 in the orchestra score.

Lucia di Lammermoor. Libretto by Salvatore Cammarano.

O Milan: G. Ricordi, n.d. Reprinted *Lucia di Lammermoor in Full Score*, Mineola: Dover Publications, 1992. IMSLP Nos. 113041, 113042, 113043.

Notes: No. 7 is not identified as such on p. 211, which also lacks a page number. The orchestra score lists a two-part Act I followed by Act II; we will keep it simple by referring to three acts as the Schirmer score does, beginning Act III with No. 11.

V Trans. Natalia Macfarren. New York: G. Schirmer, 1898. Plate 14047. IMSLP No. 409318.

M Manuscript facsimile from the collection of Senatore Conte Dott. Giovanni Treccani degli Alfieri, forward Guido Zavadini, curator of the Museo Donizettiano of Bergamo, art director Emilio Bestetti. Milan: Riproduzioni Istituto di Alta Cultura, March 1941–XIX, No. 121 of a 300-copy limited edition (in the author's private collection).

Gounod, Charles

Faust. Libretto by Jules Barbier.

O Published as *Margarete*. Berlin: Bote and Bock, n.d. [1869]. Plate 8292. IMSLP No. 98103, 98104, 98105, 98106, 98107.

Notes: The files correspond to five acts. The Act I file contains Nos. 1–4; Act II, 5–9; Act III, 10–13; Act IV, 19–26; Act V, 27–32.

V Reduction Léo Delibes, trans. H. T. Chorley, trans. revised and completed Theodore Baker. New York: G. Schirmer, 1902. Plate 16100. IMSLP No. 247609.

O The much sought-after Dover edition combines the Bote and Bock edition above with the complete ballet music (London: Chapelle and Co., Ltd., n.d.) and "Si le bonheur" from the Mapelson edition of the complete opera (New York: Mapelson, n.d.). The editors also added a substantial amount of helpful front matter. (*Faust in Full Score*, New York: Dover Publications, Inc., 1994.)

Mozart, Wolfgang Amadeus

For each opera, the first orchestra score listed below is the "urtext" edition published by Bärenreiter (Kassel, Basel, Tours, London). Reference to a BA number for an orchestra score in the following listings means that the copyrighted score is available free for non-commercial use through the Digital Mozart Edition (DME) portal (http://dme.mozarteum.at/DME/nma/nmapub_srch.php). On the portal page, icons link to either the complete score beginning with the title page (♪) or a digital table of contents (I) where smaller sections of the opera may be viewed directly or downloaded in PDF format.

Notes: The portal offers a choice of languages. Titles of works are translated accordingly. So on the Spanish page for example, *Die Zauberflöte* is *La flauta mágica*. On the English page, *Le nozze di Figaro* is listed as *The Marriage of Figaro* although it retains its original Italian name on the German page. This caveat only pertains to web site navigation, not the scores of course.

Il dissoluto punito, ossia il Don Giovanni, K. 527. Libretto by Lorenzo Da Ponte.

O Ed. Wolfgang Plath, Wolfgang Rehm, 1968. BA 4550.

V Trans. Natalia Macfarren. New York: G. Schirmer, 1900. Plate 15147. IMSLP No. 296760.

Notes: No. 10 in Bärenreiter is No. 10a in Schirmer. No. 10b in Schirmer is in the appendix of Bärenreiter as are Schirmer's Nos. 21b and 21c.

O Ed. Georg Schünemann. Leipzig: C.F. Peters, No.4505, n.d.[1941]. Plate 11456. Reprinted New York: Dover Publications, 1974. IMSLP Nos. 140963, 140964.

M Autograph facsimile from the Bibliothèque nationale, Paris. n.d. (ca. 1787). IMSLP Nos. 293277, 293279, 293281.

Notes: The preface to Bärenreiter's *Don Giovanni* identifies this autograph as the most important source for its editors.

Le nozze di Figaro, K. 492. Libretto by Lorenzo Da Ponte.

O Ed. Ludwig Finscher, 1973. BA 4565.

V Reduction Gustav Friedrich Kogel. Leipzig: C. F. Peters, n.d. Plate 8087. IMSLP No. 220533.

Notes: Bärenreiter Nos. 8 and 9 are here combined as No. 8. So Act I in Peters closes with No. 9 rather than Bärenreiter's No. 10. Thereafter musical numbers are lower by one until the end of Act III. Then Bärenreiter's No. 23 is split into Nos. 22 and 23 in Peters so that both scores end Act III with No. 23. In Act IV, numbering is the same in both scores, and both end with No. 29.

Die Zauberflöte, K. 620. Libretto by Emanuel Schikaneder.

O Ed. Gernot Gruber, Alfred Orel, 1970. BA 4553.

V Ed. Berthold Tours, trans. Natalia Macfarren. London: Novello, n.d. IMSLP No. 225842.

Notes: The index of musical numbers is in the back, physical p. 185.

Puccini, Giacomo

Notes: For all of these works, the orchestra and piano-vocal scores share rehearsal numbers, which restart at [1] with each act.

La bohème, SC 67. Libretto by Giuseppe Giacosa and Luigi Illica.

O Milan: G. Ricordi and C., n.d. (1920). Plate 115561. *Reissue* - n.d. (ca.1950). Plate P.R. 110. IMSLP No. 43676.

V Reduction Carlo Carignani, trans. William Grist and Percy Pinkerton. Milan: G. Ricordi, 1917. Plate 115494. IMSLP No. 164041.

Gianni Schicchi, SC 88. Libretto by Gioachino Forzano.

O Milan: G. Ricordi, 1918. Reprinted, Mineola: Dover Publications, 1996. IMSLP No. 524344.

V Reduction Carlo Carignani. Milan: G. Ricordi, 1918. Plate 117408. Reprinted, Mineola: Dover Publications, 1996. IMSLP 524345.

Madama Butterfly, SC 74. Libretto by Giuseppe Giacosa and Luigi Illica.

O Milan: G. Ricordi, 1907. *Reissue* (new engraving), 1920. Plate P.R. 112. IMSLP Nos. 43383, 43384.

V Third Italian edition. Reduction Carlo Carignani. Milan: G. Ricordi and C., 1907. Plate 110000. IMSLP No. 23356. (NB: p. 98 in this file should be 99, and p. 99 should be 98.)

Manon Lescaut, SC 64. Libretto by Ruggiero Leoncavallo, et al.

O Milan: G. Ricordi, 1915. Plate 115300. Reprinted, Mineola: Dover Publications, 1995. IMSLP Nos. 43385, 43386, 43387, 43388.

V Reduction Carlo Carignani. Milan: G. Ricordi, 1893. Plate 95567. IMSLP No. 416194.

La rondine, SC 83. Libretto by Giuseppe Adami.

O Milan: Casa Musicale Sonzogno, 1917. Reprinted, Boca Raton: Edwin F. Kalmus, n.d. (after 1993), Catalog A 7853. IMSLP Nos. 48414, 48415, 48417.

V Reduction Carlo Carignani. Milan: Casa Musicale Sonzogno, 1917. Plate 2022 S. IMSLP No. 23368.

Tosca, SC 69. Libretto by Giuseppe Giacosa and Luigi Illica.

O Milan: G. Ricordi, n.d. (1900). Reprinted *Tosca in Full Score*, Mineola: Dover Publications, 1991. IMSLP Nos. 43370, 43371, 43372.

V Reduction Carlo Carignani, trans. William Beatty-Kingston. Milan: G. Ricordi, 1905. Plate 109916. IMSLP No. 21958.

Il tabarro, SC 85. Libretto by Giuseppe Adami.

O Milan: G. Ricordi, n.d. (1918). Reprinted, Mineola: Dover Publications, 1996. IMSLP No. 48473.

V Milan: Ricordi, 1918. Plate 117404. IMSLP No. 161910.

Turandot, SC 91. Libretto by Giuseppe Adami and Renato Simoni. Completion and arrangement by Franco Alfano.

O Milan: G. Ricordi, 1926. Plate P.R. 117. IMSLP No. 167895.

V Reduction Guido Zuccoli. Milan: G. Ricordi & C., 1929. Plate 121329. IMSLP No. 35165.

Rossini, Gioachino

Il barbiere di Siviglia. Libretto by Cesare Sterbini.

O Milan: G. Ricordi, (ca.1920). Reprinted Mineola: Dover Publications, 1989. IMSLP Nos. 116374, 116375.

V Sesto San Giovanni, Italy: Casa Editrice Madella, 1913. IMSLP No. 280516.

M Manuscript facsimile from Bologna, Civico Museo Bibliografico Musicale, 2 vols., introductory essay by Philip Gossett. Lucca: Libreria Musicale Italiana, 1993.

O Ed. Alberto Zedda. Milan: G. Ricordi, 1969.
Notes: The 1969 Zedda edition pagination is identical to that of the older Ricordi score reprinted by Dover (cited above) and Broude Bros. (New York, n.d. [before 1970]), with the addition of rehearsal numbers. Its nineteen musical numbers are slightly different from Schirmer's twenty: Zedda combines Schirmer's Nos. 1–3 into No. 1. Thereafter, Zedda's musical numbers are 2 lower (e.g., Schirmer's No. 4 is Zedda's No. 2 and so on) until the end. At the end, Zedda makes Nos. 17–19 out of Schirmer's Nos. 19–20, with the finale beginning after the recit "Insomma io ho tutti i torti!" Schirmer's No. 20 encompasses that recit and the finale.

O Ed. Alberto Zedda, 2009 edition, vol. 17 in *Edizione critica delle opere di Gioachino Rossini*. Milan: Fondazione Rossini Pesaro - Ricordi, 2009.
Notes: The 2009 Zedda edition is newly typeset and has many more pages; it also organizes the opera into 18 musical numbers rather than the 19 of 1969; but it retains the rehearsal numbers of the 1969 edition and adds measure numbers.

O Ed. Patricia B. Brauner. Kassel: Bärenreiter, 2008 (TP 411).

La Cenerentola. Libretto by Jacopo Ferretti.

O Milan: G. Ricordi, n.d. Reprinted New York: Edwin F. Kalmus, n.d. (after 1933). Catalogue A 3031. IMSLP Nos. 114606, 114607, 114608.

V Milan: G. Ricordi, n.d. (1878). Plate 45707. IMSLP No. 111966.
Notes: The Ricordi piano-vocal score and Kalmus orchestra score share rehearsal numbers, which re-start at [1] for Act II (designated Act III in Kalmus).

O Ed. Alberto Zedda, vol. 20 in *Edizione critica delle opere di Gioachino Rossini*. Milan: Fondazione Rossini Pesaro - Ricordi, 1998.

Saint-Saëns, Camille

Samson et Dalila, Op. 47. Libretto by Ferdinand Lemaire.

O Paris: Durand and Cie., n.d. (ca.1929). Plate D. and F. 11,945. Reprinted Boca Raton: Edwin F. Kalmus, n.d. (after 1987). IMSLP Nos. 25920, 25921, 25922.

Notes: This score has twelve sets of rehearsal letters beginning with [A] and one beginning with [Aa] . The start of a new set almost coincides with the start of scenes named in the table of contents. We will use page numbers primarily and use the rehearsal letters to add direction.

V Trans. Nathan Haskell Dole. New York: G. Schirmer, 1892. Plate 40163. IMSLP No. 104974.

Notes: The breakdown of scenes is the same as in the orchestra score. The rehearsal letters are almost the same but not reliably so.

Strauss, Richard

For all of these works, the orchestra and piano-vocal scores share rehearsal numbers, which restart at [1] with each act.

Ariadne auf Naxos, Op. 60. Libretto by Hugo von Hofmannsthal.

O Berlin: Adolph Fürstner, 1916. Reprinted Mineola: Dover Publications, 1993. IMSLP Nos. 46019 (Vorspiel [Prologue, p. 1–88c]), 46020 (*Oper* overture and scenes [p. 89–151]), 46021 (Zerbinetta's aria and scenes [p. 152–200]), 46022 (*Oper* finale [p. 201–299]).

Notes: Rehearsal numbers restart at [1] with the overture to the *Oper*. We will refer to the Prologue as such and the remainder as Part II (i.e., material with the second set of rehearsal numbers).

V Reduction Otto Singer II, Berlin: Adolf Fürstner, 1916. Plate A. 6368 F. Reprinted London: Boosey and Hawkes, n.d. (after 1940). Plate B. and H. 15781. IMSLP No. 44688.

Elektra, Op. 58. Libretto by Hugo von Hofmannsthal.

O Berlin: Adolph Fürstner, 1916. IMSLP No. 24779.

V Reduction Carl Besl, trans. Alfred Kalisch. Berlin: Adolph Fürstner, 1910. Reprinted London: Boosey and Hawkes, n.d. (after 1943). Plate H. 15780. IMSLP No. 33694.

Der Rosenkavalier, Op. 59. Libretto by Hugo von Hofmannsthal.

O Berlin: Adolph Fürstner, 1910. Plate 5900. Reprinted London: Boosey and Hawkes, 1943. IMSLP Nos. 31872, 31873, 31874.

V Reduction Carl Besl, trans. Alfred Kalisch. Berlin: Adolph Fürstner, 1910, 1912. Plate F. 500. Reprinted London: Boosey and Hawkes, n.d. (after 1945). IMSLP Nos. 117568, 117569, 117570.

Salome, Op. 54. Libretto by the composer.

O Berlin: Adolph Fürstner, 1905. Plate A. 5500 F. Reprinted Mineola: Dover Publications, 1981. IMSLP Nos. 01663, 01664.

Notes: The "Dance of the Seven Veils" has its own rehearsal letters [A] through [Z] followed by [A] through [K]. The dance begins after twelve measures of [247], and singing resumes at 5 measures before [248].

V Reduction Otto Singer II, trans. Alfred Kalisch. Berlin: Adolph Fürstner, 1905. Plate A. 5503 F. Reprinted London: Boosey and Hawkes, 1943. Plate H. 15570. IMSLP No. 422501.

Verdi, Giuseppe

Aida. Libretto by Antonio Ghislanzoni.

O Milan: G. Ricordi, n.d. [1913]. Reprinted Mineola: Dover Publications, 1989. IMSLP Nos. 42193, 42194, 42195, 42196.

Notes: In places, rehearsal letters are mixed up. (At the end of Act II, for example, the sequence is T, U, Z, Y, X, W.) Reconciling all of this for the purpose of reading this book would seem to be an unnecessary burden. We therefore refer to the rehearsal letters exactly as printed and supply page numbers where it seems helpful to do so.

In Act I, rehearsal letters restart at [A] on p. 65, near the end of Scene 1; and Scene 2 starts on p. 73. In Act II, Scene 1 uses rehearsal letters [A] through [L]; Scene 2 starts on p. 144, and rehearsal letters restart with [A] on p. 148. Act III has one scene and one set of rehearsal letters. And Act IV has one set of rehearsal letters, with Scene 2 beginning with [Q] on p. 413.

V Trans. Mrs. G.G. Laurence. New York: G. Schirmer, 1897. Plate 13573. IMSLP No. 09436.

Notes: Act I's scenes begin on p. 1 and p. 60; Act II, 79 and 111; Act IV, 258 and 296. Act III, beginning on p. 204, has one scene.

Un ballo in maschera. Libretto by Antonio Somma.

O Milan: G. Ricordi, 1914. Plate 3031279. Reprinted *Un Ballo in Maschera in Full Score*, Mineola: Dover Publications, 1996. IMSLP Nos. 48142, 48143, 48144.

Notes: Rehearsal numbers restart at [1] in each act.

V Reduction Arthur Sullivan and Josiah Pittman, trans. Charles Lamb Kenney. London: Boosey and Co., n.d. [1871]. IMSLP No. 142308.

Falstaff. Libretto by Arrigo Boito.

Notes: These scores share the same rehearsal numbers, which restart at [1] in each act.

O Milan: G. Ricordi, n.d. [1893]. Reprinted *Falstaff in Full Score*, Mineola: Dover Publications, 1980. IMSLP Nos. 42197, 42198, 42199.

V Reduction Carlo Carignani. Milan: Ricordi, 1893. Plate 96000. IMSLP No. 141079.

Messa da Requiem

O Leipzig: Ernst Eulenburg, n.d. (ca.1910). Plate E.E. 4864. IMSLP No. 407348.

V Reduction Michele Saladino. Milan: G. Ricordi and C., n.d. [1875]. Plate 44004. IMSLP No. 306329.

Otello. Libretto by Arrigo Boito.

O Milan: G. Ricordi, n.d. [1913]. Plate 113955. Reprinted *Otello in Full Score*, Mineola: Dover Publications, 1986. IMSLP Nos. 48188, 48189, 48190, 48191, 48192.

Notes: After [Z] in Act I, rehearsal letters continue with [AA] on p. 71; Act II, [A] on 250: Act III, [A] on 389; Act IV, [AA] on 497. In addition, in Act III, the first rehearsal letter [J] on p. 331 is misidentified as [I].

V Reduction Michele Saladino. Milan: Ricordi, n.d. (1886). Plate 51023. IMSLP No. 24575.

Notes: The orchestra and vocal scores share rehearsal letters. In Act I, [AA] starts on p. 47; Act II second [A], 171; Act III second [A], 252; Act IV [AA], 344.

Rigoletto. Libretto by Francesco Maria Piave.

O Milan: G. Ricordi, 1914. Reprinted Mineola: Dover Publications, 1992. IMSLP Nos. 46110, 46111, 46112.

Notes: This score has one set of rehearsal numbers, [1] through [59], running continuously through fourteen musical numbers.

V Reduction Luigi Truzzi [uncredited], trans. Natalia Macfarren. New York: G. Schirmer, 1902. Plate 15959. IMSLP Nos. 65742, 65743, 65744.

O Ed. Martin Chusid, vol. 17 in Edizione critica delle opere di Giuseppe Verdi. Chicago: The University of Chicago Press; Milan: G. Ricordi & C., S.P.A., 1983.

V Reduction Martin Chusid, based on the critical edition of the orchestra score, trans. Andrew Porter. Chicago and London: The University of Chicago Press; Milan: Ricordi, 1985.

La traviata. Libretto by Francesco Maria Piave.

O Milan: G. Ricordi and C., 1914. Plate 113958 (P.R. 157). Reprinted Mineola: Dover Publications, 1990. IMSLP Nos. 113749, 113750, 113751.

Notes: The musical numbers are **Act I:** No. 1, p. 1; No. 2, 7; No. 3, 80. In **Act II:** No. 4, 108; No 5, 133; No. 6, 181; No. 7, 224. In **Act III:** No. 8, 342; No. 9, 360, No. 10, 366; No. 11, 404.

V Milan: Ricordi, n.d. Plate 42314. IMSLP No. 392068.

Notes: To reconcile with the orchestra score, the musical numbers in the table of contents may be numbered 1 through 11, including the prelude as No. 1 and the combination of "Ah no, severo scritto mi lasciava" and "Di Provenza il mar, il suol" as No. 6.

O Critical edition, ed. Fabrizio Della Seta, v. 19 of *Le opere di Giuseppe Verdi*, coordinating ed. Philip Gossett. Chicago and London: The University of Chicago Press; Milan: Ricordi, 1996.

V Reduction Fabrizio Della Seta, based on the critical edition of the orchestra score, 2 vols. Chicago and London: The University of Chicago Press; Milan: Ricordi, 2001.

Il trovatore. Libretto by Salvatore Cammarano.

O Milan: G. Ricordi, n.d. Reprinted Mineola: Dover Publications, 1994. IMSLP Nos. 48611, 48612, 48613, 48614.

V Trans. Natalia Macfarren. New York: G. Schirmer, 1898. Plate 14140. IMSLP No. 408629.

Wagner, Richard

Der fliegende Holländer, WWV 22. Libretto by the composer.

O Ed. Felix Weingartner. Berlin: Adolph Fürstner, n.d. (ca.1887). Plate A. 2760 F. Reprinted Mineola: Dover Publications, 1988. IMSLP Nos. 63866, 63867, 63868, 63869.

V Reduction Gustav Friedrich Kogel. Berlin: Adolph Fürstner, 1909. Plate A. 5777 F. IMSLP No. 330647.

Tristan und Isolde, WWV 90. Libretto by the composer.

O First edition (reprint), Leipzig: Breitkopf und Härtel, n.d. [1860]. Plate 10000. Reprinted New York: Edwin F. Kalmus, n.d. (after 1933). IMSLP No. 66167.

V Reduction Felix Mottl and Gustav Friedrich Kogel. Leipzig: C.F. Peters, n.d. (ca.1914). Plate 9815. IMSLP Nos. 330635, 330636.

Die Walküre, WWV 86B. Libretto by the composer.

O Ed. Felix Mottl. Leipzig: C.F. Peters, n.d. (ca.1910). Plate 10170. Reprinted New York: Dover Publications, 1978. IMSLP Nos. 36269, 45323, 45496.

V Reduction Felix Mottl. Leipzig: C.F. Peters, Ed. 3404, 1914. Plate 9803. IMSLP No. 316546.

Endnotes

Notes for Preface

1. James Harding, *Saint-Saëns and His Circle* (London: Chapman & Hall, 1965), 209.
2. Leonard Bernstein, *The Joy of Music* (New York: Simon & Schuster, 1959), 149.
3. Aaron Copland, *What to Listen for in Music*, rev. ed. (New York: Mentor, 1999), chapter 2.
4. Philip Gossett, "The Romance of the Critical Edition," in *Divas and Scholars: Performing Italian Opera* (Chicago: Univ. of Chicago Press, 2006), chapter 5.

Notes for Chapter 1

1. Felix Weingartner, *On Conducting*, trans. Ernest Newman (London: Breitkopf & Härtel, 1906), 43.
2. Discussing *Symphony of Psalms* in Igor Stravinsky and Robert Craft, *Dialogues and A Diary* (Garden City: Doubleday and Company, Inc., 1963), 76.
3. Normally, a fermata should only appear over a single note. The large fermata in m. 3 of Example 1.1 (based on Bärenreiter) is something different, more like an indication. It reminds us that there is time for improvisation; it invites decoration. It is only fair to add that while most scores have some fermata somewhere in this measure (see vocal score), there is none in the manuscript available for download (which Bärenreiter's editors identify as their most important source).
4. Erich Leinsdorf, *The Composer's Advocate: A Radical Orthodoxy for Musicians* (New Haven: Yale Univ. Press, 1981), chapter 4.
5. Leonard *Slatkin, Conducting Business: Unveiling the Mystery Behind the Maestro* (Milwaukee: Amadeus Press, 2012), 264–270.
6. Hector Berlioz, *The Orchestral Conductor: Theory of His Art*, trans. unidentified (New York: Carl Fisher, Inc., 1900), 18.

Notes for Chapter 2

1. To his father, quoted in *Mozart: The Man and the Artist, As Revealed in His Own Words*, ed. Friedrich Kerst, trans. Henry Edward Krehbiel (New York: B. W. Huebsch, 1905), 26.

2. Leinsdorf, 102–126.
3. There is a similar relationship in Beethoven's Ninth Symphony at the end of the last movement, and few attend to this detail in this case either. The violins' eighth notes of the PRESTISSIMO (p. 267, 𝅗𝅥 = 132) equal the thirty-second notes of the MAESTOSO (p. 273, ♩ = 60), and that relationship continues into the final PRESTISSIMO (p. 274) where the passage is again written in eighth notes.

Notes for Chapter 3

1. "To the Young People's Society, Greenpoint Presbyterian Church, Brooklyn," Feb. 16, 1901, quoted in John Bartlett, *Familiar Quotations*, 15th and 125th anniversary edition, revised and enlarged, ed. Emily Morison Beck (Boston and Toronto: Little Brown and Co., 1980), s.v. "Twain, Mark."
2. Gossett, 293.
3. Note that when the aria and the faster cabaletta that follows are discussed as a single musical form (the "aria-cabaletta") the first part may also be referred to as the "cantabile."
4. The complicated history of performing pitch is beyond the scope of this book. For a look at its seemingly endless variability over four centuries, see Bruce Haynes, *A History of Performing Pitch: The Story of "A"* (Lanham, MD: The Scarecrow Press, 2002).
5. To Count Leopoldo Cicognara, quoted in Sam Morgenstern, ed., *Composers on Music: An Anthology of Composers' Writings from Palestrina to Copland* (New York: Pantheon Books, 1956), 104.
6. From an 1834 letter to the librettist of *I puritani*, Carlo Pepoli, in *Corrispondenze Epistolari di Carlo Pepoli: Lettere di Vincenzo Bellini*, vol. 2 of *Ricordanze Biografiche* (Bologna: Tipografia Fava e Garagnani, 1881 [300-copy limited edition]), 30.
7. Giuseppe Verdi, *I Copialettere di Giuseppe Verdi*, ed. Gaetano Cesari and Alessandro Luzio (Milan: Commissione Esecutiva per le Onoranze a Giuseppe Verdi nel Primo Centenario della Nascita, 1913), 416.
8. Gossett, 301.
9. Gossett, 590, note 49. Also p. XLVIII in the front matter of the critical edition regarding the first performance.
10. To Giuseppina Appiani, quoted in Morgenstern, 112.
11. Gossett, 394ff.
12. Gossett, 434, including note 75.
13. *Spinto* comes from the Italian verb *spingere*, and there is no English equivalent for its use with respect to voices. It means to push, in the sense of pushing something out of the way, stepping on a car's accelerator,

or carrying a joke too far. By extension, especially in entertainment, it can be used to mean hot or sizzling. It is perhaps most commonly heard paired with *lirico*. A *lirico spinto* voice is a lyric voice with a bit more power than average for the lyric category.

Notes for Chapter 4

1. To Giulio Ricordi, quoted in Martin Chusid's "Verdi's Own Words: His Thoughts on Performance, with Special Reference to *Don Carlos*, *Otello*, and *Falstaff*," in *The Verdi Companion*, ed. William Weaver and Martin Chusid (New York: W. W. Norton, 1979), 178.
2. George Martin, *Verdi: His Music, Life and Times* (New York: Dodd, Mead & Company, 1963), 460.
3. Martin, 311.
4. In more technical terms: The E-flat is part of either key (first C minor and then A-flat major). This is why it does not sound wrong and connects the sections beautifully. But the written C is the tonic of C minor and thus brings resolution. On the other hand, the E-flat, while only a mediant in C minor, is the dominant of the new key. Thus, the interpolated high note thwarts the intended resolution and creates a "false dominant" leading to the A-flat tonic.
5. The history of the editing and printing of this score is beyond the scope of this book, but we know that Verdi had little involvement, and it presented many questions and problems to scholars and performers alike from its birth. A critical edition was released in 1997 and, for all its contributions, we still see a relatively light load of expressive indications and the same sameness in repeated music. Also see Gossett, 554, note 7.

Notes for Chapter 5

1. Richard Wagner, *On Conducting*, trans. Edward Dannreuther, 2nd ed. (London: William Reeves, 1897), 20.
2. Richard Wagner, "Bellini: A Word in Season," in *Posthumous, Etc.*, vol. 8 of *Richard Wagner's Prose Works*, trans. William Ashton Ellis, 2nd ed. (London: Kegan Paul, Trench, Trubner & Co. Ltd., 1899).
3. Wagner to Franz Liszt, Zurich, 13 January 1853, in *The Correspondence of Wagner and Liszt*, vol. 1, trans. Francis Hueffer (New York: Scribner and Welford, 1889), 249.
4. There is an anomaly in some scores, including the Dover orchestra score, at the chorus's entrance after the third verse of Senta's

BALLADE. The anomaly is at the MOLTO PIÙ LENTO, 88 dotted quarter notes a minute, which is considerably faster than what has come before. The indication of 88 eighth notes in the vocal score is correct (p. 185 [vocal 118]).

Notes for Chapter 6

1. Charles Gounod, *Memoirs of an Artist: An Autobiography*, trans. Annette E. Crocker (Chicago: Rand McNally & Company, 1895), 196.
2. Camille Saint-Säens, *Outspoken Essays on Music*, trans. Fred Rothwell, The Musician's Bookshelf, ed. Claude Landi (London: Kegan Paul, Trench, Trubner & Co.; New York: E. P. Dutton & Co., 1922), 72.
3. Saint-Säens, *Outspoken Essays*, 64, 70.
4. Saint-Säens, *Outspoken Essays*, 60.
5. Letter to Madame Halévy, quoted in Gertrude Norman and Miriam Lubell Shrifte, *Letters of Composers: An Anthology* (New York: Alfred A. Knopf, 1946), 247.
6. To Camille Bellaigue, quoted in Morgenstern, 231.
7. Camille Saint-Säens, *Musical Memories*, trans. Edwin Gile Rich (Boston: Small, Maynard and Company, 1919), 45.
8. Saint-Säens, *Musical Memories*, 23.

Notes for Chapter 7

1. To librettist Giuseppe Adami during their collaboration on *Turandot*, quoted in *The Letters of Giacomo Puccini*, ed. Giuseppi Adami, trans. Ena Makin (New York: J. B. Lippincott, 1931, and Vienna House, 1973).
2. Mary Jane Phillips-Matz, *Puccini: A Biography* (Boston: Northeastern Univ. Press, 2002), 86. The author cites Herbert Handt, "Bohemian Quartet," *Opera News* (January 11, 1997): 10–12+ [ProQuest web, September 1, 2019].
3. Phillips-Matz, 266.
4. Don V. Moses, Robert W. Demaree, Jr., and Allen F. Ohmes, "Conducting Three Baroque Masterworks," Part 2 in *Face to Face with Orchestra and Chorus: A Handbook for Choral Conductors*, 2nd expanded ed. (Bloomington: Indiana Univ. Press, 2004).
5. W. Anthony Sheppard. "Music Box as Muse to Puccini's 'Butterfly,'" *The New York Times*, June 17, 2012, AR1.

Notes for Chapter 8

1. "Ten Golden Rules" by Richard Strauss was written in the 1920s. It appears in a large number of books with small variations in the text, the title, and the year cited. Elliott W. Galkin cites the 1949 Betrachtungen und Erinnerungen and other sources in The History of Orchestral Conducting: Its Theory and Practice (New York: Pendragon Press, 1988), back flyleaf, verso.
2. *Style and Idea: Selected Writings of Arnold Schoenberg*, trans. Leo Black, ed. Leonard Stein, 1st pb ed. with revisions (Berkeley: Univ. of California Press, 1984), 137.
3. Henry T. Finck, *Richard Strauss: The Man and His Works* (Boston: Little, Brown, and Company, 1917), 38.
4. Michael Kennedy, *Richard Strauss: Man, Musician, Enigma* (Cambridge: Cambridge Univ. Press, 1999), 394.
5. Finck, 40.

Note for Acknowledgments

1. Letter to *The New Masses*, an American Marxist magazine that published 1926–1948, quoted in Norman and Shrifte, 406.

Literature Cited

Many of these books are available for download or borrowing on line. In such cases, the file identifier below completes the URL that begins with https://archive.org/details/.

Bellini, Vincenzo. *Corrispondenze Epistolari di Carlo Pepoli: Lettere di Vincenzo Bellini*. Vol. 2 of *Ricordanze Biografiche*. Bologna: Tipografia Fava e Garagnani, 1881 (300-copy limited edition). Download: lettere-00bellgoog. (Vol. 2 begins on physical p. 31.)

Berlioz, Hector. *The Orchestral Conductor: Theory of His Art*, trans. unidentified. New York: Carl Fisher, Inc., 1900. Download: orchestralconduc00berl.

——— *Le Chef d'orchestre: théorie de son art*. Paris: Henry Lemoine & Cie., ca. 1855. Download: lechefdorchestre36978gut.

Bernstein, Leonard. *The Joy of Music*. New York: Simon & Schuster, 1959. Borrow: joyofmusic00bern.

Chusid, Martin. "Verdi's Own Words: His Thoughts on Performance, with Special Reference to Don Carlos, Otello, and Falstaff." In *The Verdi Companion*, ed. William Weaver and Martin Chusid. New York: W. W. Norton, 1979. Borrow: verdicompanion00weav.

Copland, Aaron. *What to Listen for in Music*. Rev. ed. New York: Mentor, 1999. Borrow: whattolistenfori00copl_0.

Finck, Henry T. *Richard Strauss: The Man and His Works*. Boston: Little, Brown, and Company, 1917. Download: in.ernet.dli.2015.151772.

Galkin, Elliott W. *The History of Orchestral Conducting: Its Theory and Practice*. New York: Pendragon Press, 1988.

Gossett, Philip. *Divas and Scholars: Performing Italian Opera*. Chicago: Univ. of Chicago Press, 2006.

Gounod, Charles. *Memoirs of an Artist: An Autobiography*, trans. Annette E. Crocker. Chicago: Rand McNally & Company, 1895. Download: memoirsanartist00goungoog.

Harding, James. *Saint-Saëns and His Circle*. London: Chapman & Hall, 1965.

Haynes, Bruce. *A History of Performing Pitch: The Story of "A."* Lanham, MD: The Scarecrow Press, Inc., 2002.

Handt, Herbert. "Bohemian Quartet." *Opera News* (January 11, 1997): 10–12+ [ProQuest web, September 1, 2019].

Kennedy, Michael. *Richard Strauss: Man, Musician, Enigma*. Cambridge: Cambridge Univ. Press, 1999.

Leinsdorf, Erich. *The Composer's Advocate: A Radical Orthodoxy for Musicians*. New Haven: Yale Univ. Press, 1981. Borrow: composersadvocat00eric.

Martin, George. *Verdi: His Music, Life and Times*. New York: Dodd, Mead & Company, 1963. Borrow: verdihismusiclif010397mbp.

Meier, Gustav. *The Score, the Orchestra, and the Conductor*. New York: Oxford Univ. Press, 2009.

Morgenstern, Sam, ed. *Composers on Music: An Anthology of Composers' Writings From Palestrina to Copland*. New York: Random House, Pantheon Books, 1956. Borrow: composersonmusic0000morg.

Moses, Don V., Robert W. Demaree, Jr., and Allen F. Ohmes. "Conducting Three Baroque Masterworks." Part 2 in *Face to Face with Orchestra and Chorus: A Handbook for Choral Conductors*, 2nd exp. ed. Bloomington: Indiana Univ. Press, 2004. Borrow: isbn_9780253216991.

Mozart, Wolfgang Amadeus. *Mozart: The Man and the Artist, As Revealed in His Own Words*, ed. Friedrich Kerst, trans. Henry Edward Krehbiel. New York: B. W. Huebsch, 1905. Download: mozartmanartista00moza.

——— *The Letters of Wolfgang Amadeus Mozart*, 2 vols., trans. Lady Wallace. New York: Hurd and Houghton; Philadelphia: Frederick Leypoldt, 1866. Download Vol. 1: lettersofwolfgan01moza, Vol. 2: lettersofwolfgan02moza.

Norman, Gertrude and Miriam Lubell Shrifte. *Letters of Composers: An Anthology*. New York: Alfred A. Knopf, 1946. Download: in.ernet.dli.2015.177640.

Phillips-Matz, Mary Jane. *Puccini: A Biography*. Boston: Northeastern Univ. Press, 2002.

Puccini, Giacomo. *The Letters of Giacomo Puccini*, ed. Giuseppe Adami, trans. Ena Makin. London: George G. Harrap & Co Ltd, n.d. Download: in.ernet.dli.2015.62075. However, this file has a number of defects. The book was reprinted in New York: J. B. Lippincott, 1931 and Vienna House, 1973.

Rudolf, Max. *The Grammar of Conducting: A Practical Study of Modern Baton Technique*. New York: G. Schirmer, Inc., 1950. Borrow: grammarofconduct00rudorich.

Saint-Säens, Camille. *Musical Memories*, trans. Edwin Gile Rich. Boston: Small, Maynard and Company, 1919. Download: musicalmemories00sain.

——— *Outspoken Essays on Music*, trans. Fred Rothwell, The Musician's Bookshelf, ed. Claude Landi. London: Kegan Paul, Trench, Trubner & Co.; New York: E. P. Dutton & Co., 1922. This is a posthumous translation and publication; the author died in 1921. Download: outspokenessayso00sainuoft.

Schoenberg, Arnold. *Style and Idea: Selected Writings of Arnold Schoenberg*, trans. Leo Black, ed. Leonard Stein. 1st pb. ed. with revisions. Berkeley: Univ. of California Press, 1984. Borrow: styleideaselecte0000 scho.

Sheppard, W. Anthony. "Music Box as Muse to Puccini's 'Butterfly.'" *The New York Times*, June 17, 2012, AR1.

Stravinsky, Igor, and Robert Craft. *Dialogues and a Diary*. Garden City: Doubleday and Company, Inc., 1963. Download: dialoguesanddiar00stra.

Slatkin, Leonard. *Conducting Business: Unveiling the Mystery Behind the Maestro*. Milwaukee: Amadeus Press, 2012.

Verdi, Giuseppe. *I Copialettere di Giuseppe Verdi*, ed. Gaetano Cesari and Alessandro Luzio. Milan: Commissione Esecutiva per le Onoranze a Giuseppe Verdi nel Primo Centenario della Nascita, 1913. Download: icopialettere00verd.

Wagner, Richard. *On Conducting*, trans. Edward Dannreuther. 2nd ed. London: William Reeves, 1897. Download: cu31924022322113.

——— The *Correspondence of Wagner and Liszt*, 2 vols., trans. Francis Hueffer. New York: Scribner and Welford, 1889. Download vol. 1: correspondencew01huefgoog, vol. 2: correspondencew00liszgoog.

——— *Opera and Drama*, Vol. 2 of *Richard Wagner's Prose Works*, trans. William Ashton Ellis. 2nd ed. London: Kegan Paul, Trench, Trubner & Co. Ltd., 1900. Download: richardwagnersp00elligoog.

——— "Bellini: A Word in Season," in *Posthumous, Etc.*, Vol. 8 of *Richard Wagner's Prose Works*, trans. William Ashton Ellis. 2nd ed. London: Kegan Paul, Trench, Trubner & Co. Ltd., 1899. Download: richardwagnerspr011362mbp.

Weingartner, Felix. *On Conducting*, trans. Ernest Newman. London: W. Breitkoft & Härtel, 1906. Download: onconducting00weinuoft.

Index

Note: Page numbers in *italics* refer to tables.

A

B

C

E

F

G

H

I

J

K

L

M

N

O

Q

R

S

T

U

V

W

Z